fear of words

Censorship and the Public Libraries of Canada

Alvin M. Schrader

cla

For Lloyd
whose fierce belief in freedom has inspired and awed me

Canadian Cataloguing in Publication Data

Schrader, Alvin M.
    Fear of words : censorship and the public libraries
of Canada

Based on findings of a study of access policies and
    censorship experiences in Canadian public libraries.
Includes bibliographical references and index.
ISBN 0-88802-274-3

    1. Libraries--Censorship--Canada. 2. Public
libraries--Canada. 3. Library surveys--Canada.
I. Canadian Library Association. II. Title.

Z658.C3S34 1995   025.2'13'0971   C95-900665-6

Printed on recycled paper

The paper in this publication meets the minimum requirements of American
National Standard for Information Sciences—Permanence of Paper for Printed
Library Materials, ANSI Z39.48-1984 ∞

Copyright © 1995 Canadian Library Association
200 Elgin Street, Suite 602, Ottawa, Ontario K2P 1L5
All rights reserved
ISBN 0-88802-274-3
Printed and bound in Canada

Contents

Acknowledgements 5
Preface 7

PART 1: ISSUES OF ACCESS
1 / Introduction 11
2 / Conceptual Framework 13
3 / Study Questions 19
4 / Previous Research 21
5 / Study Design and Limitations 25

PART 2: CHALLENGES TO ACCESS
6 / Institutional Characteristics 35
7 / Access Policies and Practices 37
    A. Selection, Challenges and Donations 37
    B. Access Restrictions on Children and Young Adults 40
    C. Differential Treatment of Materials 44
    D. Collection Vulnerability 49
    E. Bill C-54, An Act to Amend the Criminal Code 54
8 / Collection Challenges 59
    A. Overview of Direct Challenges 59
    B. Profile of Challenges 62
    C. Outcomes of Challenges 83
    D. Titles Withdrawn 86
    E. Effects of Challenges 90
9 / Covert Censorship 99
10 / Acquisition Pressure 105

PART 3: THE FUTURE OF ACCESS
11 / Summary of Findings 113
12 / Conclusions 117

References 125
Appendices
    A. Survey Questionnaires & Covering Letters 129
    B. Statements on Intellectual Freedom 145
    C. Main Questionnaire: Item Responses 157
    D. Freedom to Read Week Reading List 161
    E. Materials Challenged, 1985-87 167
Index 179

Illustrations

TABLES
1. Public Library Respondents, by Governance and Jurisdiction, 1987   29
2. Survey Response Rate, based on Governance and Jurisdiction, 1987   29
3. Access Policies, by Governance, 1987   39
4. Individual Access Policies, by Public Libraries and Population, 1987   40
5. Access Restrictions Based on Age, by Governance, 1987   41
6. Controversial Materials Checklist, by Governance, 1987   50
7. Controversial Materials Checklist, by Category, 1987   51
8. Controversial Materials Checklist, by Public Library Ownership, 1987   51
9. Controversial Materials Checklist, by Titles Missing from Jurisdictions, 1987   52
10. Official Reaction to Bill C-54, by Public Libraries and Population, 1987   55
11. Collection Challenges, by Public Libraries and Population, 1985-87   59
12. Challenges, by Year, 1985-87   60
13. Challenges Annually per Library and per 100,000 Population, by Jurisdiction   62
14. Challenges per Complainant, 1985-87   62
15. Status of Complainants, 1985-87   62
16. Complainant Representation, 1985-87   63
17. Age Level of Material Challenged, by Complainants Representing Themselves, 1985-87   63
18. Publication Date of Material Challenged, 1985-87   64
19. Publication Format of Material Challenged, 1985-87   64
20. Intended Age Level of Material Challenged, by Fiction/Non-fiction Status, 1985-87   64
21. Titles Challenged, 1985-87   65
22. Authors Challenged, 1985-87   67
23. Reasons for Challenges, 1985-87   68
24. Action Requested by Complainants, 1985-87   81
25. Intended Age Level of Material Challenged, by Action Requested, 1985-87   82
26. Outcomes of Challenges, 1985-87   83
27. Library Adherence to Policy in Resolving Challenges, 1985-87   83
28. Administrative Level in Resolving Challenges, 1985-87   84
29. Reasons for Challenges to Titles Withdrawn, 1985-87   84

FIGURES
1. Percentage of Public Libraries Responding to Survey, 1987   30
2. Percentage of Canadian Population Represented by Respondents, 1987   30
3. Percentage of Public Library Circulation Represented by Respondents, 1987   31
4. Factors Influencing Outcomes of Challenges to Public Library Collections   86

Acknowledgements

I have many grateful acknowledgements to record. The original study was funded by three generous patrons: the Alberta Foundation for the Literary Arts (now the Alberta Foundation for the Arts), the Small Faculties Endowment Fund at the University of Alberta, and the School of Library and Information Studies, University of Alberta.

The School of Library and Information Studies provided administrative support, office supplies and equipment, computer services, and graduate student research assistance. The School also supported me through a six-month sabbatical in 1992 that gave me the opportunity to bring the study to fruition. I am indebted to the School's support staff, Darlene Syrotuik and Pamela Cheyne, for their assistance during various stages of this work, and to Sheila Bertram, director of the School of Library and Information Studies, for her encouragement and support.

I also want to acknowledge the encouragement I received early on to undertake this research from Nancy Fleming, executive director of the Book and Periodical Council (then the Book and Periodical Development Council), as well as from Terrence Paris of the Intellectual Freedom Committee of the Atlantic Provinces Library Association.

I am grateful to many colleagues and research assistants for their assistance and advice. Among my colleagues, I want to thank Anna Altmann, Josephine Bryant, Charles Bunge, Barry Edwards, Connie Hall, Brian Harris, Chuck Humphrey, Harvey Krahn, Janet McDonald, Luise Mendler-Johnson, Lance Nordstrom, Catriona de Scossa, Keith Walker and Mary Westcott. In addition, Judith McAnanama, chief executive officer of the Hamilton Public Library, kindly made available a copy of the 1987 statistical package produced by the Council of Administrators of Large Urban Public Libraries. Among my graduate students, I thank Laura Beswick, Don Dickson, Kevin Dodds, Roman Harrison, Michael Lesyck, Peter Ng, Yvonne Rezek, Andrea Rhodes, Sandy Stift and Marshall Sumka.

Finally, I owe a very special thanks to those loyal colleagues and friends who read drafts of the manuscript — Anna Altmann, Les Asheim, Kevin Dodds, Lloyd Houser, Sandy Stift, and Peter Wons — and to Noeline Bridge, who provided a first-class index, and to Elizabeth Morton, editor of CLA monograph publications, who provided valuable assistance in improving the manuscript.

I am grateful to Tony Thai, whose enthusiasm, interest and commitment have been a source of inspiration and reassurance during the creation of this work.

And last but not least, I wish to express my sincere appreciation to all those public library staff across Canada who participated in this study and who were concerned enough to convey their opinions and insights and thereby to give this record whatever success it might merit.

Preface

This book presents the findings of a study of access policies and censorship experiences in the public libraries of Canada. It addresses the issue of the prevailing climate of intellectual freedom in public libraries across the country. It shows just how much community pressure is brought to bear on public libraries to remove or restrict materials and how public libraries have responded to such pressure. It also makes tentative comparisons with recent events in the United States.

Fear of Words is the first attempt to document the various forms of censorship experienced by the public librarians of an entire nation. No other survey research on contemporary censorship in public libraries has been published that is comparable in scope, depth, or geographic coverage. A favourable response rate among public libraries, representing 76 per cent of all Canadian residents, assures a high level of confidence in the findings.

I begin with a selective review of recent literature about public library censorship in Canada and the U.S., focusing on the methods that have been used to study this phenomenon. Several studies of school and academic library censorship are included. I then investigate the access structures of Canadian public libraries across the country and the censorship incidents experienced in those libraries. The study focuses on institutional policies, community challenges to library materials, staff reactions, and the effects of challenges on intellectual freedom in the library.

The study shows that 70 per cent of the public libraries that responded had some or all of the basic institutional access policies that relate to intellectual freedom — a selection policy, objections policy, donations policy, an objections form, and support of the Canadian Library Association's Statement on Intellectual Freedom. Some 60 per cent reported that they did not restrict access by children and young adults.

The study also shows that during the three-year period from 1985 to 1987 an average of one direct challenge occurred every day of the year somewhere in Canada. The rate of institutions challenged across the country was approximately 21 per cent annually, and 35 per cent over three years.

Almost as many different titles were challenged between 1985 and 1987 as there were challengers: over 500 titles by fewer than 600 individuals. The most common grounds for challenges were sex, violence, and unsuitability for a particular age group. Three out of four complainants wanted the materials removed from the shelves. In 86 per cent of the cases, however, public library staff did not remove the offending items.

The study also shows that at least one in ten public libraries experienced incidents of covert censorship — theft, defacement, alteration, mutilation, or destruction of materials. This finding works out to an estimated average of one incident per week somewhere in the country. As well, one in five public libraries was pressured unduly to acquire or accept materials for their collections.

These are some of the highlights of the story that unfolds in the chapters that follow. In this story, creative tension between institutional expertise and community advocacy is revealed as a continuous thread. Public library staff consistently use challenges to their collections as opportunities for fruitful dialogue with members of the community: individuals explain their concerns and values and attitudes, and staff explain the public library's role in a democracy and the need for tolerance in communities of cultural diversity.

Fear of Words is of timely concern and will be of interest not only to those working in the field of public librarianship around the world but also to students of human freedoms, especially the freedom to receive information.

This study sheds new light on the prevailing climate of intellectual freedom in Canadian public libraries, and I hope that it will help to promote discussion about the limits on freedom of expression appropriate in a democratic society. Perhaps it will also serve as a "case study" for investigators in other democracies who might be interested in conducting similar research. The findings should be of value to public librarians everywhere in their ceaseless efforts to evaluate the adequacy and effectiveness of their own responses to censorship pressures and dilemmas.

It should be remembered that the national profile that emerges in this story is only a snapshot: every day, new twists are added that reveal how public library staff respond to the inherent tension between citizen advocacy and institutional prerogative.

Part 1

ISSUES OF ACCESS

1 / Introduction

> And who shall silence all
> the airs and madrigals that
> whisper softness in chambers?
> — Milton, *Areopagitica*

In Quebec, one of the respondents to the study reported in this book described how a parent had been scandalized to find his daughter reading a public library book on menstruation that was aimed at 10- to 14-year-olds. The daughter was 10. The father was a doctor. After staff discussed the matter with the complainant, the book was retained.

In Newfoundland, another respondent reported that a patron wanted all of Kevin Major's books removed from the children's section of the public library. The public library's reaction was to relocate his books to a newly created young adult section. But, as the respondent noted, children could still borrow materials from that area.

In Alberta, a parent wanted *Trish for President* by Lael Littke removed from the young adult section of the public library on the grounds that it was "definitely unsuitable" for a young adult. However, the real reason behind the objection, the study respondent noted parenthetically, was the liberated attitude of the female character in running for school president. In any event, after discussion with the parent, the book was retained.

In Saskatchewan, a patron objected to all adult western paperbacks in the public library on the grounds that the explicit sex in them was demoralizing to young minds. The books were removed.

In Ontario, a parent wanted Wallace Hamilton's *Kevin* withdrawn from the public library collection on the grounds that her son had been counselled "for this gay problem" that she claimed he was confused and unhappy about, and she strongly resented the content of this book, which in her view glorified homosexuality. After discussion, the book was retained.

Also in Ontario, a parent requested the removal of *Where Did I Come From?* by Peter Mayle, which she felt was too explicit and "damaging to her nine-year-old son, who was going into the priesthood." After discussion, the book was retained.

In Nova Scotia, a parent wanted the public library to remove its copy of Jack Prelutsky's *Nightmares: Poems to Trouble Your Sleep* because one poem, about a ghoul outside the school, "added to the things kids have to watch out for and be frightened of." After discussion, the book was retained.

In both Ontario and Quebec, there were various reports of public library patrons demanding the removal of all books dealing with astrology, the occult, witchcraft, magic, and parapsychology — "satanic books," as one complainant called them, and "the work of the devil," in the words of another. In all cases, the results were the same: after discussion with complainants, the books remained on the shelves.

In Alberta, a parent wanted a book removed from the public library collection so that children would not have access to the obscene words in it. The staff "relocated" it to the library's work section. The book in question? *Webster's New Collegiate Dictionary*.

In Ontario, a patron objected to the inclusion in the public library collection of Marian Engel's *Bear*. The action requested? "Removal from the collection, jail for the librarian." After discussion, the book was retained (and presumably the threat of criminal charges was withdrawn).

In Manitoba, a patron described the public library's copy of *Kansan* by Robert E. Mills as pornographic and said, "This book ought to be burned and the author gelded." After discussion with the complainant, it remained on the shelves (and I hope the threat of castration was abandoned!).

These are but a few of the hundreds of incidents that came to light in the course of this study, which was motivated by a desire to understand more clearly the climate of intellectual freedom that prevails in the public libraries of Canada. While many Canadian residents believe that they can get anything they might want to read, view or hear through their public library, the Book and Periodical Development Council (now the Book and Periodical Council) expressed a different view in the July-August 1984 issue of *Feliciter* (published by the Canadian Library Association): Canada is a nation of quiet censors. In recognizing this, the Council announced that it was sponsoring a new initiative, Freedom to Read Week, and declared that:

> While there have not been any public book burnings, a quieter form of censorship exists in Canada. Often the suppression of a book is done so quickly the public is not even aware it has happened.
>
> Censorship is becoming an acceptable way of dealing with social issues of concern to Canadians. (Book and Periodical Development Council 1984, 19)

But to what extent does this accusation apply to the nation's public libraries and public librarians? And to the extent that it does apply, what is the role of the community in bringing about this "quiet censorship"? Furthermore, does community role differ across the country?

For example, are Alberta communities, among all the provinces and territories, rampant with would-be censors? Are public libraries serving small rural communities more susceptible to censorial pressures than those serving large urban communities? Do public librarians exercise prior restraint in the selection process in order to avoid discord and rupture with public library boards which might be nervous about local controversy and volatile community support?

I was motivated to conduct this study by the realization that Canadian public librarians lacked national information on the scope and nature of community pressures to censor materials housed in the nation's public libraries. Also lacking was information on the ways in which public library staff across the country have responded to these pressures.

Published research on intellectual freedom is replete with condemnations of the censorial attitudes and self-censorship practices of librarians and with exhortations to them to resist both internal and external community censorship pressures. But there is very little research into the kinds of community pressures that contribute to such attitudes and practices or into how pervasive these censorial pressures are. And even less is known of just how frequently — or infrequently — public librarians actually remove or otherwise restrict access to materials as a result of such pressures. Studies rarely go beyond personal impressions and experiences, anecdotal accounts and sporadic press reports, and one-time surveys that are constrained by geography or methodology or both.

In an analysis of published research on censorship and intellectual freedom in public and school libraries in the United States during the decade from 1975 to 1985, the National Commission on Libraries and Information Science acknowledged that there was a public perception of increased censorship activity but also found that hard data were unavailable. The commission's report, *Censorship Activities in Public and Public School Libraries*, noted that there was no accepted and recognized "index of activity" regarding censorship (National Commission on Libraries and Information Science 1986).

A parallel situation characterizes Canadian public libraries. Until now, there has been no solid empirical basis for making generalizations about the existence or pervasiveness of community censorship pressures on public libraries across the country or for making comparisons between regions. Most of the issues involving access to Canadian public library collections remain unexplored. The study reported here, the first national survey of its kind in the world, was designed to remedy this long-standing deficiency and to shed light on the prevailing climate of intellectual freedom in Canadian public libraries.

Suggested Further Reading

Schrader, Alvin M. "Censorship Pressures on Canadian Libraries." *Newsletter on Intellectual Freedom* 40 (November 1991): 192-94.

—. "A Study of Community Censorship Pressures on Canadian Public Libraries." *Canadian Library Journal* 49 (February 1992): 29-38.

—. "Eternal Vigilance within Canadian Libraries: Price of Continuing Liberty." *PNLA Quarterly* 57 (Spring 1993): 14-15.

2 / Conceptual Framework

QUESTIONS ABOUT THE PRACTICE OF PUBlic library censorship raise important social policy issues. Public libraries, by virtue of institutional precedent and social evolution, are increasingly sensitive to their client communities. This sensitivity issues from both legal and philosophical imperatives. In Canada, public libraries exist by virtue of provincial or territorial legislation that empowers them to provide public access to a wide variety of materials deemed useful to a mass audience.

The purpose of the public library is to facilitate community access to cultural records. More precisely, the challenge that has evolved over the past century or so is to make available an unbiased, "balanced" and "representative" collection — an optimal range and diversity of informational, educational and recreational resources that represent many points of view of possible interest to the community at large. These resources are made available to the community for each individual's own personal pleasure, education, critical review, and general self-enhancement.

To the extent that public librarians succeed in providing access to these resources, they have the opportunity — and the power — to promote public awareness of diverse points of view and thereby to affect public attitudes. To the extent that public librarians deny such access, the power to promote public awareness is thereby impaired, and the potential benefit of the public library to each member of the community is diminished and its worth trivialized.

But for public librarians, the philosophical imperative that gives shape and substance to client sensitivity is double-edged: responsiveness to community demands for more access to various points of view can conflict with other community demands for less access or no access at all. The public library is a collection of competing users and competing communities. As an agent of the people and an institution of cultural transmission, which of these communities should the public library serve? Can it serve both communities? Does it not only select but also censor?

While some commentators in library and information studies, including some librarians, have asserted that there is no philosophical difference between the act of selection and the act of censorship, most have argued otherwise. Judith Serebnick, for example, who was on the faculty of the School of Library and Information Science at Indiana University in Bloomington until 1994, has written extensively about public library censorship issues. In a review of the research published up to 1979, she concluded, "Though definitions of censorship differed, in general selection was considered an activity governed by professional standards, and censorship was a rejection of materials for nonprofessional reasons" (Serebnick 1979, 102).

Almost thirty years earlier, in 1950, Leon Carnovsky, then a member of the faculty of the Graduate Library School at the University of Chicago and a long-time leader in the fight for intellectual freedom, argued:

> We must clearly distinguish between identical effects that result from altogether different causes, and we shall never face the censorship problem squarely and honestly until we see that book selection (which implies book rejection) and censorship are not identical. (Carnovsky 1950, 21)

Lester Asheim is another educator and researcher who has provided further insights into the difference between library selection and censorship. In reaction to Senator Joseph McCarthy's anti-Communist campaign, which silenced most of America in the early 1950s, the American Library Association sponsored the Second Conference on Intellectual Freedom, in 1953. Asheim, then dean of the Graduate Library School at the University of Chicago, delivered a paper about the nature of censorship that has become a landmark in the professional literature. Asheim argued that the act that must be examined is the rejection of items that occurs as part of the library's selection process. He posed the question: How does this kind of rejection differ from the censor's rejection?

Asheim held that the key characteristic that distinguishes selection from censorship can not be found in the criteria by which judgements are made, but rather in the motivation for judging. He argued that the selector's motivation is positive while the censor's is negative. This difference in motivation transforms the entire act of rejection:

> ... to the selector, the important thing is to find reasons to keep the book. Given such a guiding principle, the selector looks for values, for strengths, for virtues which will overshadow

minor objections. For the censor, on the other hand, the important thing is to find reasons to reject the book; his guiding principle leads him to seek out the objectionable features, the weaknesses, the possibilities for misinterpretation.... And since there is seldom a flawless work in any form, the censor's approach can destroy much that is worth saving. (Asheim 1954, 66)

Asheim noted that the censor sees nothing wrong with making judgements about a whole work on the basis of isolated parts that are taken out of context and given a weight completely out of keeping with their contribution to the overall work. To the censor, single words and unrelated passages are sufficient to damn a book — four letters of the alphabet can outweigh 500 pages (Asheim 1953, 66).

In Asheim's view, selection is democratic, and the social responsibility of the public library is to defend freedom of choice so that the individual can pursue whatever intellectual matters are of interest. In contrast, the censor's negative orientation leads to a search for reasons to ban and hence to take away the individual's right to choose freely.

Asheim summed up his views in this way:

> Selection, then, begins with a presumption in favor of liberty of thought; censorship, with a presumption in favor of thought control. Selection's approach to the book is positive, seeking its values in the book as a book, and in the book as a whole. Censorship's approach is negative, seeking for vulnerable characteristics wherever they can be found — anywhere within the book, or even outside it. Selection seeks to protect the right of the reader to read; censorship seeks to protect — not the right — but the reader himself from the fancied effects of his reading. The selector has faith in the intelligence of the reader; the censor has faith only in his own. (Asheim 1953, 67)

In arguing this position, however, Asheim also acknowledged the legitimacy of intellectual conflict between the library selector and the library user:

> It is important to note here that, whether they annoy us or not, some pressures are legitimate and our patrons have every right to exert them, *so long as they are pressures on opinion, not on the expression of opinion.* So long as the opposing point of view may be expressed, the reader has a right to reject it, to take issue with it, and even to try to convince others of its falsity. Unfortunately, the methods taken to convince others often introduce elements which limit by intimidation the freedom to arrive at an honest judgment on the merits of the case alone.... (Asheim 1953, 66-67; italics in original)

Thirty years later, in a reappraisal of his original paper, Asheim reaffirmed his view that the ultimate issue is the defence of access to ideas, to information, to aesthetic pleasure, to recreation, and to knowledge and of the process that leads to knowledge. He wrote, "I still believe that the best solution to the problem of access is to add positively to the store of ideas, not negatively to reduce it" (Asheim 1983, 184).

In 1970, LeRoy Charles Merritt's *Book Selection and Intellectual Freedom* was published. Merritt, then dean of the School of Librarianship at the University of Oregon, underscored Asheim's distinction between selection and censorship. His argument was that any librarian who understood the distinction need have no fear of a censor's success in the courts. He quoted approvingly an argument advanced by a speaker at the Washington Conference on Intellectual Freedom in 1965:

> It is my opinion that under present law no book selected by a librarian for his shelves can constitutionally be found obscene. Why? Because any such book must have at least some slight redeeming social importance. The very act of library selection testifies to and engrafts such importance upon it.... Any material selected by a librarian, in the exercise of his function as a librarian, is protected. The protection extends both to his acquisition and retention of the material, and also precludes any valid prosecution of the librarian for acquiring or retaining it. (Merritt 1970, 22-23)

Like all individuals and institutions, the public library functions within a context of conflicting political values and changing social constraints. In this context, the process of selecting materials for public library collections can be viewed as a balancing act between community demands and institutional perspectives, and the censorship phenomenon as an inherent tension between citizen advocacy and institutional autonomy. In these struggles, what is at stake is political and social power, the power to control which points of view will be made available through the institution to the community, the power to determine whose voices will be heard.

As Marjorie Fiske, a social psychologist who was a visiting professor and research director with the School of Librarianship at the University of California at Berkeley, noted in 1959,

> The basic function of librarians — to bring people and books together — is deceptive in its apparent simplicity. If we conjure up a library

Garden of Eden with a librarian who has had the best available training, has overcome all personal prejudices, is supported by a capable board, and is unhampered by financial stringencies, we still should find a far from idyllic situation. Librarians must interpret and anticipate the needs of a vast, uncoordinated and unpredictable assortment of human beings. They must evaluate and select the material to meet these needs from an overwhelming mass of publications that include numerous items about which no two people are likely to agree. The librarian, in short, is the matchmaker in a continual marriage of diversity and disparity. (Fiske 1959, 7)

Presumably there exists a continuum of community reactions to intellectual freedom ranging from legitimate expressions of personal opinion to oppressive infringements on the institutional mandate to serve all of the people. When the balance moves too far in the direction of either protagonist, the potential for intellectual abuse exists: for the public library, the danger is alienation from its community; for the citizen advocate, the danger is arrogance and intolerance.

Intellectual freedom has two sides, the freedom to disseminate ideas and the freedom to receive them, and in the end it is the librarian and the board of trustees who must assume responsibility for serving all the interests of the public library's public, not just those of the vocal minority or of the intimidating majority. For librarians involved in selecting materials, there is a simple principle to adopt that is never simple to follow: Do your selection decisions increase the potential for community access to more points of view, or do they help to maintain the *status quo*?

There have been many *ad hoc* attempts to establish guidelines for the selection and acquisition of materials by public libraries, including guidelines for potentially controversial materials. But what has been lacking in the professional literature is a systematic analysis of precisely what happens when public library acquisitions elicit strongly negative reactions from individual members of the community. Without such knowledge, public librarians may ignore or misread important forces in the body politic. They may overestimate the power of some subgroups in the community, and they may ignore the needs of the voiceless individual.

In general terms, the censorship phenomenon may be viewed as both a process and a product: it is a process that occurs over time, and it is also an outcome. For a standard definition of a "censor," I consulted *The Concise Oxford Dictionary* (1990): a censor is, to paraphrase, one who suppresses, and the verb "to censor" means to make deletions or changes in. In another source, to "censor" is to attempt to influence human thoughts by limiting or designating what humans read, see, or hear (Poppel and Ashley 1986, 39). Still another source describes censorship as "silencing": to censor is the process or act of silencing the expression of ideas (Dochniak 1986, 71).

This process concept is also reflected in the definition of censorship that appears in the *Intellectual Freedom Manual* published by the American Library Association. There, censorship means "not only deletion or excision of parts of published materials, but also efforts to ban, prohibit, suppress, proscribe, remove, label, or restrict materials" (Krug and Harvey 1992, xiv).

Another definition that appears in the *Manual* was first developed in 1986 by the Intellectual Freedom Committee of the American Library Association as part of an effort to standardize relevant terminology. The current wording of this definition of censorship is:

> A change in the access status of material, based on the content of the work and made by a governing authority or its representatives, including: exclusion, restriction, removal, or age/grade level changes (American Library Association. Office for Intellectual Freedom 1992, 65).

At the same time, four other terms are defined there:

> Expression of concern: an inquiry that has judgmental overtones.
> Oral complaint: an oral challenge to the presence and/or appropriateness of the material in question.
> Written complaint: a formal, written complaint filed with the institution (library, school, etc.), challenging the presence and/or appropriateness of specific material.
> Public attack: a publicly disseminated statement challenging the value of the material, presented to the media and/or others outside the institutional organization in order to gain public support for further action. (American Library Association. Office for Intellectual Freedom. 1992, 65)

Several terms — "challenge," "complaint" and "objection" — are used to refer to actions designed to deny or restrict access to materials. Standard dictionary definitions suggest that these terms are similar if not identical in meaning. To paraphrase *The Concise Oxford Dictionary*, for example, a "challenge" is defined as a summons to prove or justify something or a call to respond, a "complaint" is a grievance or an expression of dissatisfaction, and an "objection" is an expression or feeling of opposition or disapproval, or an adverse reason or statement.

Frances M. Jones, a public library supervisor with Hennepin County (Minnesota) Library and long-time censorship workshop planner and presenter, wrote in her book *Defusing Censorship: The Librarians' Guide to Handling Censorship Conflicts* that an essential distinction exists between a patron "question" and a patron objection or complaint. While a question is a non-judgemental inquiry about the reasons for material being in the library's collection, an objection or complaint is a judgemental expression that the library's inclusion or exclusion of certain material is incorrect, unsuitable, inappropriate "or just plain bad" (Jones 1983, 130).

Previous censorship studies, however, have sometimes made rather arbitrary distinctions among these terms, such as taking a challenge to be "a written complaint" and a complaint to be "a verbal charge." This conceptual inconsistency in the foundations of censorship research is cause for concern, because differences in findings may be the result of differences in definitions, rather than an accurate reflection of social reality.

Dianne Hopkins, a member of the faculty of the School of Library and Information Studies at the University of Wisconsin-Madison, recognized this danger in her comprehensive national study of censorship pressures on secondary school libraries in the United States, completed in 1991 and a landmark work. In this research, Hopkins focused on the outcomes of challenges and the factors influencing outcomes. She treated "challenge" and "complaint" synonymously: any oral or written complaint questioning the presence or appropriateness of library media material. I have elaborated on the issue of terminology in Chapter 4.

In summary, "censorship" encompasses both intent — censorial pressures, challenges, complaints, objections, requests or demands for review or reconsideration — and outcome. That is to say, it encompasses both successful and unsuccessful efforts to alter the composition of a library collection according to non-professional criteria, criteria that are extraneous to the library's formal collection management policies and informal conventions.

However, overt censorship is not the only strategy by which members of the community can exercise power to influence the content of a collection and thereby control public access to certain points of view. While both removal and restriction are actions designed to alter the content of a collection through subtraction, challenges to the appropriateness of materials can also imply pressure to add materials in such a way that the traditional selection policy goals of balance and representativeness are compromised.

Pressure to add, rather than to subtract, materials has the same effect on the collection: criteria outside those found in approved policy are invoked to alter the make-up of the collection, to move its content in a partisan direction. Covert censorship — unilateral acts of theft, defacement and the like intended to deny access to others — is similar in both motive and result. Hence, I would argue that an adequate conception of censorship taken as pressure to alter collection composition should encompass several forms of censorial pressure: direct challenge, covert censorship, and acquisition pressure. All of these constitute challenges to the collection.

No framework has been constructed to help understand the censorship phenomenon in public libraries that is comparable in scope to the conceptual model developed for school libraries by Hopkins, in which she sets out the path that leads to the outcome of a challenge to materials. In her model, whether the outcome is retention of challenged materials or their withdrawal depends upon some combination of the following determinants: a) school district selection policy; b) school librarian characteristics and values; c) school environment; d) community environment; e) initiator of a challenge; and f) complaint background (Hopkins 1991, 6-7).

I constructed a conceptual framework for investigating and understanding censorship in public libraries based in part on the work of Serebnick (1979) and Hopkins (1989) and supplemented by the concepts of process and feedback as derived from general systems theory (Schrader 1983). The censorship phenomenon as it affects the public library occurs within a context that has several primary dimensions:

1) political and constitutional factors, including library governance and relationships with political entities such as municipal council,
2) social and community factors, including individual and group initiators of challenges, and
3) institutional factors, including library policies and practices and librarian attitudes, values and behaviours.

In looking at the censorship phenomenon in public libraries as a process over time, I identified three stages. The first stage, the censorial occurrence itself, raises the question: Why do some public libraries experience pressure to alter their collections in one way or another while others do not?

The second stage is the resolution or outcome of a censorship incident. In the case of direct challenges to withdraw materials or restrict their access, the question is raised: Why are some challenged materials retained on open shelves, while others are restricted in access, and still others are removed altogether? In the case of covert incidents of censorship, the question is similar: Why are some materials replaced on the shelves, while others are restricted in access, and still others are not replaced at all? In the case of acquisition pressure, the question is: Why are some materials acquired or accepted as a result of external pressure while others are not?

The third stage, the feedback or impact stage, raises the question: What is the effect of a collection challenge on public library policies and practices? And, in particular, is there a "chilling effect" — a reluctance born of fear to honour the public library's mandate to serve all of the people all of the time, so that increasingly conservative policies and practices are adopted in order to avoid potential conflict in the future with individuals or groups in the community?

These three stages of the censorship phenomenon can be summarized as follows:

1) the likelihood and nature of censorship pressure,
2) the outcome of censorship pressure, and
3) the effect of censorship pressure.

Within each of the three groupings of political, social and institutional factors, a number of variables can be identified that help to predict the various stages of a challenge. Not all of these factors, however, were investigated in the present study, and indeed not all of them can be quantified easily for either descriptive profiling or hypothesis testing. Quantitative descriptive study based on a questionnaire methodology dictated the final selection of operational variables in this work.

Nonetheless, an overall conceptual framework for systematic inquiry is needed in order to understand the dynamic political, social and administrative circumstances within which the censorship phenomenon occurs in public libraries. Such a framework provides a guide for formulating good research problems into access and censorship issues, as well as a context for interpreting the results of research.

Suggested Further Reading

For a broad view of censorship issues, see Appendix D, which contains a suggested reading list for research that is part of the annual Freedom to Read Week Kit published by the Book and Periodical Council.

Hopkins, Dianne McAfee. "Challenges to Materials in Secondary School Library Media Centers: Results of a National Study." *Journal of Youth Services in Libraries* 4 (Winter 1991): 131-40.

3 / Study Questions

THE OBJECTIVE OF THE STUDY WAS TO gather information about censorship pressures on Canadian public librarians during the three-year period from 1985 to 1987. Of particular interest was the identification of factors that predict the final outcomes of such pressures. As well, I was attempting to provide some insight into the effects that censorial pressures have had on public library staff and on their institutional policies.

Research questions were devised for the mail questionnaire within five main areas of interest:

a) institutional characteristics;
b) access policies and practices related to intellectual freedom;
c) direct challenges to collections and their effects on access policies and practices;
d) covert censorship; and
e) acquisition pressure.

Specific research questions were constructed in order to provide insight into these five areas:

1) How many Canadian public libraries have a written selection policy?
2) How many Canadian public libraries endorse the Canadian Library Association (CLA) Statement on Intellectual Freedom?
3) How many Canadian public libraries have policies that restrict access or borrowing privileges by age?
4) How many Canadian public libraries have a written policy and an official form for dealing with challenges to materials? Was either or both used in the actual cases which occurred?
5) How many Canadian public libraries received requests of any kind during the study period to remove, restrict, relocate, reclassify, label or expurgate materials?
6) How many such requests were received by each library during the study period?
7) Was the incidence of requests constant over the study period, or were there variations by year or by month?
8) Were the requests verbal or written?
9) How many titles were involved in each request? And what were the titles?
10) What type of material did each request involve in terms of:
    a) format (books, magazines, videocassettes, films, etc.),
    b) content (fiction or non-fiction), and
    c) audience (children, young adults or adults)?
11) What types of individuals and groups made these requests? Were they acting on their own behalf or on behalf of someone else, such as their children? Were they registered borrowers?
12) What reasons were given for the requests and what actions were requested?
13) What was the final outcome of each request, that is, was the material in question retained, restricted or removed? Who was involved in the process of resolving the request? How much time elapsed from initial request to final outcome?
14) Were the requests reported in the local press or through any other medium of mass communication?
15) What effect did these requests have on the polices, procedures, practices or attitudes of public library staff and trustees? In particular, was a "chilling effect" at work in affected institutions, such that more conservative policies and practices were adopted in order to avoid potential conflict in the future with individuals or groups in the community?
16) How many titles that had previously been challenged in Canadian public libraries were owned by public libraries at the time of the study? And were these titles also challenged during the study period?
17) How many Canadian public libraries treat certain materials considered to be potentially controversial differently from other materials?
18) How many Canadian public libraries experienced patron actions during the study period that were suspected to be attempts to prevent or restrict access by others? What were these actions and what titles were involved?
19) How many Canadian public libraries experienced pressure to accept or acquire certain titles or types of materials during the study period?

For a copy of the questionnaire and covering letter in English and French, see Appendix A.

In examining factors that might explain or account for the likelihood of censorial pressure on a public library, I analyzed several variables for their value as predictors. Several variables were also analyzed in regression models for their value as predictors of the final outcome of direct challenges to library collections. In this study, inferential patterns of association and regression models were tested at the .01 level for statistical significance (this reference is omitted from the body of the text in order to avoid endless repetition). The .01 level of significance was chosen as a more rigorous test of patterns and relationships than is obtained at the conventional .05 level in human science research, a level which tolerates more risk of coming to the wrong conclusions than I wished to accept.

Readers interested in the details of the extensive statistical analyses performed on the study data are encouraged to write to the author for a copy of the 96 tables prepared in the course of the research.

I hoped that the information thus gathered would permit me to develop a national picture of how pervasive censorial pressures have been on public libraries across the country and of the ways in which public librarians have responded to these pressures.

I also hoped that the answers to these questions would refine and extend our understanding of the issues of access that constrain intellectual freedom in Canadian public libraries. I anticipated that the study would have useful implications for those concerned with collection management and patron access policies, as well as for those concerned with public awareness and educational programs to promote the value of the public library in the life of the individual and the community.

More broadly, I hoped that the study would stimulate discussion about the limits on freedom of expression that are appropriate in a democratic body politic.

4 / Previous Research

A SEARCH OF THE PREVIOUSLY PUBLISHED research reveals very few empirical investigations of the actual experiences of public librarians in dealing with censorial pressures: a few questions within a larger study of library-publisher relationships in English-language Canada commissioned by the Canadian Book Publishers' Council, province-wide surveys of Alberta and Manitoba, and a handful of state-wide surveys in the United States.

In the academic library sector, only one empirical study has been done, and it was limited to the three prairie provinces in Canada. Among school libraries, there have been a small number of province-wide and state-wide studies, as well as the recently published landmark study by Hopkins of U.S. secondary school libraries. There is also the personal reflection written by David Booth, a member of the Faculty of Education at the University of Toronto and general editor of the *Impressions* reading program series. Booth's *Censorship Goes to School* chronicles school censorship and the remarkable furor over the *Impressions* series during the past decade or so.

At the the same time, the professional publications contain many exhortations, especially to public librarians, to uphold the principles of intellectual freedom. These statements of principle include the formal statements on intellectual freedom of various local, regional and national associations. Readers may consult Appendix B for the statements of the Canadian Library Association, the library associations of the provinces of Quebec, Ontario, Sakatchewan, and British Columbia, the Book and Periodical Council, and the American Library Association (the latter is included because so much of Canadian public library philosophy and practice with respect to intellectual freedom emanates from the United States).

Although the exhortations have been many, empirical investigations that would assess the relevance of these statements of principle to professional practice have been few. Following the landmark studies of self-censorship by Marjorie Fiske in 1959 and by Charles Busha in 1972 (Busha 1972a,b), much of the subsequent censorship research also concentrated on librarians and their practices of self-censorship. Such research has generally taken as its unit of analysis the individual practitioner, not the institution, focusing on personality characteristics and attitudes and how these affect selection practices.

It was not until the early 1980s that the focus of research shifted from public librarians themselves to the broader social and political environments within which their decisions are made and their actions carried out. In these later studies, the unit of analysis has generally shifted. In some, it has been the public library as an institution, focusing on formal policies and procedures and other institutional variables. In others, the unit of analysis has been the censorship incident itself, sometimes including the attendant characteristics of the would-be censor.

Claire England, who is a member of the Faculty of Information Studies at the University of Toronto, managed to include both perspectives in her 1974 study of attitudes and perceptions that might explain the personal "censoriousness" of public librarians in selected Ontario cities. She related these dimensions to the nature of library collections, the role of public demand, the role of the public library board, and personal experience of a censorship incident.

On the basis of previous studies of censorship incidents in public libraries, I refined and broadened the focus of the present study to take account of earlier strengths as well as limitations. One type of limitation in past research that has constrained not only comparisons among studies but also the ability to generalize from these studies has been geography. In Canada, the public libraries of only two provinces have been surveyed: Alberta and Manitoba.

In the United States, public libraries in at least fourteen states have been investigated, most in the 1980s and a few since then: Alabama, Arkansas, Delaware, Florida, Georgia, Idaho, Indiana, Louisiana, Minnesota, Missouri, Nebraska, Oregon, Tennessee, Vermont and Washington. An entirely different kind of limitation in this research has been its very limited dissemination — several of these studies remain unpublished in somebody's office.

Another type of limitation in past censorship research has been its focus. In a study of relationships between libraries and publishers in Canada commissioned by the Canadian Book Publishers Council, coverage was restricted to English-language Canada. David Jenkinson, a member of the Faculty of Education at the University of Manitoba, limited his study of challenges in Manitoba public libraries to materials for children and teenagers of school age (Jenkinson 1985; Jenkinson 1986).

Another limitation has related to time coverage. Some studies asked for information covering a one-year period, some for two years, one for one and a half years, another for two and a half years, another for four years, and still another for five years. These variations in time coverage make comparisons more or less impossible, particularly in terms of attempting to standardize the rates of censorship incidents per selected time period.

For example, a difference in time coverage is the most likely explanation for the lower rate of challenges found in the Alberta public libraries survey by Keith Walker, who undertook his study while a student in the Master of Library Science program at the University of Alberta in 1984 (Walker 1984; Schrader and Walker 1986). The rate in Alberta was 22 per cent, compared to the Manitoba rate of 37 per cent found by Jenkinson. The difference in rates between these two provinces is not necessarily a reflection of differences in community attitudes towards public library collections. Rather, the difference is at least in part an artifact of the dissimilar time periods adopted by the researchers, two years in the Manitoba survey, one year in Alberta.

Two years of censorship incidents can not be reduced to a per annum basis simply by arithmetic averaging. In the present study, for example, the three-year rate was 34 per cent of all respondent public libraries, but the annual rate was an estimated 21 per cent.

While these limitations in research design make comparison among the previous studies difficult, more serious still are the substantial differences in the kinds of censorial events that were investigated. The most specific concept of censorship was reflected in the survey commissioned by the Canadian Book Publishers' Council of English-language public libraries in Canada, which asked for information about "demands to withdraw specific titles from circulation" (Beta Associates 1982). A slightly broader definition appeared in Walker's survey, which asked if the library had been requested to remove any book or other material from the collection.

In contrast to these "action" approaches, many other studies took a "substantive" approach, asking for information about a named thing, which in most cases was something called a "challenge." This approach, unfortunately, invites considerably more variation in what respondents perceive should fall within the concept of a challenge. Following the lead of the Missouri study (Engelbert 1982), a challenge was usually defined as "any complaint about, or objection to, or request for the removal or restriction of any resource." Somewhat broader still were the definitions adopted by other researchers, who included requests for the "review" of any resource. These conceptions of censorship are arguably broader in scope than what is reflected in the "action" approaches of both Beta Associates and Walker.

The danger of these broader notions of censorship is that they may overstate the rate of occurrence in a particular jurisdiction compared with the rate that would be obtained if an action approach were used instead. This difference in what should be studied as "censorship" may explain in part the higher rate of challenges in Manitoba public libraries compared to the Alberta rate.

Earlier, England warned readers about this definition problem in describing her own approach, which was simply to ask whether respondents had personally been involved in or cognizant of a "censorship incident." She had anticipated that defining the term would impose the interviewer's perception of those events that should be reported. Survey participants confirmed her view. They did not consider complaints at the desk as incidents, and she speculated that an incident was "perhaps a more memorable or an acrimonious occasion involving argument and strong feeling" (England 1974, 145).

Others, however, distinguished between "challenges" and "complaints." The 1985 report of a survey by the Delaware Library Association's Intellectual Freedom and Open Access Committee defined a "challenge" as "a formal written complaint filed with the library questioning the presence and/or appropriateness of specific material," while a "complaint" was defined as "a verbal charge against the presence and/or appropriateness of the material in question" (Delaware Library Association 1985, 5).

Other studies have limited their coverage to written communications. In the first annual report for 1987-1988 of the Oregon Intellectual Freedom Clearinghouse, information was requested about "formal challenges," and a formal challenge was defined as "a written 'Request for Reconsideration' or 'Statement of Concern' submitted by a group or individual" (Ginnane 1988, 1).

A study of Washington state public libraries also requested information about formal challenges, which were defined as "any formal written request to remove materials from the collection, or otherwise restrict access to, any book, video, magazine or other material" (Heuertz 1993, 7). Other studies asked for information about "challenges" but provided no definition of the term.

One study asked for information about "patron complaints" (Swan 1986, 3). A study of British Columbia public school censorship distinguished between objections to materials, "informal complaints which may or may not result in censorship," and challenges, "formal expression of objections with the complainants asking for specific action from the recipients of the challenges which may also result in censorship of the material." The author wrote that an act of censorship occurs when material is removed, restricted or altered (Poole 1986, 4-5).

In Hopkins' study of factors influencing the outcome of library media centre challenges at the secondary public school level, she used "challenge" and "complaint" synonymously: for purposes of the study a challenge was defined as "an oral or written complaint about the appropriateness of school library material" (Hopkins 1991, 1:1).

My own solution to the problem of defining censorial events was to adopt and extend the action model favoured by Beta Associates and Walker.

Another important limitation of research design in censorship surveys relates to the validity of making generalizations based on varying levels of the information collected about challenged titles. While a few studies asked for information about all censorship incidents experienced during a designated time period, many others requested information for one incident only, regardless of how many had occurred in a library. One author asked for information about "the single most crucial or significant challenge" (Engelbert 1982, 6).

Similarly, others asked for information about "the most crucial, significant single challenge," or if only one challenge had occurred, for information about it. It is evident that findings based on crucial incidents are not comparable to findings based on all incidents experienced by public libraries. "Crucial" incidents do not necessarily represent the range and nature of all incidents, nor do they permit the investigator to develop a full picture of the frequency of challenges to each particular title.

Still another limitation in the research designs of some previous studies is the population and unit of analysis selected for coverage. In several studies, questionnaires were mailed to public librarians and respondents are referred to as "public librarians," while in others the references are to "public libraries." It is unclear from the information provided in published reports whether the population was indeed librarians rather than institutions; if the former was the case, the research design is seriously at fault.

Also unclear, in those studies that clearly focused on libraries, was the treatment of multi-branch libraries: was the unit of analysis the system or each branch of the system? This issue was rarely addressed in the published reports.

A related limitation in previous research is the fact that the rates of censorship incidents are only reported in terms of the overall proportion of libraries affected and, possibly, the number of incidents per affected library. These figures are never related to other institutional characteristics, such as the proportion of municipal populations affected or the number of incidents per so many thousands of circulations.

To illustrate, research may show that 20 per cent of the libraries in a particular jurisdiction experienced censorship incidents — but does this 20 per cent represent a similar percentage of the population, or does it represent, say, 80 per cent of the population? Presumably, in the absence of such information, the researcher's assumption is that the proportions of both libraries and populations affected are the same. Such an assumption is quite unwarranted anywhere in Canada, with its typically dense concentrations of people in just a score or so of urban centres across the country and concomitantly few people scattered in many smaller centres.

In addition to the geographic and methodological limitations described above, it is impossible in several of the U.S. studies to separate public library data from aggregated results for several types of libraries that might have been included in the surveys.

In spite of these types of constraints, the previous studies represent a promising start in the search for a comprehensive picture of the patterns and trends in community challenges to the holdings of public libraries. The present study benefited from the previous research, and I made every effort to avoid the kinds of limitations described above.

Suggested Further Reading

American Civil Liberties Union. *Censorship in the South: A Report of Four States, 1980-1985.* Atlanta, Ga.: American Civil Liberties Union, 1986.

Booth, David. 1992. *Censorship Goes to School.* Markham, Ont.: Pembroke, 1992.

Budlong, Tom. "Censorship in Georgia." *The Georgian Librarian* 25 (Fall 1988): 61-64.

Chepesiuk, Ron. "On Assignment. Censorship in the South; A Report of Four States, 1980-85." *Wilson Library Bulletin* 61 (September 1986): 49-50.

Florida Library Association. "Florida Library Censorship Survey." *Newsletter on Intellectual Freedom* 39 (November 1990): 228.

Gardner, Charles A. "The Censorship Climate in Nebraska Libraries." *Nebraska Library Association Quarterly* 14 (Summer 1983): 3-11.

Geller, Evelyn. *Forbidden Books in American Public Libraries, 1876-1939: A Study in Cultural Change.* Westport, Conn.: Greenwood Press, 1984.

Herring, Margaret. "The Effectiveness of Written Selection Policies in Preventing Censorship in Academic Libraries in the Prairie Provinces since 1980." Unpublished M.L.S. project, University of Alberta, 1986.

Johnson, Ellen. "Stalked by the Censor: Intellectual Freedom in Arkansas Libraries — 1992." *Arkansas Libraries* 50 (June 1993): 13-17.

Kerns, Bettye and Linda Bly. "Lust in the Dust: Are Our Selections Just?" *Arkansas Libraries* 44 (December 1987): 14-17.

McDonald, Fran[ces Beck]. *A Report of a Survey on Censorship in Public Elementary and High School Libraries and Public Libraries in Minnesota.* Minneapolis, Minn.: Minnesota Civil Liberties Union, 1983.

McDonald, Frances Beck. *Censorship and Intellectual Freedom: A Survey of School Librarians' Attitudes and Moral Reasoning.* Metuchen, N.J.: Scarecrow Press, 1993.

McDonald, Frances Beck, Matthew Stark, and William Roath. *A Report of a Survey on Censorship in Public School Libraries and Public Libraries in Minnesota, 1993.* Minneapolis, Minn.: Minnesota Civil Liberties Association, 1993.

Morse, Susan Mignon. "Censorship in Louisiana Public Libraries." Unpublished Master's project, University of Southern Mississippi, 1985. Available ERIC ED269029.

Oregon Intellectual Freedom Clearinghouse. "Library Censorship in Oregon." *Newsletter on Intellectual Freedom* 39 (January 1990): 4-5.

Oregon Intellectual Freedom Clearinghouse. "Oregon IF Clearinghouse Issues Annual Report." *Newsletter on Intellectual Freedom* 39 (January 1990): 229.

Reiss, Joe. "Intellectual Freedom Committee Survey Results." *Idaho Librarian* 44 (October 1992): 122-123.

Schrader, Alvin M., Margaret Herring, and Catriona de Scossa. "The Censorship Phenomenon in College and Research Libraries: An Investigation of the Canadian Prairie Provinces, 1980-1985." *College and Research Libraries* 50 (July 1989): 420-32.

Swan, John. "Vermont School Libraries: 1990 Intellectual Freedom Survey." *Newsletter on Intellectual Freedom* 39 (July 1990): 124.

Wiegand, Wayne A. *"An Active Instrument for Propaganda": The American Public Library During World War I.* Westport, Conn.: Greenwood Press, 1989.

5 / Study Design and Limitations

THE STUDY WAS CARRIED OUT IN EARLY 1988 by means of a mail questionnaire, which asked for information from all public libraries across Canada for the three years 1985-87. At the time of the survey, there were 998 autonomous institutions (public libraries and systems) in Canada with a total of just over 3,000 service points.

Survey Questionnaire

The survey questionnaire consisted of two parts. The main survey contained a series of questions about institutional access policies and practices related to intellectual freedom issues, including questions about the incidence of various kinds of collection challenges between 1985 and 1987. The second part of the questionnaire was a "history sheet," a series of detailed questions about each challenge that had occurred during the time period covered by the study. See Appendix A for a copy of the questionnaire and covering letter sent to the public libraries.

The survey instrument reflected the overall project objective by posing questions in the five areas detailed in Chapter 3:

a) institutional characteristics, including type of governance (single-unit or multi-branch library), province, municipal or service area population served, number of registered borrowers, circulation, hours per week of service, whether school-housed, language of questionnaire response, and language of acquisitions;
b) access policies and practices related to intellectual freedom in the areas of selection, handling of challenges, donations, endorsement of the CLA Statement on Intellectual Freedom, access restrictions on children and young adults, treatment of potentially controversial materials, vulnerability to censorship as measured by means of a checklist of controversial materials, and public library board reaction to the proposed Bill C-54, a federal legislative proposal to redefine the obscenity provisions in the Criminal Code of Canada;
c) direct challenges to collections and their effects on access policies and practices;
d) covert censorship; and
e) acquisition pressure.

The survey questionnaire was based as much as possible on survey instruments used in previous censorship studies in Canada and the United States, in particular, the questionnaires used in the Alberta and Manitoba surveys. While the focus was on public library instruments, the questionnaires used in studies of school and academic library censorship were also reviewed.

A number of innovative questions were devised for the survey instrument used in the present study. These questions attempted to go beyond the level of information collected in previous research and related to the following areas of interest:

- access restrictions on both in-house use of materials and lending,
- library treatment of potentially controversial or questionable materials,
- pressures to accept or acquire titles or types of materials,
- covert or subtle censorship activities, such as mutilating passages of text and theft of library materials suspected of having been motivated by censorial attitudes,
- effects of direct challenges on library selection, classification, shelving, access or circulation,
- qualitative commentary on the reason(s) given for direct challenges, including direct quotation of complainant wording if possible, rather than the inclusion of a forced-choice set of checklist reasons or subjects, and
- duration of direct challenges, from initiation to resolution.

Controversial Materials Checklist

The survey also included a controversial materials checklist. Although the controversial materials checklist is not an original approach to quantitative measurement, designing an impartial checklist based on past history was something of an experimental idea for the present study.

The overall purpose of the checklist was to determine how likely it would be that a library was vulnerable to future censorship pressures. The more checklist titles in the collection, the more controversial the collection, and hence the more likely it would be for a library to experience censorship pressures in the future. In the same way that past use of library materials is the best predictor of future use, I assumed that past trouble over library materials would be the best predictor of future trouble.

The checklist consisted of 30 titles that could be deemed potentially controversial since they had drawn public criticism during the previous four or five years as reported in other public library censorship studies in Canada. The checklist was designed to "normalize" challenges to a given public library collection on the basis of how controversial its materials were at the time, irrespective of such factors as size of community served, size of collection, or annual acquisitions budget.

The checklist was also designed to indicate how similar public library collections are across the country in terms of per capita availability of potentially controversial materials. If rates of checklist materials are appreciably lower in some political jurisdictions than in others, then one would expect fewer censorship challenges in those jurisdictions because their collections are already more conservative in content.

I hoped that the checklist would serve as a barometer of the likelihood of a public library being subjected to censorial pressure in the future. The checklist was not designed to measure self-censorship, which, according to Serebnick (1982), was the goal of previous checklist-based research, and I was not implying that public libraries ought to own all of the checklist titles.

The checklist was developed from the lists of challenged items identified in three previous publications about Canadian public library censorship incidents: the Alberta study, the Manitoba study, and the Book and Periodical Development Council's "Freedom To Read Week Kit" for 1986, which identified books challenged or banned in the 11-year period 1974 to 1985 (Book and Periodical Development Council 1986).

Items from these surveys were excluded from the checklist if the challenge occurred in an institution other than a public library, if the bibliographic data provided for an item were insufficient for specific title identification, if an item was of purely local interest, or if it could not be found in the collections of both the Edmonton Public Library and the Toronto Public Library.

Two titles by Judy Blume, *Forever* and *Wifey*, appeared in all three surveys. One title by Maurice Sendak, *In the Night Kitchen*, appeared in two of the three surveys. The remaining 27 titles appeared only once among the three survey lists. The resulting checklist consisted of 30 titles.

These 30 titles were classified into five standard categories: adult fiction, adult non-fiction, juvenile fiction, juvenile non-fiction, and picture books and easy reading. Those titles identified in the Alberta survey were classified according to information provided by questionnaire respondents, while the remaining titles were assigned classifications used in the catalogue of the Edmonton Public Library.

The proportion of titles in each category (total 30 titles) is shown below:

Adult fiction — 10 titles
Adult non-fiction — 4 titles
Juvenile fiction — 7 titles
Juvenile non-fiction — 4 titles
Picture books and easy reading — 5 titles

Questionnaire Pre-Testing

The survey questionnaire was pre-tested extensively with the staff of five public libraries. Three of these were major systems serving municipalities of more than 500,000 people in Ontario and Alberta, and two were smaller public libraries in Alberta serving municipalities of approximately 10,000 people. Approximately ten senior staff in two of the major systems were involved in pre-testing the questionnaire. The questionnaire and covering letter were reviewed with six other colleagues, both academic and professional, who had expertise in either questionnaire design or censorship issues.

Three versions of the covering letter were prepared, one for the chief executive officers of multi-branch library systems, one for the managers of individual branches within such systems, and one for the chief librarians of single-unit libraries. Sufficient copies of the questionnaire for all branches in multi-branch systems were mailed together to the chief executive officer, with a request in the accompanying covering letter to distribute the questionnaires to individual branch managers.

The covering letters and questionnaire were translated into French. All public libraries in Quebec received the French version of the questionnaire, and those in Ontario and New Brunswick that had French names and/or addresses received the questionnaire in both French and English.

In Quebec most public libraries are municipal administrative units that do not have boards of trustees. In the French version of the questionnaire, the term "conseil d'administration de votre bibliothèque" was used to recognize this difference in municipal governance systems.

Survey Population

The identification of Canadian public libraries to be included in the survey was based on a set of 1987 address labels purchased from Micromedia Limited. The list was examined to determine single-unit libraries and the total number of service points within each multi-branch library system, as well as the chief executive officer of each multi-branch system.

Survey Response

On February 16, 1988, questionnaires were mailed to the chief executive officers and chief librarians of all public libraries and public library systems across Canada that could be identified on the purchased mailing labels. Returns were requested by March 11, slightly more than three weeks from the mail-out date.

Response rates were calculated in two ways: a) returns by institution per province; and b) returns by municipal population per province (for these figures, the 1988 edition of the *Canadian World Almanac and Book of Facts* was used).

Respondent Follow-Up

Between February 23 and March 31, 520 usable responses, based on public library governance units, were received. A total of 6 questionnaires were returned undelivered by the post office. Follow-up was pursued with selected non-respondents (multi-branch systems serving approximately 50,000 people or more) by means of questionnaires and telephone interviews in April and May 1988. Further follow-up telephone calls were made at the end of July to those that still had not responded, and a reminder letter and copy of the questionnaire were sent. The questionnaires of three large regional systems that had substantial amounts of information missing were returned, with a letter asking for the missing information if it was available.

After the follow-up initiatives of April through July, 40 more usable responses were received, accounting for an additional municipal population of 4 million people. With the last response of November 1, 1988, there were 560 usable questionnaires. The survey response rate is discussed later in this chapter.

Editing and Processing the Responses

In order to tabulate and analyze the quantitative component, an SPSS program was used. This tabulation and analysis required the creation of a coding structure for quantitative questions on the survey instrument. In fact, two interconnected coding structures and two interconnected computer files were devised, one for the main body of the questionnaire and a second for the "history sheets" which asked respondents for in-depth information about any censorship incidents they had experienced.

Coded responses representing the quantitative information on the questionnaire were recorded on optical machine-readable sheets for entry into the respective computer files (data coding required 2 to 4 minutes per questionnaire to fill in an estimated 100,000 circles on the optical scanning forms, and consumed 12 pencils!). Once the forms were completed and read into the computer files, SPSS was then used for the data analysis and hypothesis testing.

Where responses from the individual branches of a multi-branch system were received, they were compared for consistency of response. In some cases, branch respondents gave contrary answers to factual questions (for example, question 1, "Does your library have a written selection policy?"). In such instances, the affirmative response was selected as the system response in the survey data.

In order to deal with the qualitative information collected on the survey instrument, authority files were set up for the open-ended questions on both the main questionnaire and the history sheets. The categories into which reasons for challenges were classified were derived from the descriptions as given by survey respondents; a predetermined, forced-choice checklist of categories was not superimposed on public library respondents (and through them, therefore, on complainants). Other qualitative information that could not be transformed into coding schemes for quantitative analysis was recorded manually and patterns discerned.

For the authority file of challenged titles identified on the history sheets, a card file was created that consisted of a title card for each unique title reported by respondents. A numerical code was then assigned to it for purposes of coding identification in the history sheet computer file. The title cards were filed alphabetically by author in the card file and were reviewed for variant entries to ensure that there were no duplicates.

Most of the quantitative questions proved to be straightforward and unambiguous. To ensure internal consistency and conformity with question intent, questions eliciting a dichotomous "yes" or "no" response were carefully reviewed in light of written elaborations and explanations.

There was a minor problem concerning interpretation of some checklist responses to question 16, which concerned ownership of titles on the controversial materials checklist. In instances where respondents indicated that items were on order or being ordered, these responses were treated as ownership. There were two other checklist ownership problems that could not be resolved. One of these was the presence in public library collections of uncatalogued paperbacks. In interpreting the ownership of materials as reported by respondents, therefore, it should be kept in mind that, in many cases, the rates calculated may tend to understate actual ownership levels.

The other ownership problem was the reporting of French translations of the English-language titles on the checklist. In the time available for this project, it was not possible to verify the existence of all French translations, largely because no comprehensive publication of such translations exists. As a consequence, ownership rates for French-language public libraries may be understated if respondents did not report their French-language equivalents.

French translations of the titles for the controversial materials checklist were verified by consulting *Les Livres Disponibles 1987, Canadian Translations*, the catalogue of the Library of the Faculté Saint-Jean at the University of

Alberta, and a languages specialist at the Metropolitan Toronto Reference Library. Through these sources, 11 French translations were identified.

A few challenges reported as having been initiated after the end of 1987 were eliminated from the analysis, as were challenges initiated and resolved completely by the end of 1984. Only challenges in process during 1985, 1986, or 1987 were included.

The development of satisfactory classification systems of responses on a number of history sheet questions proved difficult, in particular the question relating to reasons for objections. There were minor difficulties with the questions relating to the intended age level of the challenged item, actions requested by complainants, final outcomes of challenges, and administrative levels at which objections were resolved. In addition, a few respondents categorized novels, poetry, and even picture books as non-fiction if they were given Dewey Decimal classification numbers in their particular library collections.

Once the qualitative coding was complete and the computer files created, data error checks and logical consistency checks were undertaken. The questionnaires for all system responses and for a random sample of single-unit library responses were compared to the computer data file for accuracy. Very few coding errors were found, and I decided that no additional checking was necessary.

Finally, missing data were identified and every effort was made to find relevant information from published and unpublished sources, including direct follow-up by telephone or mail with respondents. The annual public library statistics for 1987 or 1988 that are published by the various provincial library services were consulted extensively for missing institutional data, such as number of registered borrowers, circulation, number of service points in systems, and weekly hours of service.

Item Response Rate

In part as a result of these measures and in part because of the care respondents took in answering questions, there were few missing values: response rates on individual questions were very high, averaging 98 per cent on the main questionnaire and 91 per cent on the history sheets. (For response rates to selected questions on the main questionnaire, see Appendix C.)

A lower response rate on history sheet questions is reasonable in light of the high proportion of verbal challenges for which satisfactory records would not normally be kept; indeed, one respondent commented that only written complaints were filed, and their responses to the survey questions would therefore not deal with verbal ones.

One respondent refused outright to complete the history sheet questions, explaining that details about censorship incidents were considered to be confidential data — a position apparently unique among Canadian public libraries and disturbing. In their capacity as agents of the public, librarians should recognize that such secrecy is misguided and can only be greeted with censure.

There was also one poorly structured question on the main questionnaire that resulted in an anomalous response rate. This question investigated institutional endorsement of the CLA Statement on Intellectual Freedom, but it was the second part of a nested question on the existence of institutional policy for handling objections (see Appendix A). This placement may have obscured the question; as well, for many others who did not have a written objections policy, it meant that the CLA question was not logically relevant to them at all. Nonetheless, these same respondents may have endorsed the CLA Statement on Intellectual Freedom through some other institutional policy mechanism, such as a mission statement, a written selection policy, or a written donations policy. Unfortunately, the survey instrument was not structured in such a way that it would elicit this information.

In addition, before the questionnaire was distributed, I was unaware of the existence of a Quebec counterpart of the CLA Statement on Intellectual Freedom, the Charte des droits du lecteur (see Appendix B), adopted by three Quebec organizations: l'Association des bibliothécaires du Québec/Quebec Library Association, l'Association pour l'avancement des sciences et des techniques de la documentation, and la Corporation des bibliothécaires professionnels du Québec. While it should not come as a surprise that few Quebec public libraries would endorse a unilingual English-language statement on intellectual freedom, only two respondents mentioned the Quebec document in its place.

As a result of these weaknesses both structural and conceptual in the questionnaire, the survey data on institutional endorsement of intellectual freedom may understate Canadian public library support for a formal policy statement in this regard. These deficiencies seem to form the most plausible explanation for the low response rate to the survey question regarding the CLA Statement; a total of 266 respondents, or 47 per cent, did not answer, while the non-response rate for similar questions was on average 2 per cent (see Appendix C).

Survey Response Rate

The overall response rate for the survey was calculated from several different vantage points in order to assess how representative of all Canadian public libraries the study's findings and conclusions were. The power to generalize research findings is easy to determine where a survey response rate is based on a relatively straightforward and consistent unit of analysis, such as individuals or households. However, the primary unit of analysis in the present study, the public library as an autonomous institution, does not meet this criterion of consistency; it is not the same concept everywhere in Canada.

It may come as a surprise to many, but at the level of governance, the legal concept of a "public library" varies widely from one political jurisdiction to the next in Canada.

This is because very different kinds of structures have been adopted by the various provinces and territories for the governance and delivery of public library services.

In Prince Edward Island, Yukon, and Northwest Territories, for example, there is only one governance structure in each jurisdiction — in effect, each province/terrritory has one vast system that is responsible for public library services, and this system comprises many geographically dispersed service points, which are variously called branches, branch libraries or just public libraries.

In Nova Scotia and New Brunswick, the primary governance structure is the multi-branch regional system. In Newfoundland, Quebec, Manitoba and Saskatchewan, there are both urban and regional multi-branch systems. Just to complicate the picture further, in Manitoba there are even single-library regional systems; however, for purposes of the present study, such regional organizations were treated as single-unit libraries unless they operated more than one service point.

In Ontario, in addition to single-unit municipal libraries, there are regional, county, and township systems that are multi-branch systems. In British Columbia, there are also regional (consolidated) and urban systems in addition to single-unit municipal libraries. Only in Alberta is the primary governance structure the single-unit municipal library, but, even there, two large urban multi-branch systems, Edmonton and Calgary, serve half of the population of the province and therefore dominate the provincial picture. Finally, most provinces provide direct lending and reference services for those rural areas where local public libraries have not been established.

All of these types of institutional structures can be grouped into two primary categories: single-unit libraries and multi-branch systems.

Table 1 shows the overall geographic distribution of respondents according to primary type of governance structure.

Table 1. Public Library Respondents, by Governance and Jurisdiction, 1987

Province/Territory	Single No.	Single %	System No.	System %	Total No.	Total %
British Columbia	35	8	13	11	48	9
Alberta	120	27	2	2	122	22
Saskatchewan			9	8	9	2
Manitoba	11	2	11	9	22	4
Ontario	211	48	49	41	260	46
Quebec	58	13	8	7	66	12
New Brunswick			5	4	5	1
Nova Scotia			11	9	11	2
Prince Edward Island			1	1	1	<1
Newfoundland			7	6	7	1
Yukon			1	1	1	<1
Northwest Territories			1	1	1	<1
Unidentified	7	2			7	1
National	442	100	118	100	560	100

This table shows that the 560 survey respondents consisted of 442 single-unit libraries and 118 multi-branch systems. Ontario public libraries, with 46 per cent of the respondents, outnumbered all other jurisdictions. Alberta accounted for 22 per cent, Quebec 12 per cent, and British Columbia 9 per cent.

Table 2 shows the questionnaire response rate by province/territory, based on the number of autonomous institutions.

Table 2. Survey Response Rate, based on Governance and Jurisdiction, 1987

Province/Territory	Libraries* (Census)	Questionnaire Returns	Response Rate in %
British Columbia	69	48	70
Alberta	144	122	85
Saskatchewan	10	9	90
Manitoba	37	22	59
Ontario	556	260	47
Quebec	153	66	43
New Brunswick	6	5	83
Nova Scotia	12	11	92
Prince Edward Island	1	1	100
Newfoundland	8	7	88
Yukon	1	1	100
Northwest Territories	1	1	100
Unidentified	—	7	—
National	998	560	56

*Source: 1987 Statistics Canada data, in *Canadian Library Yearbook 1990*, p. 49.

The data show that, based on institutions, the response rate was 56 per cent of all Canadian public libraries reported in the 1987 Statistics Canada census data. By political jurisdiction, this rate ranged from less than 50 per cent in Quebec and Ontario to 85 per cent or more in Alberta, Saskatchewan, Nova Scotia, Prince Edward Island, Newfoundland, and the two territories.

Figure 1 gives a visual picture of the pattern of survey responses based on governance units across the country.

However, basing provincial and national response rates solely on institutional frequencies presents a methodological problem: each responding institution, whether it serves a community of 500 people or 500,000, is counted as one unit. This problem is especially obvious where units differ substantially from one another. Table 1 demonstrates this point: Alberta respondents consisted of 2 systems and 120 single-unit libraries, while in Saskatchewan, with half the population of Alberta, there were 9 systems and no single libraries. In British Columbia, which has 35 per cent more people than Alberta, respondents consisted of 13 systems and only 35 single libraries. While Alberta public libraries accounted for 22 per cent of all institutions in the study, British Columbia public libraries accounted for only 9 per cent.

Relying exclusively on the number of responding public libraries does not reveal the whole story about the survey

Figure 1. Percentage of Public Libraries
Responding to Survey, 1987

response rate. What is needed is a weighting factor that would differentiate institutions on the basis of other characteristics. A more complete picture of the survey response rate emerges when the rate is based on municipal population, registered borrowers, or library circulation. These measures provide more meaningful comparisons across municipalities and provinces. They also provide better indicators of the impact of public library policies and practices on client communities. However, for purposes of the present study, census figures are available only for municipal population and public library circulation.

The study represented 76 per cent of all Canadian residents in 1987 based on responses from 29 of the 31 largest communities in Canada with populations of more than 100,000 (excluding the Metropolitan Toronto Reference Library). Figure 2 shows that Quebec residents, at 45 per cent of the provincial population, were under-represented in the study, while the residents of predominantly English-language provinces were much better represented, with the exception of Manitoba at 71 per cent.

Figure 2 shows the geographic pattern by province and territory of municipal populations represented in the study.

However, even municipal population figures have limited methodological meaning because they do not represent a survey response rate based on actual demand for public library services. Demand is traditionally — though imperfectly — reflected in the borrowing of library materials. Therefore, the impact of public library policies and practices on the most visible sector of its client community is reflected in the circulation of materials.

The study represented 83 per cent of all public library lending in Canada in 1987. By political jurisdiction, response rates based on circulation were uniformly high across the country, with one exception: only about half of Quebec circulation was represented by the respondents to the study.

Figure 3 gives a visual picture of this lending pattern across Canada.

A comparison of these three rates of overall participation reveals that while 56 per cent of all public libraries across Canada responded to the questionnaire survey, they served municipalities containing 76 per cent of the total population and accounted for 83 per cent of all circulation in 1987.

Looking at survey participation rates on all three indicators, nine jurisdictions reported consistently high response rates which ranged from 70 to 100 per cent: British Columbia, Alberta, Saskatchewan, New Brunswick, Nova Scotia, Prince Edward Island, Newfoundland, Yukon, and the Northwest Territories. Response rates for Manitoba and Ontario were high from the vantage point of both municipal population and library circulation, but low in terms of governance units. At the other extreme, Quebec experienced consistently low response rates on all three indicators, between 43 per cent and 52 per cent.

The response to the survey by public librarians across the country was very positive, indicating solid support among them for this type of research. With such high coverage, the study represents both sparsely populated areas and the large urban centres. Similarly, by whatever measure — governance units, population, or circulation — the level of response was sufficiently high that generalizations can be made with confidence from the study data to the Canadian community at large. As well, the per capita circulation rate of the respondents was typical of the overall national rate, another factor supporting the appropriateness of projecting the findings of this study to the communities and public libraries of Canada as a whole.

Figure 2. Percentage of Canadian Population
Represented by Respondents, 1987

Figure 3. Percentage of Public Library Circulation Represented by Respondents, 1987

Survey Non-Respondents

Which institutions did not respond to the questionnaire? In general, they were single-unit libraries located in Ontario and Quebec that served small communities and circulated few items in 1987. Only 2 out of the 31 urban systems across Canada that served more than 100,000 people failed to respond to the study.

Altogether, 438 public libraries did not respond, 44 per cent of the total. However, although non-respondents accounted for 44 per cent of public libraries across the country, in 1987 they served only 24 per cent of the total population (6.2 million people) and circulated only 17 per cent of all items (30.2 million items). In contrast, while public library respondents accounted for 56 per cent of all institutions, they served 76 per cent of the total population and circulated 83 per cent of all items.

Study Limitations

In terms of research delimitations, the study did not set out to investigate broad social and economic factors such as publishing industry forces and constraints, or government legislation and regulations. Also excluded were the complex matters of self-censorship in the public library selection process, both practices and attitudes, and of how staff attitudes towards censorship influence diverse aspects of institutional policy and activity.

Although the questionnaire asked whether or not public libraries owned certain previously challenged titles and whether or not their access policies and practices involved age-related restrictions or special treatment of certain materials, there was no direct attempt to investigate the phenomenon of prior restraint in the selection process. (An interesting question in this regard that might have been asked, but did not surface until after the questionnaire had been distributed, was whether there had been instances in which the controversiality of an item or an author had resulted in a decision not to purchase.)

Another limitation of study methodology relates to bounded recall or recall loss, that is, the possibility of the under-reporting of past events because records are not readily available and as a consequence respondent memory is the only source of information. A reference period of three years for censorship pressures and their effects is probably too long for accuracy, especially when, as it turns out, about half of all direct challenges were made only verbally. These limitations may account for the overall item response rate on history sheet questions of 91 per cent compared to 98 per cent on the main questionnaire. Even though the calendar year was used as the reference period, some degree of recall loss may mean that the study understates the incidence of various kinds of censorship pressures, notably those without formal documentation.

Keeping these limitations in mind, there is no doubt that the present study has revealed a wealth of information that was previously unavailable. But it should also be remembered that any questionnaire survey gives only a snapshot of reality, a snapshot that reflects numerical social patterns at a particular point in time and place.

Suggested Further Reading

Hupp, Stephen L. "The Left and the Right: A Preliminary Study of Bias in Collection Development in Ohio Libraries." *Collection Management* 14 (1991): 139-54.

Szuchewycz, Bohdan. "New Right Publications: A Survey of Public and Academic Libraries in Metropolitan Toronto." *Canadian Library Journal* 47 (February 1990): 17-25.

Woods, L.B. and Claudia Perry-Holmes. "'The Flak if We Had The Joy of Sex Here'." *Library Journal* 107 (September, 15, 1982): 1711-15.

Part 2

CHALLENGES TO ACCESS

6 / Institutional Characteristics

WHAT WERE THE PREDOMINANT DEMOgraphic characteristics of the public libraries that responded? This chapter develops a profile of institutional patterns according to the following variables: type of governance structure (single-unit library or multi-branch library system); number of service points operated by systems, including number of school-housed facilities; provincial or territorial jurisdiction; municipal population; registered borrowers; annual circulation; weekly hours of service; languages of library acquisitions; and dominant language of the community (English or French).

Overall, 560 public libraries and public library systems across Canada responded to the survey, accounting for 56 per cent of the 998 autonomous institutions in 1987. They served more than 19.4 million Canadian residents, or three out of every four people in the entire country. The libraries also reported 7.5 million registered borrowers and circulated almost 144 million items. Some 36 per cent of all residents accounted for in the study were registered borrowers.

Single-unit libraries predominated. Out of 560 respondents, 442 (79 per cent) were one-library institutions, while 118 (21 per cent) were multi-branch library systems. The 118 multi-branch systems in the study consisted of both urban and regional governance arrangements. They operated 1,249 service points, including 83 school-housed facilities (which accounted for 7 per cent of all outlets).

Of the 118 systems represented in the study, 53 systems, or 45 per cent, reported one or more school-housed facilities. The majority of them had only one such operation, but 15 per cent had between 2 and 10 each.

If we turn again to the broader picture of all study respondents, the data show that multi-branch systems were demographically very different from single-unit libraries. Though far fewer in number, multi-branch systems were many times larger than single libraries. The typical system served 129,000 residents, reported 52,000 registered borrowers, and circulated over 1,000,000 items. In contrast, the typical single library reported 9,000 residents, 3,000 borrowers, and 59,000 circulations.

Statistical analysis reveals significant differences between systems and single libraries in these demographic variables. While multi-branch systems represented only 21 per cent of institutional respondents, they accounted for 79 per cent of all municipal residents in the study. Conversely, single libraries, while representing 79 per cent of all respondents, accounted for only 21 per cent of municipal residents.

Both sparsely populated areas and the large urban centres were well represented in the study. Respondent public libraries served municipalities with populations ranging from 100 people to almost 1,000,000. Registered borrowers varied from 17 patrons to almost 400,000, and annual circulation varied from 243 items to almost 8,000,000. Public service availability ranged from 1 hour per week for the smallest single-unit library to almost 2,000 hours per week for the largest system. In numerical terms alone, because small public libraries far outnumbered large ones in the study, the survey data tend to reflect the characteristics of small institutions across the country.

Generally speaking, then, lower demographic figures describe single-unit libraries in the study, and higher figures describe systems. However, the differences between mean and median demographic features indicate highly skewed patterns of municipal residents, registered borrowers, library circulation, and library hours among respondent public libraries. Indeed, fully half of all responding public libraries served municipalities with 6,000 or fewer residents, reported 2,000 or fewer registered borrowers, circulated 36,000 or fewer items annually, and provided 33 hours or fewer of public service per week.

Because of these significant demographic differences among respondents, it is somewhat misleading to speak of a "typical" public library in the study. Rather, the data describe two patterns of institutions in the study, the single-unit library and the multi-branch system. This bimodal character is largely explained by the numerical preponderance of single-unit Ontario public libraries in the study. They accounted for 38 per cent of all respondent institutions across the country (Table 1). In contrast, single libraries in Alberta accounted for only 21 per cent of all respondent institutions and in Quebec, 10 per cent. Hence, the data analysis tends to reflect the characteristics of Ontario public libraries.

In addition to these demographic characteristics of interest, two linguistic features of respondent public libraries were also documented: dominant language of the community (English or French) and languages of library acquisitions. Dominant language was not specifically identified in the study questionnaire, but it is assumed throughout the chapters that follow to be the language that was used by respondents in completing their return. Such a linguistic correspondence between community speech and questionnaire response may not, of course, hold true 100 per cent of the time. Nonetheless, insofar as respondent language on the questionnaire did reflect the majority language of the community, English predominated: 492, or 88 per cent, of the questionnaire responses were in English. By municipal population served, the proportion of English-language responses was similar, 84 per cent, thus representing over 16 million Canadian residents in the study.

French was the dominant language for 68, or 12 per cent, of the respondents. Nine out of 10 French-language responses (61 out of 68) came from Quebec; 5 were from Ontario, 1 was from New Brunswick, and 1 was unidentified. On the basis of both institutions and municipal population, therefore, the results of the present study tend to reflect the characteristics of English-language public libraries across Canada.

In spite of the numerical preponderance of English-language public libraries in the study, however, the size of municipal populations served by both French- and English-language respondents was similar. English-language public libraries served an average 34,000 residents, while French language public libraries served 45,000 residents. The median population of French-language municipalities was three times higher than that of English-language municipalities, implying that disproportionately fewer small French-language public libraries responded to the questionnaire survey than English-language ones. However, statistical analysis reveals no significant differences between the two dominant linguistic groupings with respect to population, borrowers or circulation.

Two-thirds of all public libraries in the study reported that they acquired materials in both French and English, and in many cases in other languages as well. This proportion was similar for both English- and French-language public libraries across the country. At the same time some 30 per cent of all respondents reported unilingual acquisitions — that is, materials acquired in either French or English.

Summary

The survey data reveal the following demographic snapshot of public library respondents — though it is more like a "double exposure." Among single-unit libraries, which accounted for 79 per cent of all institutions in the study, the typical respondent:

- was located in Ontario,
- served a predominantly English-speaking community,
- collected materials in both French and English,
- provided 29 hours of service per week,
- served a small municipality of 9,000 people,
- reported 3,000 registered borrowers, and
- circulated 59,000 items annually, for a ratio of 23 items per borrower, or just under 7 items per capita.

Among multi-branch systems, which accounted for 21 per cent of all institutions, the typical respondent:

- was located in Ontario,
- served a predominantly English-speaking community,
- collected materials in both French and English,
- operated 11 service points, including 1 school-housed facility,
- provided 292 hours of service per week in total, or 27 hours per service point,
- served a large municipality of 129,000 people,
- reported 52,000 registered borrowers, and
- circulated over 1 million items annually, for a ratio of 19 items per borrower, or just over 7 items per capita.

These general patterns show that public libraries serving both sparsely populated areas and the large urban centres were well represented in the study. However, overall numerical findings reflect the characteristics of smaller public libraries across Canada, and more specifically those of English-language public libraries situated in Ontario — just because so many more small public libraries are located there and responded to this study. Nonetheless, users of single-unit libraries and multi-branch systems were alike in certain respects: circulation per capita and circulation per borrower were about the same, and borrowers constituted similar percentages of the municipal population.

7 / Access Policies and Practices

DO CANADIAN RESIDENTS ENJOY UNFETtered, unrestrained access to published materials through their public libraries? The answer is much more complex than the question.

The focus of the present study was on tangible barriers to patron access. Survey questions were designed to elicit a portrait of existing institutional policies, procedures and practices that affect patron access to public library materials across Canada.

The areas selected for investigation were these:

a) the presence of formal, written policies and procedures for selection, challenges and donations,
b) age-related restrictions on the use of materials,
c) differential treatment of certain materials,
d) susceptibility of the institution to censorship, and
e) reaction to Bill C-54, a federal legislative proposal to redefine the obscenity provisions in the Criminal Code of Canada.

The resulting portrait reveals in general terms the extent to which Canadian public libraries have adopted sound and consistent management practices that relate to intellectual freedom. A consideration of such practices furnishes the context for examining the scope, nature, outcome and effects of collection challenges, including not only direct and covert incidents but also pressure to acquire materials. These themes — access policies and collection challenges — form the major chapters in the present work.

A. Selection, Challenges and Donations

With regard to the presence of formal policies and procedures that have an impact on access by patrons to materials, five kinds of policy issues were investigated:

o Does the library have a written selection policy?
o Does the library have a written policy for handling objections?
o Does the library endorse the Canadian Library Association Statement on Intellectual Freedom (CLA Statement)?
o Does the library have a written form for registering objections?
o Does the library have a written donations policy?

Although the existence of formal policy will not guarantee the public library's freedom from censorship pressure, policy is imperative for rational and consistent organizational response to such pressure. It is also essential for staff guidance and for the protection of the public. As one respondent observed:

o We have found that suggesting that the complainant read the library's selection policy and then put their complaint in writing helps to give the patron a cooling-off period. Reading the policy seldom makes them change their minds, but it does put the procedure on a more businesslike basis. In the written reply, the library quotes from the policy, may quote from reviews, and mentions any awards the author has received. In *Fairy Tales of New York*, for example, we explained that the author was attempting satire, not condoning behaviour. We try not to sound condescending but simply factual.

And another commented:

o We have found that clear policies and a well-trained staff provide a solid basis for responding to a range of patrons and patron demands. Perhaps the reason we have had so little trouble with our collection and service is that we try to be responsive to the community, and not to determine or set its values.

In our view, any comment or serious complaint regarding service or material is appreciated. It is both an opportunity to hear from our patrons and our public, and an opportunity to show them what we do offer and to explain Board policy. It is also a source of feedback to the Board and provides for ongoing evaluation of the policy.

Moreover, formal policies should not only be adopted, but they should be seen — literally. How many public libraries with approved access policies, and especially policies endorsing the institution's commitment to intellectual freedom, display copies prominently for patron information?

These policies should also be readily available in manuals at reference and circulation service points for both staff and patrons.

Examples of selection policies are found in a manual produced in 1991 by the Intellectual Freedom Committee of the British Columbia Library Association. This and several other practical guides are listed at the end of this chapter.

In the fourth edition of its *Intellectual Freedom Manual*, the Office for Intellectual Freedom of the American Library Association stresses the advantages of a written policy and form for handling challenges:

> o First, it encourages stability and continuity in the library's operations. Library staff members may come and go but the procedures manual, kept up-to-date, of course, will help assure smooth transitions when organization or staff changes occur. Second, ambiguity and confusion are far less likely to result if a library's procedures are set down in writing.
>
> . . . .
>
> Having a prepared form is not just an additional piece of record keeping. There are a number of advantages in having a complaint procedure available. First, knowing that a response is ready and that there is a procedure to be followed, the librarian will be relieved of much of the initial panic which inevitably strikes when confronted by an outspoken and perhaps irate library patron. Also important, the complaint form asks complainants to state their objections in logical, unemotional terms, thereby allowing the librarian to evaluate the merits of the objections. In addition, the form benefits the complainant. When citizens with complaints are asked to follow an established procedure for lodging their objections, they feel assured they are being properly heard and that their objections will be considered. (American Library Association. Office for Intellectual Freedom 1992, 205, 215)

The purpose of a procedure and form for handling challenges, then, is to facilitate dialogue in case of a dispute and to provide a defined course of action for both patron and staff to follow.

Several respondents commented on book selection policies and practices in their libraries (respondent comments in French have been translated throughout the text):

o Since book selection can not be a science, we can only hope to *guard* against our biases warping our collections. Changing staff doing the selection is probably the most *palatable* solution. Diversity of selectors *should* help provide balance. Please note that not only are there controversial and/or questionable books we do not buy, but also non-controversial, non-questionable books that we do not buy! [Emphasis in original]

o I feel selection of materials is getting more and more complex each year. Adults want mass market books on horror, violent crimes, sex, murder, etc. What is disturbing is young adults are starting to pick up their reading habits — they're into V.C. Andrews, Stephen King, Dean Koontz, etc. They're also into Sweet Valley Highs and will read very few hard copy books at all. You either provide the service — or have lots of books on shelves that look nice and never circulate. With dollars so tight, you're "damned if you do and damned if you don't."

o Books in our library are chosen by committee (a children's book committee and an adult book committee). Each committee is chaired by a member of the library board. Committees are composed of members of the library. Each committee member serves for two years only. Sometimes the head librarian is a member, but mostly not. As head librarian, I find this method of choosing books is excellent. The reading public gets to read books of their choice and, because members change frequently, a variety of interests are represented. It also takes all pressure off the head librarian.

o Libraries must make it clear to staff when hiring what their policy is. Our policy is that a public library should contain material for all interests and beliefs, and access to all materials is open to all.

o Very occasionally an adult, usually a parent or teacher, will suggest that an individual title is inappropriate for a public library, in their view. We always thank them for their concern and examine the book or material in question. We refer to our policy and, usually, send the item back to the shelves. Inaccurate materials, out of date, etc., are removed.

o We believe receiving complaints in written form and responding with information on our policy, provides a consistent method of addressing "complaints."

o This brings up the basic problem of trying to reconcile the Canadian Library Association's

Statement on Intellectual Freedom with library book selection policies. Most librarians and library boards understand that the two work in concert — the Statement on Intellectual Freedom ensures that material will not be excluded because of its subject matter, but at the same time the material must also meet the criteria of the book selection policy, such as demand and literary quality. Others, however, interpret the Statement on Intellectual Freedom to mean that libraries must accept all materials. I would be very interested to hear some discussion on how other librarians and boards have dealt with these issues.

o As librarian, I generally select books for the library. I do consult with my board and with the patrons as to what should be added to our collection. We try to choose wisely, given a very limited budget. I tend to stay clear of controversial books that might offend, but if a book is requested I do try to obtain it for the patron, not necessarily by purchasing it. Selection, on a small budget, is not necessarily censorship.

Table 3 shows how many access policies were endorsed by respondent public libraries, according to their governance structure.

Table 3. Access Policies, by Governance, 1987

Extent of Policy Coverage*	Governance Structure					
	Single		System		Combined	
	No.	%	No.	%	No.	%
All	91	21	60	51	151	27
Some	195	44	48	41	243	43
None	156	35	10	8	166	30
National	442	100	118	100	560	100

*policies for selection, objections, donations, endorsement of the CLA Statement, and form for objections

Overall, 70 per cent of the public libraries in the study reported having some or all of these access policies in place (including here as "policies" the endorsement of the CLA Statement on Intellectual Freedom and the existence of a form for handling objections). Fewer single-unit libraries had some or all of them than did multi-branch systems, 65 per cent compared to 92 per cent. A total of 151 respondents, or 27 per cent, had all five of these policies. Another 43 per cent said that they had one or more but not all. At the other extreme, 30 per cent, or 166 respondents, reported that their libraries had none of these policies.

Among the 151 respondent public libraries with all five access policies, there were 60 multi-branch systems and 91 single libraries. Systems were disproportionately represented among respondents with inclusive policy coverage — half of all systems in the study, compared to only 21 per cent of single libraries. Partial policy coverage was approximately the same for both groups, 44 per cent among single libraries and 41 per cent among systems. Statistical analysis confirms that systems had a significantly higher level of access policy coverage than did single libraries.

While inclusive policy coverage was reported by only one out of four respondent public libraries, these institutions accounted for over half of all municipal residents, registered borrowers, and library circulations reported in the study. These libraries served almost 10 million Canadian residents, recorded over 4 million registered borrowers, and circulated 81 million items. Another 7 million residents, 35 per cent of the total, were served by the 243 respondents reporting partial policy coverage. Respondent public libraries with no access policies at all served municipalities with just under 3 million people in total, or 14 per cent.

What these figures mean is that respondents serving larger municipal populations were far more likely to have all five access policies than those serving smaller populations. The typical public library with all five policies served a municipality with 65,000 municipal residents, 28,000 registered borrowers, and 536,000 library circulations. Those with partial policy coverage were half as large, on average serving a municipality with 28,000 residents, 11,000 borrowers, and 208,000 circulations. Those with no access policies were smaller still: on average they reported 17,000 residents, 4,000 borrowers, and 81,000 circulations.

Statistical analysis confirms that access policy coverage was significantly linked to municipal population, registered borrowers, and library circulation. That is to say, the larger the municipality — whether in terms of population, borrowers, or circulation — the more likely it was to have all five policies.

Among the respondent public libraries with inclusive policy coverage, all but one were English-language institutions. Partial policy coverage was similar for both linguistic groups, just over 40 per cent of respondents. At the other extreme, over half of the French-language public libraries had none of these access policies, compared to 26 per cent of the English-language respondents. Statistical analysis confirms that English-language institutions were significantly more likely to have comprehensive access policy coverage than were their French-language counterparts.

While only one French-language respondent reported having inclusive policy coverage, among the 30 French-language respondents with at least one of the five access policies were the following: 24 institutions had a written selection policy, 9 had a written policy for handling objections, 6 had a form for registering objections, 18 had a donations policy, and 6 endorsed the CLA Statement on Intellectual Freedom or its Quebec counterpart.

Although inclusive policy coverage characterized 27 per cent of the respondent public libraries across the country, there were wide variations among political jurisdictions:

from under 30 per cent of the public libraries in Alberta, Ontario, Quebec, New Brunswick and the Northwest Territories, to more than 85 per cent in Saskatchewan, Prince Edward Island, Newfoundland and Yukon. Since this study was conducted, the Northwest Territories has also implemented all five policies. Alberta public libraries were required by provincial regulation in 1984 to develop written policies for selection and donations (Alberta. Culture and Multiculturalism, 1988), but it is apparent from the study results that many had still not complied by 1987.

Table 4 shows how many public libraries had each type of access policy in 1987, together with the number of residents that they served. Overall, each policy had been adopted by about half of the respondent public libraries across the country, and these institutions served approximately 75 per cent of all Canadian residents represented in the study. The contrast with school libraries is striking. In Hopkins' nation-wide study of challenges to U.S. secondary school library materials, 72 per cent of the respondent institutions indicated that there was a written, board-approved selection policy (Hopkins 1991, 4:28).

Table 4. Individual Access Policies,
by Public Libraries and Population, 1987

Type of Policy	Public Libraries		Population	
	No.	%	(000s)	%
Selection policy	293	54	15,344	80
Objections policy	278	50	12,681	65
Endorse CLA Statement				
on Intellectual Freedom	258	46	13,861	71
Objections form	234	43	12,571	69
Donations policy	310	57	14,481	80

Somewhat curiously (to me, at least), 22 public libraries reported having a form for handling objections but no written objections policy. Also, 33 respondents reported that they endorsed the CLA Statement on Intellectual Freedom but had none of the other four policies of interest.

Table 4 shows that the CLA Statement on Intellectual Freedom was endorsed by 258 respondents, representing 13.9 million Canadians. However, as noted earlier in Chapter 5, it is likely that this finding under-represents institutional endorsement because of the way in which this question was structured on the survey instrument and because there was no reference to the Quebec counterpart of the CLA Statement, Charte des droits du lecteur. Only two Quebec respondents voluntarily mentioned this document in place of the CLA Statement.

Overall, the present study has revealed a considerable amount of variation in the kinds of policies and practices that public libraries across Canada have adopted in relation to intellectual freedom and access. While most of the multi-branch systems reported having at least some of the relevant policies and practices in place, there were still a few systems, as well as a very large number of smaller institutions, that did not have all of them: 16 out of 94 respondent public libraries serving populations of 50,000 or more did not have a selection policy; 26 did not have a policy for handling challenges or a form; 4 did not endorse the CLA Statement; and 17 did not have a donations policy. French-language public libraries are particularly noticeable for their lack of access policies.

B. Access Restrictions on Children and Young Adults

Another dimension of public library access policies involves the presence of constraints based on patron age or school grade level. These constraints generally take one of two forms: a) restrictions on access to the institution, typically achieved by restricting borrowing privileges by age or school grade level, and b) restrictions on access to the collection, by requiring minors to have written parental or guardian consent to consult or borrow certain materials, either individual titles or types.

The study reveals that 334 respondent public libraries, or 60 per cent, reported no age-based access restrictions at all. At the same time, a considerable number of Canadian young people did not enjoy unfettered access to public libraries in 1987: overall, 221 institutions, or 40 per cent, either restricted borrowing privileges on the basis of age or required minors to have consent for the use of certain library materials, or both.

One hundred and sixty-six respondents (30 per cent) restricted borrowing by age, while 125 respondents (23 per cent) required consent for the use of certain materials. A total of 70 institutions, or 12 per cent, reported both forms of restriction.

While at the time of the study most public libraries allowed patrons who were over the age of 12 or 13 or in junior high school to borrow adult fiction, adult non-fiction, and sexually explicit books and comics, others limited borrowing privileges for these materials to patrons over the age of 14, 15, 16, 17, or even 18. Restricted access was frequently accomplished by having separate borrower cards for children or juveniles, or by discreetly marking certain titles for staff alert.

Some institutions restricted borrowing according to age, but not in-house consultation of materials. Some institutions issued adult borrower cards to children who had parental permission. Another way that some public libraries restricted access was through separate areas for children's materials, young adult materials, and adult materials. As one respondent noted, some took this separation of materials even further:

> o The youngsters do not have the right to access adult books, even if they are placed on the same shelf but in a different section.

Some respondents restricted access to specific titles or authors. Among the restricted works reported in the survey were "Judy Blume adult titles," *Wifey, Forever, The Joy of*

Sex, The Hite Report, You and Your Child, Boys and Sex, Girls and Sex, and *Our Bodies, Ourselves: A Book by and for Women*. Sometimes there was a provision for access to young adult or adult materials if written consent was provided by parents or teachers, or if parents were present.

In many other cases, access was not restricted unless parents provided written instructions or library staff were otherwise aware of the views and wishes of the patron's parents. Some respondents mentioned that they would phone parents for permission if they thought a patron was too young to have certain materials.

A sizeable minority of respondents also restricted access to certain categories of materials, variously described as "questionable" adult material, books of "doubtful morality," adult fiction, adult type of material, sexually explicit material, adult comics, erotic comics, sexual enjoyment guides, books on sexuality, sex education books, books on childbirth, "pornographic" materials, "some controversial reference material (sex)," violent material, certain art and science books, or, in one case, "anything that is not housed in the children's room." One public library respondent in Quebec sent a copy of their access policy, which reads:

> o Minors entering the "adult" section must be accompanied by a parent if they wish to consult or borrow items dealing with the following subjects:
> — books dealing exclusively with violence and destruction (e.g., Rambo)
> — books dealing with horror, esotericism, the occult, various religious prophecies, cults (e.g., *The Exorcist*)
> — books of an erotic nature
> — adult comics are restricted to adults (not available to persons under 16, even with parental consent).

A few respondents indicated that it was left to the discretion of the library staff member to decide whether to allow a young patron to consult or borrow a "questionable" item. Various factors in the decision might be the maturity or comprehension level of the prospective borrower, appropriateness or suitability of a book, "a child's level — emotional, mental or other," availability of children's material on a topic, referral from the children's department, and "what the book is needed for." Some respondents also restricted access to certain forms of publication, such as film and video; presumably, these latter restrictions issued from the laws and regulations imposed by provincial governments.

Table 5 shows the incidence among respondent public libraries of both forms of access restriction based on patron age, by type of governance structure.

Among the 166 respondent libraries with restricted borrowing privileges, there were 52 multi-branch systems and 114 single-unit libraries. These systems accounted for 44 per cent of the systems in the study, compared to only 26 per cent of the single-unit libraries. Statistical analysis shows that multi-branch systems were significantly more likely than single libraries to restrict borrowing privileges of minors.

Table 5. Access Restrictions Based on Age, by Governance, 1987

Form of Restriction	Governance Structure					
	Single		System		Combined	
	No.	%	No.	%	No.	%
Borrowing privileges	114	26	52	44	166	30
Consent requirement	87	20	38	32	125	23
Borrowing &/or consent	154	35	67	57	221	40
Neither	283	65	51	43	334	60

While respondent public libraries with restricted borrowing privileges were more likely to be multi-branch systems than single-unit libraries, the municipal populations that they served also differed. However, they were not different in terms of registered borrowers or circulated items.

By linguistic grouping, French- and English-language public libraries were similar in their approach to borrowing restrictions on minors: 43 per cent of the French institutions in the study, 28 per cent of the English. Statistical analysis shows that there was no significant difference between French- and English-language institutions in their rates of borrowing restriction.

There were mixed patterns among institutions that required minors to have consent for access to certain titles or types of materials. Among the 125 respondents reporting a consent requirement for minors, there were 38 multi-branch systems and 87 single-unit libraries. Institutions with this form of restriction on collection access accounted for one-third of the systems in the study, compared to only 20 per cent of the single-unit libraries. Statistical analysis shows that multi-branch systems were significantly more likely than single libraries to have consent requirements for minors.

While respondent public libraries with a consent requirement were more likely to be multi-branch systems than single-unit libraries, all institutions were similar in terms of municipal population, registered borrowers and circulation.

French- and English-language public libraries differed in their approach to the treatment of minors. By dominant language of the community, significantly more French- than English-language institutions required minors to have consent to use certain public library materials: 49 per cent of the French institutions in the study, 19 per cent of the English.

For a substantial minority of public libraries at the time of the study, age-related access restrictions appeared to go hand in hand with support for intellectual freedom principles. Many respondents who reported that their institutions endorsed the CLA Statement on Intellectual Freedom also reported one or both forms of access restriction on minors. Of the 258 institutions supporting the CLA Statement, 77 (30 per cent) restricted borrowing privileges on the basis of age and 51 (20 per cent) reported consent requirements for minors; 32

institutions reported both forms of restriction. However, statistical analysis reveals that the overall difference between support for the CLA Statement and the presence or absence of age restrictions was not significant. That is to say, respondent public libraries were just as likely to restrict access based on age, whether or not they endorsed the CLA Statement.

It should not be surprising, then, to discover that for a substantial minority of respondents, the presence of patron access policies was no guarantee against age-related access restrictions. Among the 151 respondents who had all five of the access policies discussed in the previous section, 43 (28 per cent) restricted borrowing privileges on the basis of age and 33 (22 per cent) required minors to have consent for access to certain materials; 19 institutions with inclusive policy coverage had both forms of age-related access restriction. However, statistical analysis reveals that the overall difference between inclusive policy coverage and the presence or absence of age restrictions was not significant. That is to say, respondent public libraries were just as likely to restrict access based on age whether they had all five access policies or not.

Verbatim comments by many respondents indicated a wide range of attitudes and policies among respondents concerning intellectual freedom issues involving minors. Several respondents mentioned the particular circumstances of public library service to small communities:

> o In a small town library, if you allow youngsters to take out questionable material, you may soon find the parents upset and stop the children from borrowing. Everyone knows everyone here and most people believe if you take a book from the library it should be suitable. Adults' values are already formed and they should be free to read anything.

> o Our library is very small as is our community; therefore, the Librarian is in a position to watch everyone in the library and see to it that children are not exposed to adult reading.

> o Being a small village we know our patrons and will tell children that such a book is not to be taken out by them. If I think a book might offend an older patron I will tell them it is violent or sexually explicit.

> o I don't believe the library as such should have to remove or restrict an item unless it's pornographic. The library has all kinds of reading for the public. We have never refused anyone any kind of material — except for a school age child, say 10 to 12, wanting to read some adult novel that they wouldn't understand. I just tell them when they're older they can read it. Our village is only 300 so you know everyone and sometimes you have to refuse (for own peace of mind) a youngster, but I always get him another book and they're happy.

> o We restrict to the point that we know patrons and families (small town) and are able to monitor books taken out quite well. If in doubt, we phone the parents.

> o Library assistants monitor the 14 and under age group and make suggestions if they feel a book is inappropriate. (We are a small local library.)

One respondent suggested that age-related access restrictions had a positive effect on library use:

> It happens that the parents are sensitive to book illustrations: naked women, naked breasts in comics. It goes without saying that they pay attention to our collection of films and videocassettes. We only loan films to adults, who will decide whether the whole family should see them. That implies the intellectual and material responsibility of the parents. A great advantage is that the young people bring their parents to the library.

Other respondents gladly acted *in loco parentis* to monitor and control children's access to library materials, or otherwise aligned themselves with parents:

> o No restrictions, but I did deny *Wifey* to a 12-year-old who thought it was a YA book. She took it out while I was on holidays! I withdrew it!

> o If the borrower is juvenile and taking an adult book we question them to find out if their parents are aware of what they are reading.

> o Loose control only, by staff, for example if a minor brought, for example, *Wifey* to the desk to sign out, we would discourage the young patron if possible and question the reading of an adult book. Usually this works but if a teenager was to insist on borrowing it we would allow it to go out.

> o Although our policy states no age restrictions, I think there still may be some residual "control" of this by wily staff.

> o Parents must approve certain individual titles that may not be suitable for that child. We do not

want to make that decision if the title is a controversial one.

o Young boys can not look at or borrow books in our reference area, i.e. *Our Bodies, Ourselves,* which is a woman's reference manual.

o Judy Blume adult titles require written consent from a parent when requested by borrowers under 14 (mostly to protect us from angry mothers).

o In our case, certain art, science and sex education books would be restricted from a child's use; if it was not to be used constructively, we would contact parents.

o Some books have a notice on the front that parental discretion is suggested for readers under (x years of age).

o Nothing formal — common sense and parental permission.

Other respondents commented on the additional role that school teachers played in promoting policies and practices on age-related access restrictions:

o Since the library is in the school, the teachers sign out the books for the children and know exactly what they are reading.

o Due to pressure from teachers (we are at present located in a public school) certain materials (*You and Your Child*) have to have parental consent to be viewed by children.

One respondent took social responsibility further, seeing in age-related access restrictions the opportunity to play a didactic role in parent-child relationships:

o Not written, just verbal consent. We have several *very* graphic "Facts of Life" books which parents should be aware their younger children have, so that they can discuss the material with them. [emphasis in original]

One respondent's comments revealed no concern about the very likely negative impact of restricted access policies on public library use by children and young adults:

o Our library is very distinctly divided and until children go into grade 7 their nook is the children's room. They are not "banned" from the adult room but unless parents are with them it's rare they venture into the adult section.

Another's comments revealed no concern about the likelihood that special shelving might constitute an important barrier to access:

o In the children's section, books on childbirth are kept behind the counter. But any children can take them out (staff uses their judgement).

In contrast, other respondents were clearly uncomfortable acting *in loco parentis* and eschewed responsibility for monitoring children's materials, although some noted the dilemma in which they found themselves:

o We have had parents who put the onus on the librarian.

o Part of the problem about censorship is a lack of education — somehow parents feel it is the job of the public library to "censor" material for their children rather than take the responsibility themselves.

o We *suggest* that younger patrons take out Jr. books. Responsibility for what children read rests with their parents or legal guardians. [emphasis in original]

o Sometimes we feel certain books should be restricted, particularly at the Junior level, but don't feel we have the right to tell an individual he shouldn't take out a certain book. We feel this is the parents' responsibility to screen what books their children are reading.

o On joining the library, parents are told, in writing, that every effort will be made to ensure that children take only appropriate materials, but responsibility lies ultimately with parent. Up to junior high, children take only from children's area.

o I started out thinking this [parental consent] might be a good idea, but it's cumbersome and actually unnecessary. The kids control their own reading, know what suits them, and the parents who care come with their kids or make an effort to read their books themselves.

Many respondents also reported age-related access restrictions because of costs and ability to handle properly certain types of materials such as records, films, videos, VCRs, CDs, and film projectors.

In many instances where parental consent was required by the public library in order to extend borrowing privileges to a minor, the motivation was as much or more a concern about legal liability for the loss or damage of materials or for the payment of fines as it was a concern about parental responsibility for their children's reading. A typical rationale for this policy was reflected in one respondent's comments:

> o All children must have their parents authorize their membership application. This is to ensure that parents are aware that their child is borrowing library materials rather than any subtle form of censorship.

Overall, the present study has revealed a great deal of variation in age-related access restrictions in Canadian public libraries. The evidence from this study suggests that, among respondent public libraries, there appears to be a fairly common qualification to the principle of unrestricted choice for children. However, public librarians did not have a consistent approach in their policies on institutional and collection access for children and young adults. At the time of the study, minors experienced unpredictable and unsystematic treatment by public librarians across the country, even in large urban centres.

C. Differential Treatment of Materials

Institutional policy is one thing; practice is another; and reported practice is still another. In a study of this kind, which relies on respondent self-disclosure for all information, reports of practice were the only means of gaining additional insights into patron access.

Respondents were asked if they treated potentially controversial or questionable materials differently from other collection holdings in terms of selection, classification, shelving, access or circulation. They were also asked if they restricted in-house access or borrowing privileges to certain titles or types of materials, other than by patron age or school grade level.

Overall, 424 public libraries, or 79 per cent, said that they did not treat potentially controversial or questionable materials differently in any way, while 114 respondents, or 21 per cent, said they did. Among those reporting differential treatment, there were 32 multi-branch systems and 82 single-unit libraries, 28 per cent and 24 per cent, respectively. Statistical analysis shows that there was no significant difference between systems and single libraries in their treatment of potentially controversial or questionable materials.

Statistical analysis also shows that there were no significant differences in municipal population, registered borrowers, or library circulation between respondents treating certain materials differently and those not doing so.

Analysis by linguistic grouping reveals that respondents reporting differential treatment of certain materials were just as likely to be in English- as in French-language institutions, 20 per cent compared to 28 per cent, respectively.

The evidence from this study reveals that public libraries reporting differential treatment of these controversial or questionable materials also tended to support public library restrictions based on patron age. Among the 113 respondents reporting differential treatment of some materials, 50, or 44 per cent, also restricted the borrowing privileges of minors. In contrast, only 109, or 26 per cent, of respondents without differential treatment did so.

Similarly, among the 113 respondents reporting differential treatment of materials, 39, or 35 per cent, also required minors to have consent for the use of the collection. Only 81, or 19 per cent, of respondents without differential treatment had a consent requirement. Statistical analysis shows that the overall difference between institutions reporting differential treatment of potentially controversial or questionable materials and the presence or absence of age restrictions was significant. That is to say, respondent public libraries tended to restrict access based on age if they also treated such materials differently in selection, classification, shelving, access or circulation.

However, the study showed that public libraries reporting differential treatment of materials were just as likely to support the CLA Statement on Intellectual Freedom as not. Among the 56 institutions that treated these materials differently in one way or another, 86 per cent also endorsed the CLA Statement. Among those that did not report differential treatment, 88 per cent still endorsed the CLA Statement.

Moreover, institutions with differential treatment of controversial materials were just as likely to have some or all of the five access policies explored earlier, including support for the CLA Statement, as not to have any formal access policies. Among respondents treating certain materials differently in one way or another, 68 per cent had all or some of these access policies; but 71 per cent of respondents not doing so had them too. Statistical analysis shows that the overall difference between institutions reporting differential treatment of some materials and the presence or absence of access policies, including support for the CLA Statement, was not significant. That is to say, respondent public libraries tended to treat potentially controversial or questionable materials differently in terms of selection, classification, shelving, access or circulation even if they had access policies.

Respondents' explanations indicated that most of the differential treatment of such materials involved selection, classification, physical location, or labelling. The materials affected were usually sexually explicit fiction, sex education books, or books on the occult.

Several respondents commented on the question of differential selection of potentially controversial or questionable materials. Some reported that, if a book was "pornographic" or too controversial, they would not buy it. Others, in contrast, said that no title would be rejected merely because it was likely to offend someone. Several noted that they would select controversial titles if there was a need to balance the collection and if there were favourable reviews or there was sufficient patron demand. Of those admitting to self-censorship during the selection process, the following statements by respondents are typical:

o As a small library with limited funds, we simply do not purchase items of a controversial nature.

o A book will be rejected during selection if it seems overly or needlessly violent or pornographic. The books rejected are those which, according to the judgment of the librarian, could offend the majority of patrons and not a minority. It is therefore uncommon enough that the books are rejected due to this criteria.

o No, but we do not select materials we know to be pornographic.

o In as much as selection is a type of censorship in that we do not order materials that the majority of readers in our community would find objectionable, then we do censor. We feel finances are limited and we should meet the demands of the majority, not the minority. Controversial materials may still be obtained through interloan.

o Selection policy is very conservative. For example, a gay magazine that I wanted purchased was put "on hold." No Nancy Drews, etc., in system.

o Some branches are used by more conservative people than others. We are careful about what we send to some rural areas.

o The only restriction I can recall is no books on religion pertaining to a certain faith, but general religion gladly accepted.

o At the selection stage, when illicit illustrations are found, chiefly on covers of comic books.

o Adult comics occasionally raise some comments, above all if they have drawings that are erotic or tendentious. The only book not acquired, or censured, was the well-known French book *Suicide: Directions*.

o In selection of records, we attempt to avoid music which has a strong sexual message, or material in which the language would not be acceptable to the majority of our patrons (e.g., some of Eddie Murphy's comedy routines).

Several respondents noted that their selection policy did not endorse differential selection of any materials, but added that the reality was not perfect:

o By policy, no; in practice, yes, especially in the children's area, which can state the budget is too small to buy everything and thus they must buy only materials which meet what they believe to be community standards. I suspect that this is the rationale most of us use.

o I don't think that we do discriminate but of course in selecting books I use my own judgement, and that can be a pretty subjective area.

Several respondents noted that reviews were important in the selection of potentially controversial or questionable materials:

o If a reviewer says that a book is likely to be controversial, staff who do selection will certainly discuss the purchase. If it is a favourable review overall, we will probably order one copy so that we know what is being published, what is being reviewed, etc. It keeps us knowledgeable about new materials for children, even those that are controversial.

o Seek reviews from reputable reviewing sources prior to purchase.

o We make sure we have several reviews to back our selections.

o Religious materials — restricted to favourably reviewed materials or to materials carefully examined. Medical — the library system adds only materials which have favourable reviews or which have been carefully examined.

o Selection — attempt to purchase recommended, basic titles. Wait and see if specific titles or subjects requested, e.g., gay rights/erotica/cults.

Others noted that patron demand was a factor in acquiring certain materials:

o If a book is questionable (for example sexually explicit) and is on a best-seller list, we wait until two patrons ask for the book before purchasing.

o If I judge that a book could bring about controversy, I avoid buying it unless a patron suggests buying it.

Still other respondents stressed the goal of collection balance in the process of selecting materials on controversial topics:

o If issues are seen as controversial, the library will take particular care to ensure that the collection represents all points of view (e.g., abortion).

o At the selection stage we think about these materials more carefully, spend more time weighing their pros and cons, but no title will be turned down just because it is likely to offend someone.

o Controversial titles are purchased only if the subject matter demands it — if the collection needs a title on that subject and if the book itself is of high quality — writing, coverage of subject, in good taste, etc.

o Only in the sense that we try to select controversial materials which reflect both sides of the argument. More obscure issues or perhaps questionable materials are simply not purchased, but we would make no restrictions on obtaining such information for a patron via interlibrary loan.

A second way in which some respondents treated certain materials differently was in classification and shelving. Some said that they occasionally used classification as a means of restricting physical access to certain categories of materials. One example mentioned was sex education books written for children but classified and shelved as adult books. Explicit comics were also treated this way on occasion. In other public libraries, certain materials were classified in the conventional manner but kept, variously, on a separate shelf, behind the reference or circulation desk, in an office, or in a store room and had to be asked for. These items were available upon request to adults or to children with parental permission.

Items typically targeted for differential shelving were sex education manuals, other sexually explicit materials, those dealing with cults or horror, and some health and diet books. In several libraries, new books bypassed the "New Book" shelf if they were potentially controversial.

Respondent comments reveal how public library staff used classification and shelf location as means of controlling and restricting access to certain materials or titles:

o If a particular picture book is very controversial, it may be catalogued in a particular place, e.g., *Slugs*. We had so many complaints about *Slugs* when it was classified in the picturebook collection that I had it reclassified to poetry; but it still remained in the children's area of the library.

o We do have objections to certain books being recommended for junior high, for example, which when we catalogue them we feel are inappropriate — and end up including them with adult fiction. Would like to see more careful screening/selection of these age recommendations, e.g., Norma Klein's *Love is One of the Choices*, Brancato's *Facing Up*.

o We did have a written complaint about *Then Again, Maybe I Won't* by Judy Blume a number of years ago. At a senior staff level, it was decided to recatalogue from juvenile to adult.

o *Very* rarely, the library has classed and shelved in the adult section a title that ordinarily would be classed as "young adult" due to frank treatment of controversial subjects. However, no attempt is made to limit its use by the age of the patron.

o All material dealing with sexual education is classified as adult material.

o Books for children and teens about sex and growing up are put in adult non-fiction. The parents can take the books out for their children. Teens are also allowed to sign them out. For example: *Knowing about Sex* by Dr. James Hemming, *Growing and Changing* by Kathy McCoy.

o As quite young teens (or even younger children) often read books from our young adult section, I try to be careful about what is there. If I have doubts about a book, I usually put it in the adult section.

o In the children's collection, some titles are placed on "Parent's shelf"; otherwise everything is shelved.

o Comics are examined carefully as much as possible and placed in adult section if the theme is found too violent or characters pornographic. This category of books causes some problems with the users, but here the problem of censorship is not serious.

o I am somewhat careful in which area I place fiction material, particularly in the Young Adult and Juvenile sections.

o Special treatment, i.e., placing material in special collections, has occurred with books dealing with Canadian history that portray Native Indians in a very negative light. This has occurred with *Little Black Sambo* and with a diet book that was deemed dangerous by medical authorities. The books can still be accessed by patrons through the main catalogue and can be borrowed, but a special request is required to bring them to the branch.

o Materials for children which are no longer acceptable to the community or are of historic interest only are housed in the Children's Historical Collection shelved in the children's coordinator's office. They are available for borrowing, and location is identified in the catalogue. This is the only instance of which I am aware.

One respondent forwarded a copy of an information sheet, "Notice to all parents and adults":

"If you or your children happen to find a book that is classified in the children's department, but that you find morally or sexually offensive, please signal it out to me so that we can make the necessary changes. I am sorry if this is happening, but I do not have the time to read every book that comes in here. They say you can't judge a book by its cover and I guess this is quite true as in one particular case that was pointed out to me. Thank you."

Some respondents noted that access to certain materials was controlled by means of shelving location. Often the concern was access by children.

o Books on drawing, adult, not suggested for children; supplied others for children's shelf; placed adult ones higher up on shelf.

o We have a high shelf for sexual or horror type books.

o Juvenile Parent section is housed on a top shelf.

o Occasionally we will bypass the prominently displayed new books shelf and place a book immediately on the regular shelves so that the book is available for those who need it, but it escapes the attention of the casual browsers, who may object to it, e.g., *Safe Sex* by John Prestin.

In some cases, respondents went further in their efforts to control the use of public library materials. They reported that selected items were shelved in non-public areas to prevent unauthorized access by patrons (usually children and young adults). While it goes without saying that such items were only available to those patrons willing to disclose their personal interests to staff members, respondents did not appear to view this practice as a barrier to "legitimate" use of materials.

o Only children's books dealing with sex education/abuse are housed in office but are freely accessible if asked for.

o Some librarians keep the racier titles behind the desk.

o The librarian before me bought erotic books which she would keep hidden in the library.

o Twenty-four titles are shelved in a non-public area and must be requested. They contain visual representations of sexual activity.

o Only one book — *The Joy of Sex* by Alex Comfort — is behind the desk and has to be asked for. (Because we were tired of the giggling Jr. boys.)

o One volume only, *The Illustrated Joy of Sex*, has written on top of catalogue cards, "Please ask for at counter" due to easy access by children.

o Just one book, *The Joy of Sex*, has "store room" on the catalogue cards. This is so children won't have access to it.

o *Joy of Sex*, due to continual theft, is kept at the Reference desk and patrons must leave their card to use it.

o *Joy of Sex* and *More Joy of Sex* are shelved behind circulation desk; card catalogue directs borrower to this location and tells them to "Ask staff."

o We use dummy books on shelf that have a note which directs patrons over 16 years to ask librarian for access to restricted book section (sex manuals, etc., that have very intimate detail and pictures).

o Adult books are in a locked shelf.

o Books describing adult sexuality are in a place different from other publications and are accessible only upon request.

o Two titles are shelved in librarian supervisor's office with a note directing browsers to ask for them. One is a nutrition book for pregnant women (Adelle Davis, *Let's Have Healthy Children*), the other *Why Men Rape: Interviews with Convicted Rapists*, edited by Sylvia Levine and Joseph Koenig. Placement is to ensure a librarian talks to the potential borrower about seeing a doctor before starting the diet or about the explicit descriptions and attitudes of the people interviewed. Both were treated in this manner after complaints about content of titles within our materials selection policy.

o "Denial of the Holocaust" type of material is kept in the closed stacks — but catalogued in the public catalogue and marked "stacks."

o Books such as O'Huigin's *I'll Belly Your Button in a Minute*, Macklem's *Jacques the Woodcutter*, and Musgrave's *Hag Head* have been placed on restricted shelves in HQ but may be circulated on request. Often, books published in a picture book format can be quite offensive in the wrong hands. We have found that American reviewers often find acceptable books which are too violent for our young readers. Normally the selection policy precludes purchase of questionable material on the basis of quality, reliability/accuracy of content, and suitability for the intended audience.

o Material such as dictionaries of slang are kept behind the desk because of the coarseness of many of the phrases.

o Only one book, Will McBride's *Show Me*, is restricted to two copies in the system. One copy is in stacks at central, which circulates to anyone who wishes to borrow it. The other copy is in the Juvenile coordinator's office, for use in lecture talks on censorship. All our other sex education books are in open stacks.

o Some materials (Blume's *Forever*) are kept off the shelves and given out only if the person asking for it is mature enough to handle the information.

o Some health and books dealing with cults are shelved in back room.

o No general restriction, although on occasion we remove problem material to our reference office, e.g., about 10 years ago a police officer informed us that a book on locksmithing was a "how to" primer for a burglar.

o Since children have access to adult books for school projects, erotic or potentially erotic material is shelved separately in an adults-only area.
a) Nude photography books, techniques and how-to
b) *Joy of Sex* and *More Joy of Sex*
c) *Men in Love*, Nancy Friday
d) *Tales from the Smokehouse*, Herbert T. Schwartz
e) *Man and Woman: Encyclopedia of Adult Relationships,* volumes 1-6
f) *Woman Alive* series, *The Sexual Side of Love*
g) *Woman's Experience of Sex* by Sheila Kitzinger.

o We get a magazine from Russia which we don't put out and also magazines from various religious organizations which we don't put out, mainly because we don't get all of them.

o A Communist newspaper was kept in cupboard, now on shelf.

One respondent noted the political difficulties associated with access to materials housed in a joint facility:

o One of our branches shares facilities with an elementary school. We find we sometimes have to house explicitly sexual material off shelf for awhile if visiting classes become "inappropriately" (the word is the school's, not ours) interested in it. We have never really resolved this problem since our staff is not present during class visits, the branch site is important to the community, and we are willing to live with a less-than-perfect situation in order to offer library service to the public there. One of the problems of shared facilities — to date we feel the advantages outweigh the disadvantages, although we are uncomfortable with this issue.

In several instances, respondents noted that access restrictions were imposed in order to prevent theft or defacement of materials:

o When we have to replace a title umpteen times because it has been stolen, we shelve the replacements beside the circulation desk, under the eyes of staff but accessible to users. The designation "Ask at Desk" is added to the call number. The collection is a strange mix of auto repair manuals, sex manuals if well illustrated, a certain local history and its separately published index, pharmacopoeia, GED study programs, and *Mr. Chips 101 Plans* (a favourite woodworking title).

o *Guns, Knives Illustrated, Digest,* etc., have been placed behind the counter because pages are often removed from them. Patrons can borrow them but they have to ask.

o A very few titles, among them *The Joy of Sex*, are retained in basement storage and must be requested to circulate. The book is a high-risk theft item and will be returned to the open stacks after we have installed a security system.

o Certain materials are stored in reference office due to theft. Patrons must ask staff.

o I think some staff may restrict access in spite of my warning. I cannot be 22 places at once. We have some branches that keep *Joy* and *More Joy* under the counter, more to prevent theft and mutilation.

A few respondents dealt with controversial materials by labelling them for the benefit of patrons. This differential treatment was explained as follows:

o Notations are on library cards received with talking books, e.g., "explicit descriptions of sex." Copies of these are being placed on containers themselves for staff/patron information when selecting for themselves or others.

o This is a small town — we occasionally put a small label in a book "Portions of this book may be offensive to some readers." We may suggest that certain books chosen by a patron may not be what they would enjoy! Rare.

o We had public concerns about some books, but no real complaints. Some patrons took offence at "dirty language" in books and mentioned it. We put a note into two paperbacks warning "language may be offensive."

o Potentially controversial 16mm films have a message on the can that prior screening is important so as to ensure best use of film.

o All materials describing violence, horror, esotericism, science occults [?], sects with erotic characteristics are indicated with a yellow binding for loan.

o Certain pocketbooks such as *Valley of the Horses* (Auel) and *Wifey* (Blume) are marked "Adult."

o A couple of children's books on homosexuality had Young Adult stickers applied.

These respondent comments indicate a fascinating variety of attitudes and practices regarding access to materials housed in the nation's public libraries. While most public libraries that participated in the study selected and shelved all materials on a similar basis, among the minority which did not, differential shelving practices ranged from the purely pragmatic (to prevent theft) to the cautious ("We wait and see if specific titles or subjects are requested, for example, gay rights/erotica/cults") and the openly censorious ("We attempt to avoid music which has a strong sexual message, or material in which the language would not be acceptable to the majority of our patrons").

Summary

Overall, institutions that treated potentially controversial or questionable materials differently in way one or another shared the same demographic features as those that did not treat controversial materials differently. Differential treatment by certain institutions did not depend on type of governance (system or single unit), linguistic grouping (French or English), size of municipal population, number of registered borrowers, number of circulations, or the presence of access policies (including support for the CLA Statement on Intellectual Freedom). However, institutions with differential treatment did tend to restrict access based on age. Most differential treatment involved selection, classification, physical location, or labelling. Judging by respondent comments in the study, I concluded that most staff who engaged in these practices viewed them as responsible and positive actions designed to honour majority standards and norms.

D. Collection Vulnerability

In order to try to predict how vulnerable a public library might be to complaints about its collection, I devised a "controversial materials checklist" for the study. This checklist consisted of 30 titles that had been subjected to censorship pressure during the previous four or five years as reported in three recent public library censorship studies in Canada (see Chapter 5 under "Controversial Materials Checklist" for more information about how the list was created). The thinking behind the checklist was that the more checklist titles in a collection, the more likely the collection would include still other potentially controversial titles, and hence the greater the risk of future conflict with somebody in the community.

For example, in an institution with a low rate of ownership of checklist materials, one would expect fewer calls for censorship because the collection contained fewer controversial materials — was possibly more conservative — than those collections containing a high proportion of the checklist materials. The checklist would indicate overall collection vulnerability on the assumption that past trouble with collection holdings in public libraries somewhere in Canada would be the best predictor of future trouble in a given institution. Hence, I hoped that the checklist would serve as a barometer of the likelihood of a public library's being subjected to censorship pressure. The hypothesis of a link between checklist materials and experiences of censorship is discussed in Chapter 8.

Table 6 summarizes respondent holdings of the checklist titles by type of governance unit.

Table 6. Controversial Materials Checklist, by Governance, 1987

Titles Owned	Governance Structure					
	Single		System		Combined	
	No.	%	No.	%	No.	%
0	10	2	0	0	10	2
1-5	79	18	1	1	80	14
6-10	160	37	7	6	167	30
11-15	113	26	17	15	130	24
16-20	54	12	26	22	80	14
21-25	18	4	41	35	59	11
26-30	5	1	25	21	30	5
National	439	100	117	100	556	100

Overall, half of the public libraries in the study owned 11 or more titles on the checklist. Only 10 out of 556 respondents owned none of the titles at all. At the other extreme, 30 respondents owned 26 or more. Mean ownership was 12.5 titles per respondent, or 42 per cent of the checklist. In other words, a patron would have about a 40 per cent chance of obtaining a checklist title through any Canadian public library in the study. It should be kept in mind, however, that shelf availability for high-demand materials, that is, the probability that an item is immediately available in the library, is always considerably lower than the rate of ownership.

The study shows that multi-branch systems differed substantially from single-unit libraries in their ownership of titles. More than half of the systems owned 21 or more titles, while only 5 per cent of single libraries did. In fact, the typical system owned on average twice as many checklist titles as did the typical single library, 20 titles compared to 10.

The significant difference in ownership rates between systems and single libraries was also reflected in institutional characteristics. While the typical public library that owned 12.5 titles served a municipality with 35,000 residents, institutions owning 10 or fewer checklist titles served on average 7,000 residents. At the other extreme, those owning between 26 and 30 titles served municipal populations averaging almost 200,000.

Overall, then, respondent public libraries serving larger municipal populations tended to own more checklist titles than did those serving smaller populations. Statistical analysis shows that this correlation was significant; however, it explained only 23 per cent of the variation between population and checklist ownership. The correlations between registered borrowers and ownership and between library circulation and ownership were similar in magnitude.

French- and English-language public libraries also differed in ownership rates. On average, French-language respondents owned fewer checklist titles than their English-language counterparts, 8 versus 13, respectively, a difference found to be statistically significant. This difference is hardly surprising, given the English-language bias of the checklist. What is surprising is that French-language respondents owned as many of the titles as they did.

Ownership of checklist titles was also related to institutional access policies (selection policy, policy for handling objections, donations policy, an objections form, and support of the CLA Statement on Intellectual Freedom, as discussed at the beginning of this chapter). The study shows that respondents with these access policies tended to own more checklist titles than did those with none of the access policies. On average, respondent libraries with all five access policies had 17 titles each, and those reporting some access policies had 12 each. In contrast, those with no access policies had only 9 titles each. Statistical analysis shows that checklist ownership was significantly influenced by access policy coverage.

Respondent public libraries reporting more direct challenges tended to own more checklist titles than those reporting fewer challenges. Statistical analysis shows that this correlation was significant; however, it explained only 18 per cent of the variation between number of challenges and ownership of checklist titles. Similarly, ownership of controversial titles was associated with acquisition pressure. On average, respondents reporting pressure from the community to acquire items had 17 titles each while those not reporting this type of pressure had 11 titles each. Statistical analysis shows that ownership of checklist titles was significantly related to acquisition pressure. For more on acquisition pressure, turn to Chapter 10.

At the same time, however, the study found that checklist ownership was the same for both institutions with age-related access restrictions and those without restrictions. Similarly, differential treatment of controversial or questionable materials — whether in selection, classification, shelving, access or circulation — did not significantly influence checklist ownership rates. Average ownership was the same for institutions practising differential treatment as for those without this practice. Statistical analysis shows no significant difference between ownership of checklist titles and age restrictions or between ownership of checklist titles and differential treatment.

It is likely that several of these determinants are related to each other. This possibility makes it advisable to analyze the relationship of each one in the presence of all others that were statistically significant in bivariate comparisons. This procedure isolates those factors that account for the greatest influence on the ownership of checklist titles. Analysis of these several factors together reveals that public library selection of titles on the checklist was more than just a function of the size of the municipality being served. Other factors carried additional weight in the process of collection development and management.

The most important conditions relating to ownership of checklist titles were the following: number of direct challenges to institutional material, dominant language spoken in the community (English or French), possession of a selection policy, exposure to acquisition pressure, governance (multi-branch system or single unit), and municipal population (library circulation is an almost equally strong factor in place of population). Statistical analysis shows that these institutional characteristics were significant predictors of ownership of checklist titles.

So, for example, other things being equal, a French-language system that experienced three direct challenges between 1985 and 1987, had a written selection policy, was pressured to acquire or accept material for the collection, and served 100,000 residents would be predicted to own 17 checklist titles. An English-language single library that experienced no direct challenges, did not have a written selection policy, reported no acquisition pressure, and served 10,000 residents would be predicted to own 9 titles.

High ownership of checklist titles was associated with the following institutional conditions: a high number of direct challenges, service to an English-language community, possession of a selection policy, exposure to acquisition pressure, presence of a multi-branch system, and service to a large municipal population (or an institution with high circulation).

Other things being equal, the more direct challenges an institution had, the more checklist titles it owned: for every challenge experienced, an additional 0.2 checklist title was owned. English-language respondents owned more titles than their French-language counterparts, 13 titles compared to 8. Institutions with a selection policy had 15 titles each compared to 9 each among those without a selection policy. Institutions reporting acquisition pressure owned 17 titles compared to 11 among those not reporting such pressure. The typical multi-branch system owned twice as many checklist titles as the typical single library did, 20 titles compared to 10. Institutions serving more residents owned more checklist titles: for every 10,000 people, an additional 0.1 checklist title was owned. Institutions circulating more items also owned more checklist titles: for every 100,000 transactions, an additional 0.1 checklist title was owned.

When the language factor is excluded, the other determinants — direct challenges, selection policy, acquisition pressure, governance, and population — are still significant predictors among English-language institutions; however, this is not the case among their French-language counterparts.

These determinants together accounted for 52 per cent of significant influences on the selection of checklist titles for respondent collections. Other factors not identified and examined in the present study accounted for the remaining influence on checklist title selection.

Analysis of Holdings of Titles on the Controversial Materials Checklist

Analysis of ownership of checklist titles shows that collections were strongest in the adult fiction category, in which 7 out of 10 titles were owned by half or more of the respondents. At the same time, collections were weakest in juvenile non-fiction, in which none of the 4 titles was owned by half or more of the respondents.

Table 7 shows checklist ownership according to the five common categories of classification that were used in the survey questionnaire.

Table 7. Controversial Materials Checklist, by Category, 1987

Category	Total Titles	Titles Owned by Half or More Respondents	
		No.	%
Adult fiction	10	7	70
Adult non-fiction	4	1	25
Juvenile fiction	7	2*	29
Juvenile non-fiction	4	0	0
Picture books and easy reading	5	2	40
Total	30	12	40

*includes one title owned by 47% of respondents

Examination of title ownership indicates that Canadian public libraries collectively owned all 30 books on the controversial materials checklist.

Table 8 shows each checklist title by the percentage of public libraries that said they owned it.

Table 8. Controversial Materials Checklist, by Public Library Ownership, 1987

Author(s)	Title	Owning Libraries	
		No.	%
Auel, J.	Valley of the Horses	511	92
Andrews, V.C.	Flowers in the Attic	502	90
Uris, L.	The Haj	456	82
Blume, J.	Then Again, Maybe I Won't	450	81
Robbins, H.	Goodbye Janette	381	69
Blume, J.	Forever	373	67
	Wifey	339	61
Major, K.	Hold Fast	325	59
Jong, E.	Fear of Flying	326	59
Dr. Seuss	Butter Battle Book	298	54
Baigent, M.	Holy Blood Holy Grail	290	52
Sendak, M.	In the Night Kitchen	280	50
Klein, N.	It's Okay If You Don't Love Me	259	47
Suddon, A.	Cinderella	203	37
Kosinski, J.	The Painted Bird	200	36
McCoy, K. & C. Wibbelsman	The Teenage Body Book	197	35
Doerkson, M.	Jazzy	189	34
Bellairs, J.	Figure in the Shadows	182	33
Lovelace, L. & M. McGrady	Ordeal	155	28
Dayee, F.	Private Zone	131	24
Wildsmith, B.	The True Cross	126	23
Cohen, B.	I Am Joseph	124	22
Ferry, J. & D. Inwood	The Olson Murders	120	22

continued

Table 8. Controversial Materials Checklist,
by Public Library Ownership, 1987 (cont.)

Author(s)	Title	Owning Libraries No.	%
Johnson, C. & E. Johnson	Love and Sex and Growing Up	119	21
Neufeld, J.	Freddy's Book	90	16
Rockwell, T.	The Thief	88	16
Dickinson, P.	City of Gold and Other Stories from the Old Testament	82	15
Maestro, Betsy	Lambs for Dinner	64	12
Lareuse, J.	Devils in the Castle	44	8
Smedley, A.	Chinese Destiny	37	7

As the table shows, not only were all of the checklist titles available somewhere in Canada, but four were owned by more than 80 per cent of respondent public libraries: *Flowers in the Attic* by V.C. Andrews, *Valley of the Horses* by Jean Auel, *The Haj* by Leon Uris, and *Then Again, Maybe I Won't* by Judy Blume. At the same time, six titles were owned by fewer than 20 per cent of the respondents.

Checklist ownership differed widely across political jurisdictions. Respondents collectively owned all 30 titles in British Columbia, Alberta, Saskatchewan, Ontario and Quebec, while 1 to 7 titles were missing from collections in the other seven Canadian jurisdictions. It is not surprising that the collections of respondents in Yukon, the Northwest Territories, and Prince Edward Island were missing more checklist titles than anywhere else in Canada, since those jurisdictions contain the smallest population bases.

Table 9 shows titles missing by political jurisdiction.

Table 9. Controversial Materials Checklist,
by Titles Missing from Jurisdictions, 1987

Province/Territory	Items	Titles Missing
Manitoba	1	Chinese Destiny
New Brunswick	3	Chinese Destiny, Devils in the Castle, Lambs for Dinner
Nova Scotia	1	Freddy's Book
Prince Edward Island	6	Chinese Destiny, Devils in the Castle, Freddy's Book, Jazzy, Lambs for Dinner, The True Cross
Newfoundland	4	Chinese Destiny, City of Gold, Lambs for Dinner, Private Zone
Yukon	7	Chinese Destiny, Devils in the Castle, Freddy's Book, Goodbye Janette, Lambs for Dinner, The Olson Murders, The Teenage Body Book
Northwest Territories	6	Chinese Destiny, Devils in the Castle, Freddy's Book, Jazzy, Lambs for Dinner, The Thief

This table shows that *Chinese Destiny* was missing from respondent collections in six jurisdictions, *Lambs for Dinner* was missing in five, *Devils in the Castle* and *Freddy's Book* in four, *Jazzy* in two, and missing in one jurisdiction each were *City of Gold*, *Goodbye Janette*, *The Olson Murders*, *Private Zone*, *The Teenage Body Book*, *The Thief*, and *The True Cross*. The other 18 checklist titles were found in all 12 Canadian jurisdictions.

There are some limitations about the checklist concept that should be kept in mind in drawing conclusions from the analysis of findings reported above. In the first place, rates of ownership may be somewhat understated because many public libraries do not catalogue their paperback holdings. Secondly, other potentially controversial titles not included on the checklist may be owned by a public library, but such information is unavailable on a systematic basis. Thirdly, rates of ownership may not be a valid representation of controversial holdings among French-language public libraries for two reasons: a) checklist titles were English-language publications that had drawn previous criticism in predominantly English-language public libraries; and b) checklist titles were not all available in French translation (only 11 French translations among the 30 titles could be identified).

A few respondents commented on the shortcomings of the checklist for French-language collections:

> o Our library develops its collection according to the following percentages: 70-75 per cent French, 25-30 per cent English. Many books dealing with controversial subjects (*Annie on My Mind* by Nancy Garden) are unfortunately not translated into French. However, I have taken note of certain books in your list with the intention of buying them.

> o It would be preferable to make a distinctive list of titles for francophone libraries. It appears that the limited number of French titles makes it difficult to evaluate the degree of censorship in a library.

Other respondents offered comments on the overall validity of the checklist concept. One wrote as follows:

> Since you indicated [in the covering letter with the questionnaire] that the checklist is something of an experimental idea, I wanted to make a few comments with regard to our system. Perhaps other libraries will also find this list somewhat of a problem. Several of the titles on the list date from the 1960s and early 1970s. Some of these, although controversial, were never more than ephemeral titles to begin with.
>
> In the course of 20 years these titles wear out or otherwise disappear from the collections. Our Collection Development plans would not advise replacement. One example is *Freddy's Book*. All our libraries had this at one time. However, there were serious literary flaws in this book that

had nothing to do with its subject matter and therefore this title would probably not be replaced. The same is true of Harold Robbins. Since this author produces books almost yearly, and patrons want what is new, we would tend to buy multiple copies of the new titles but not replace older ones.

Another aspect which might skew the results is that many of the older titles are replaced in paperback format, e.g., Jong's *Fear of Flying*. Since paperbacks are not available in our online database, some of our libraries may not be able to establish ownership of some titles. I would hope that this list would not be used to score any library's Collection Development practices.

I applaud your attempt to produce a list. Checking it will remind our staff of some titles which perhaps should be replaced.

Other respondents wrote:

o Some of these older titles were in the branch at one time. When withdrawn as past usefulness, they were not replaced.

o As you may know, we have an extensive interlibrary loan network. Though many of these books aren't in our collection, that doesn't mean patrons don't have easy access to them through the different branches and regions by a simple order form.

o While we do not have quite a few of the books listed, we do have other books by the same authors. We are a very small library with limited funds and no room to expand.

o I'm embarrassed to see how many of your titles we don't have but that is in a collection of 8,000 and we do have free access through our county cooperative and ILLO, which we depend on for many of the popular non-fiction.

o Books not owned is due more to money problems than to censorship.

o Although we don't seem to have too many of the titles listed it's certainly not because I've been "afraid" to buy them! Being a small rural library, we have to consider each purchase very carefully in order to "get the most for our money."

o I am fascinated by this survey. The books on the checklist are a dog's dinner of titles. I am at a loss to explain why many of them have (I assume) been the focus of censorship attempts. Although we are missing a few of these in our collection, it is only omission. We are going to order the few we do not own. I cannot imagine why anyone would object to Suddon's *Cinderella*, Wildsmith's story of St. Helena, or *City of Gold* — EXCEPT that I assume you have some rabid fundamentalists on your hands. We all know about fanaticism and fear of knowledge, from Jehovah's Witnesses to Tories.

Anyway, I think the major thing missing in all these reference surveys is a clear comparison of number of incidents and social class of the library's clientele. As you can see, we never have any real complaints here (except yuppie ones about the environment) because the city of ... is the clearest class-divided city in Canada. There is a long-standing perception in this city that the library is only for educated people who live in clearly identified cultural barrios. The lower/working classes seldom cross the bisecting thoroughfare in the city for any cultural event, and they are not made welcome, of course, but politely scorned by the proprietary intelligentsia. The organized fundamentalists take on the school board over sex education and homosexuality (but they always lose, after time to rant and rave) and they ignore the public library, because it is clearly not their preserve.

Therefore — can you test for social class? I assume that many of these books [on the checklist] are perceived by lower class fundamentalists as "dangerous" politically or socially or religiously (*Holy Blood, Figure in the Shadows, The Haj*?). I assume *Lambs for Dinner* is a yuppie target (too funny — violence is a no-no, of course human beings don't hit anyone or tear the clothes off soldiers and beat them to death.... After all, the Irish are civilized, not like the Pakis...). What is the objection to the wimpy Dr. Seuss? Perhaps in the areas in which these books have been the target of censorship, somehow working class zealots have dared to enter the middle classes' private club....

I would like to see the results of your survey, and I would also like to see any articles or information on WHY these books have been attacked. There are so many much more radical books out there, why pick on these wimpy ones? [emphasis in original]

o I found it interesting that a number of books that I expected to find in our library are not in our catalogue. I suspect that we have probably had copies which are now missing and I am looking into this.

Summary

Overall, half of the public libraries in the study owned 11 or more of the 30 titles on the controversial materials checklist. Collectively, all 30 titles were owned somewhere in Canada. Analysis of checklist categories shows that collections were strongest in adult fiction and weakest in juvenile non-fiction.

To the extent that the titles on the survey checklist represent controversial library holdings, it can be inferred that controversial material tends to be acquired by English-language multi-branch systems that serve a large number of people, have a written selection policy, and experience both direct challenges and acquisition pressure.

Nonetheless, these determinants accounted for only half of the influences on the decision to acquire checklist titles; other factors not examined in the present study accounted for the rest. The value of the controversial materials checklist as a predictor of censorial pressure is explored in the chapter on direct challenges to public library collections.

E. Bill C-54, An Act to Amend the Criminal Code and Other Acts in Consequence Thereof (1987)

Both the controversial nature and the timing of this federal legislative initiative made it opportune to query respondents about it. On May 4, 1987, about nine months before this survey was undertaken, the federal government introduced new censorship legislation, Bill C-54, to replace the obscenity provisions in the Criminal Code.

The proposed legislation, promoted by the Minister of Justice of the day as an "urgent response" to child sexual abuse, child pornography, sexual violence against women, and other "hard-core pornography," drew immediate fire from virtually the entire cultural community across the country.

While critics deplored sexual abuse and sexual violence, they nevertheless charged that Bill C-54 would criminalize virtually any public reference to human sexuality — in direct opposition to the 1985 recommendations of the Fraser Committee, the Special Committee on Pornography and Prostitution that had been established by the federal government two years earlier.

Librarians, particularly public librarians, were among the leaders of the opposition. The Canadian Library Association criticized the bill in a letter to the Minister of Justice on June 29, 1987 (Canadian Library Association 1987). And over the next few months, letters and submissions were sent to him and to other federal politicians by a wide variety of library associations at the provincial, regional, and national levels, as well as by public library boards and public library trustee associations.

There were also letters, press releases, and public protests by associations representing arts and artists, art galleries and museums, art gallery and museum associations, associations representing authors and writers and poets, book and periodical publisher and marketing associations, bookseller associations, civil rights associations, university teacher associations, women's issues organizations, anti-censorship coalitions, and even governmental agencies such as the Canada Council and the Ontario Arts Council. The Intellectual Freedom Committee of the American Library Association expressed concern about the impact of the proposed legislation on libraries in Canada (Schmidt 1987).

By December 1987, Bill C-54 had quietly disappeared from the government's agenda, and the public library community, along with the rest of Canada, waited uncertainly for what would happen next. As of this date, the answer is nothing — yet.

In order to gauge the Canadian public library community's overall response to Bill C-54, I asked respondents to indicate whether their board or municipal council (in the case of Quebec) had written to the Minister of Justice about the proposed legislation or had otherwise taken a public stand on it and, if so, to note the nature of the board or council position.

The study reveals that the public library community was deeply concerned about the proposed legislation. Overall, 238 respondent public libraries, or 51 per cent, reported that their boards and councils had written to the Minister or otherwise taken a public stand on Bill C-54 by spring 1988.

Among these 238 respondents, there was near unanimity of opinion. Fully 92 per cent — 220 institutions — called for withdrawal of the bill or in a few cases for withdrawal and amendment. Only 8 per cent — 18 respondents — supported the legislation without qualification.

Those opposed to the bill served municipal populations totalling 12.3 million Canadian residents, thus accounting for 72 per cent of all Canadian residents represented in the study. In contrast, those supporting it represented only 300,000 people. Boards and councils calling for withdrawal of the bill tended to serve much larger municipalities than did its supporters, 54,000 residents compared to 17,000 residents, respectively.

The boards and councils of multi-branch systems were more likely to have taken a stand one way or another than those of single libraries, 72 per cent compared to 44 per cent. This difference was statistically significant. However, governance structure was not a factor in the proportion of systems and single libraries that called for withdrawal of the bill, 97 per cent of systems and 89 per cent of single libraries.

Although there was no difference in levels of opposition to the bill between systems and single libraries, there was a difference in municipal population served by respondents. These patterns are detailed in Table 10.

The proportion of French-language boards and councils opposed to the bill was somewhat similar to the proportion of their English-language counterparts. However, since only three French-language institutions had taken a stand one way or another on the bill, statistical comparisons are inconclusive.

Table 10. Official Reaction to Bill C-54,
by Public Libraries and Population, 1987

Official Position	Public Libraries No.	%	Population No. (000s)	%	Mean (000s)
Yes	239	45	12,273	72	51
No	233	44	3,371	20	15
Don't know	60	11	1,483	8	26
National	532	100	17,127	100	
Support	18	8	309	3	17
Withdraw	220	92	11,964	97	54
Total	238*	100	12,273	100	

*1 respondent who said the board had taken an official position did not indicate the nature of that position

Among the few respondents who supported the bill (regardless of language), written comments nonetheless indicated qualified support:

o The board supports the bill insofar as it gives some protection for children.

o Support the intent of the bill, but with the request that "public libraries" should not be included or judged on the same level as the corner store where offensive material is displayed for all to see.

o Our council supports Bill C-54 because it's completely normal to remove from our shelves books or magazines with pornographic characteristics or other since we should protect our users from this kind of reading material. If they wish, the bookstores have them.

However, the written comments of the majority of respondents indicated that many believed the definition of pornography in the bill, while superficially precise, was too broad. For others, the bill's most alarming aspect was the "reverse onus" clause, which shifted the burden of proof from the prosecutor, who normally must prove that the defendant is guilty, to the defendant, who must prove that he or she is innocent. Many asserted that this clause violated natural justice. Some respondents stated that public libraries could not effectively perform their functions while they lived under the constant threat of criminal charges. Some suggested that libraries should be exempt from the legislation.

Along with their completed questionnaires, several respondents sent copies of letters written by their public library boards to the Minister of Justice, other members of Parliament, and so on. In some cases, they also included copies of the replies that had been received. One public library board's letter to the Minister of Justice declared:

o We have been serving our community for over 100 years, and we have a great deal of experience in dealing with public response to our materials. Only a small number of complaints are received, and we, as most other libraries, have a formal review process in place. Under Bill C-54, an individual would be able to cause a criminal charge to be laid against the Library Board, its librarians, clerks, and pages (many of whom are teenagers). Bill C-54 takes the normal complaint process out of the community and political arena and into the arena of criminal law. Library workers become censors and yet may still be liable to prosecution.

Another board expressed similar views in a letter to its member of Parliament:

o The ... Public Library Board wishes to register our strong opposition to the proposed pornography legislation, Bill C-54, as it will mean radical reorganization of library services and operations in our library, and indeed in libraries across Canada. The subsequent literature separations into over and under age 18 categories; the screening processes; the subsequent staff classifications and the loss of society's freedom are particularly abhorrent to us.

One public library board followed up its earlier letter to the Minister of Justice with another submission, noting that his response had not allayed their fears.

o You note ... "that these proposals are directly aimed at hard core pornography." We do not for a moment question this intention. However, I and many others have studied the bill and come to the conclusion that this intention is not served by Bill C-54. Library material may contain descriptions of sexual activities and may also contain depictions of same. Whether such depictions are erotic or pornographic or neither, are highly debatable and subjective issues. Librarians have selected from their collections clearly innocent material that could fall within the definition of pornography in the Bill. Regardless of your good intentions, Bill C-54 if enacted will restrict artistic creativity in this country and ensnare innocent library material.

[You] go on "to point out that the detection of pornographic material and the determination of the use to which such material is put are placed in the hands of responsible persons who would be aware of these special defences available and cognizant of the guarantee of free expression including artistic expression contained in the *Canadian Charter of Rights and Freedoms*." It should be noted that the Minister of Justice will not be administering this legislation if it is enacted. It will be administered at the local level by municipal police forces. The Minister of Justice is not in a position to guarantee that frivolous or harassing charges will not be made by private individuals or publicity seeking groups.

Finally, your comments on the issue of reverse onus fail to relieve us. You have confirmed that the issue of reverse onus is real. You have confirmed that library boards and librarians may be subject to lengthy, expensive, and emotionally exhausting litigation. And you have confirmed that even after that trauma, library material may still be stigmatized as pornographic, albeit with a defense.

Written comments by questionnaire respondents provided further insights into the reaction by public librarians and public library trustees to Bill C-54. Among them were the following:

o The idea of such a bill has been received with an outburst of laughter. Even if it was passed, it would not be applied to Quebec, I'm sure of this.

o Pornography is disgusting but some parts of the bill would be difficult for small libraries to comply with. Porn should be controlled at the publishing stage.

o The ... Board was split, some feeling the books in question are not pornographic, others concerned about the availability of pornographic material to kids in other places. All were concerned about censorship.

o We are not opposed to a bill on pornography, just this one.

o Reword the bill in a more clear text so that both patrons and staff will be protected.

o Amend the bill so that the rights of the individual are respected.

o I oppose any restriction on the publication of any material in Canada, and endorse the Statement on Intellectual Freedom.

I came from Germany and have some knowledge of Hitler's Germany and East Germany, and what censorship can do to a people. I also oppose minorities, religious or moral, who try to impose their standards and values on the rest of the population. I sincerely hope Canada does not go back to the Middle Ages.

Each individual should have the right to publish, select and read what he chooses, without the government being responsible for their choice. I do not agree with everything that is published, sold or held in public libraries, but I am not arrogant enough to judge what is right for other people.

The library where I work and select books will have the widest choice of materials, opposite opinions and controversial materials.

o We have a major concern about how to operate the library should Bill C-54 be passed. It would appear we would have to restrict access to the Adult Department where most of the "controversial" material is housed and eliminate our YA collection (that is, integrate a collection presently housed separately into the restricted adult collection). It is interesting to note that no one has actually made plans to deal with the situation should, God forbid, this bill be passed.

o We have had little trouble here, so far. This is why we have not had a written policy up until now. We are educating our public to the perils of the bill, however. It is amazing that with all the media hype, people still are totally unaware that Bill C-54 even exists.

o In our small town, most people are totally unaware of Bill C-54. However, our board and I personally oppose the bill as it is presently worded. We have never had a problem with controversial materials, and have never felt any need to restrict or remove material from our shelves. The idea of being forced to do so is repugnant to us.

o The bill at present is too broad and we feel requires greater clarification in respect to libraries. We support the CLA Statement on Intellectual Freedom.

o Bill C-54 fills me with alarm and dismay. While I am familiar with the kind of mentality that supports the bill, I cannot comprehend it. Let us hope that reason prevails and the bill is withdrawn.

o Administration supports withdrawal of Bill C-54, supportive of privacy and intellectual freedom.

o We were going for a major funding increase while opposing the bill, and two members of

Council were upset by our opposition; however, the funding passed anyway.

o I am seriously concerned about the government's attempt to legislate pornography, in literature, in this manner — too much government intervention is a detriment to an open-minded, future-sighted society. I am deeply disturbed that Bill C-54 will cause extreme Victorian regression, especially in literature. As a librarian I believe only in the freedom of choice!

o The staff here is strongly opposed to Bill C-54 in its present form. We are not censors.

One respondent noted that the bill, if passed, would have a chilling effect on the selection process:

o It made me realize that even in a small library, Bill C-54, if passed in its present form, could strongly affect our library. As I select all our books and decide on access, etc., I resolved to be more circumspect than ever in the future.

The strongest reactions were from several respondents who vowed that they would resign from their public library duties if Bill C-54 became law.

o If this bill becomes legislation I will have to seriously reconsider my willingness to continue to work as a librarian. The restrictions would completely change the whole tone of my work here.

o If Bill C-54 becomes law in its present form, I am resigning. This is a small library and the wages are not worth the risks and hassle.

In addition to writing letters to politicians, some respondents reported that they had initiated a variety of public awareness campaigns to publicize their opposition to the bill. Among these were book displays, public speakers, panel discussions, press releases, interviews with the local press, newspaper columns, editorials in professional journals (see Fowlie 1988), "stop censorship" signs, printed postcards for the public to send to the Minister of Justice, and petitions for patrons to sign to be forwarded to the Minister of Justice. There was also the widely reported closing of the Toronto Public Library system on December 10, 1987, in protest over the legislation (Flavelle 1987).

The bill, which was at second reading when the House of Commons adjourned at Christmas 1987, did not appear on the government's agenda in the new year. At a meeting of the Freedom of Expression Committee of the Book and Periodical Council in June 1988, the chair of the committee suggested that widespread opposition to the bill had lowered its priority on the federal agenda, and the Council's executive director noted that "... the position taken by librarians and libraries was pivotal as government does not perceive them to be as radical as other cultural groups" (Book and Periodical Council 1988).

Suggested Further Reading

Alvin Schrader has compiled an information package on Bill C-54 consisting of letters, press releases, public announcements, newspaper reports and articles, and periodical articles in response to the Canadian government's proposed sexual censorship legislation, Bill C-54. He can be contacted at the School of Library and Information Studies, University of Alberta, Edmonton, Alberta T6G 2J4.

American Library Association. Office for Intellectual Freedom. *Intellectual Freedom Manual*. 4th ed. Chicago, Ill.: Office for Intellectual Freedom, American Library Association, 1992.

American Library Association. Subcommittee on Guidelines for Collection Development. *Guide for Written Collection Policy Statements*. 2nd ed. Chicago, Ill.: American Library Association, 1989. (Collection Management and Development Guides, 3).

British Columbia Library Association. Intellectual Freedom Committee. *Intellectual Freedom Handbook*. Burnaby, B.C.: British Columbia Library Association, 1991.

Cassell, Kay Ann and Elizabeth Futas. *Developing Public Library Collections, Policies, and Procedures; A How-To-Do-It Manual for Small and Medium-Sized Public Libraries*. New York: Neal-Schuman, 1991.

Fraser Committee. *Pornography and Prostitution in Canada; Report of the Special Committee on Pornography and Prostitution*. 2 vols. Ottawa: Minister of Supply and Services, 1985.

Lacombe, Dany. *Blue Politics: Pornography and the Law in the Age of Feminism*. Toronto, Ont.: University of Toronto Press, 1994. (See Chapter 6, "Bill C-54: The Impossible Compromise.")

Reichman, Henry. *Censorship and Selection: Issues and Answers for Schools*. Revised ed. Chicago: American Library Association; Arlington: American Association of School Administrators, 1993.

"Toronto Closes 27 Libraries in Porn Bill Protest." *American Libraries* 19 (January 1988): 4.

8 / Collection Challenges

WHILE SOME INSTITUTIONAL POLICIES INhibit or deny patron access to public library collections, community pressures and actions by members of the community are also a major source of barriers to access. These pressures and actions take one of three general forms: direct challenge, covert censorship, and undue pressure to acquire material. All of these are strategies to influence the make-up and balance of a collection on grounds other than those justified by standard professional criteria for selecting library materials.

Most people think of direct challenges as the essence of censorship activity in the public library. A "direct" or "overt" challenge refers to a specific request that is communicated to library staff to remove or restrict access to certain titles, subjects or authors. However, the issues of covert censorship activity and acquisition pressure are also part of the picture of patron access to library materials.

"Covert" or "indirect" censorship activity refers to a more subtle form of censorial behaviour — those incidents of collection loss, theft, defacement, alteration, mutilation or destruction that are, or are suspected to be, attempts to prevent or restrict access by others. "Acquisition pressure" refers to a demand that is perceived to be undue pressure to accept or acquire material for a collection.

Only 26 public libraries in the study reported experiencing all three forms of censorship pressure between 1985 and 1987. But, while these 26 libraries accounted for only 5 per cent of responding institutions, they served municipalities with 19 per cent of the study population, 3.6 million residents. Another 219 respondents, or 39 per cent, reported at least one form of censorship pressure during this period. These libraries served almost 11 million people, over half of the study population. At the other extreme, 315 public libraries, or 56 per cent, reported no pressures at all. These libraries served comparatively smaller municipalities, totalling 4.8 million people, or 25 per cent of the study population.

Table 11 summarizes these various forms of censorship pressure over the three years of the study.

In general terms, the data reveal that those public libraries reporting one or more types of collection challenge during the study period served larger municipal populations. In contrast, those experiencing no collection challenges served comparatively small populations.

What the study discovered about each of these forms of collection challenge among Canadian public libraries is treated in more detail below and in the chapters that follow.

Table 11. Collection Challenges,
by Public Libraries and Population, 1985-87

Type of Challenge	Public Libraries		Population	
	No.	%	No. (000s)	%
Direct challenges	193	35	13,632	70
Covert incidents	57	10	5,387	30
Acquisition pressures	121	22	9,845	54
All three	26	5	3,643	19
One or two	219	39	10,975	56
None	232	41	1,922	10
Don't know, no response	83	15	2,886	15
National	560	100	19,426	100

A. Overview of Direct Challenges

Respondents were asked in the survey questionnaire to indicate whether or not they had received direct challenges to their collections between 1985 and 1987, that is, requests to remove materials or otherwise restrict access to materials. If so, they were also asked to provide as much detail as possible about each occurrence. The rich snapshot of information that this study has collected about direct challenges is presented in four sections: a) overview, b) profile, c) outcomes, and d) effects.

1. Analysis of Challenge Rates

Altogether, 367 respondent public libraries, or 65 per cent, reported no direct challenges between 1985 and 1987. At the same time, 193 institutions, or 35 per cent, received one or more requests to remove or restrict materials during these three years. The annual rate of institutions challenged during this period was approximately 21 per cent.

Extrapolating from these data to the whole population of Canadian public libraries, I estimated that one challenge occurred somewhere in Canada every day of the year between 1985 and 1987. And every week, as many as four different institutions across the country were involved in these disputes.

Table 12 shows the incidence of challenges reported by respondents according to calendar year.

Table 12. Challenges by Year, 1985-87

Challenges	Public Libraries (n=167)	Percentage of Respondents (n=560)
1985	81	15
1986	82	15
1987	115	21

As this table indicates, among respondents who reported challenges by calendar year, 15 per cent experienced at least one challenge in 1985, 15 per cent in 1986, and 21 per cent in 1987 (an additional 118 incidents were listed but not by year of occurrence). The higher rate of institutions challenged in 1987 may be more apparent than real, however. In all probability, it is due to better respondent memory and better library records for those events immediately preceding the questionnaire survey.

As about half of all challenges during the study period were communicated verbally, the only available "records" were the memory of public library staff. Even when cases were documented, the policy at some institutions was to keep written records for one year only, thus necessitating reliance, again, on memory recall for incidents in the earlier years.

Furthermore, an additional 118 challenges for which year of occurrence was not provided by respondents was noted above. It is plausible that many of these challenges were experienced in the earlier years, and that, as a consequence, the overall rate of affected institutions remained relatively stable over the three-year period of the study.

The challenge rate of 21 per cent per year between 1985 and 1987 is remarkably similar to the rates reported in two previous one-year studies, the Alberta study and the one of English-language Canada. In the latter, which focused on large English-language public libraries across Canada, 27 per cent of the respondents received requests to withdraw titles from circulation during the one-year period from September 1981 to August 1982 (Beta Associates 1982). In the Alberta study, 22 per cent of that province's public libraries said that they had been asked to remove materials from their collections during 1983 (Walker 1984).

In an earlier study of six medium-sized Ontario public libraries, 15 per cent of the public librarians said that they personally had been involved in a censorship incident, while another 20 per cent said that they had worked in an institution where there had been a censorship incident within the previous 10 years (England 1974). It should be remembered, however, that England did not limit responses to a one-year period and, because the unit of analysis was the individual rather than the institution, some librarians may have been reporting the same incident.

In the present study, respondent public libraries reported 687 challenges to well over 500 different titles. Overall, half of the respondents who reported challenges were involved in 2 or more disputes. A total of 72 out of 188 respondents experienced only one challenge in three years, while another 80 experienced one or more every year. At the other extreme, a small number of public libraries across the country were fairly busy dealing with challenges: 16 institutions reported involvement in 3 or more disputes per year. One respondent was involved in as many as 15 challenges per year.

Among only those respondents reporting disputes, the mean was 3.6 challenges over three years, or 1.2 per year. Among all respondents in the study, the mean was 1.2 challenges over three years, or 0.4 per year.

The pattern of challenges documented in the present study is somewhat different from the pattern for secondary school libraries that Hopkins found in her nationwide U.S. study covering the three school years 1986-87 through 1988-89. Among respondents experiencing one or more challenges, just over half of the U.S. school libraries reported one challenge each during this three-year period, while among Canadian public libraries only 38 per cent had one challenge each during a similar three-year period (Hopkins 1991, 3:8).

The overall rates of challenge among all survey respondents, however, were similar for the two studies, 36 per cent of American school libraries compared to 35 per cent of Canadian public libraries. While some readers may question the validity of making comparisons between public libraries and school libraries, I think that selected similarities and differences are useful benchmarks for gauging how widespread censorship pressures are on the major educational institutions of North American communities.

2. Factors Influencing Challenge Rates

The present study shows that institutions challenged were much more likely to be multi-branch systems than single-unit libraries. Two out of three systems experienced challenges, compared to only 25 per cent of all single libraries. Statistical analysis shows that this difference was significant. Among multi-branch systems alone, respondents reporting challenges had twice as many service outlets as those not reporting any challenges, 13 outlets versus 5 outlets, respectively. This difference was also significant.

While public libraries involved in disputes represented only one out of three respondents between 1985 and 1987, they accounted for 70 per cent of all Canadian residents served by survey respondents, and even higher proportions of registered borrowers and library circulation, 77 per cent and 79 per cent, respectively. In 1987, these libraries served 13.6 million people, recorded 5.7 million registered borrowers, and circulated 114.2 million items. In general terms, what these figures imply is a potential denial of access to particular public library materials for 7 out of every 10 Canadian residents in the study population.

The significant difference between systems and single libraries was also reflected in institutional characteristics. Respondent public libraries serving larger municipalities were far more likely to experience challenges than those serving small centres. The typical public library involved in challenges served a municipality with 71,000 people, and had 30,000 registered borrowers and 595,000 library circulations in 1987.

Those that did not report experiencing challenges served an average municipality of 16,000 people and had 4,900 borrowers and 83,000 circulations. Statistical analysis shows that institutions challenged during the study period served significantly larger municipalities in terms of residents, borrowers and circulation than did those with no reported challenges.

Respondent public libraries serving larger municipalities tended to experience more challenges than those serving smaller municipal centres. Statistical analysis confirms the existence of a moderately positive correlation between municipal population and direct challenges. Similar correlations were recorded between registered borrowers and direct challenges, and between library circulations and direct challenges. These correlations were significant; however, they explained only 24 per cent of the variation between challenges and population, borrowers, and circulation.

French- and English-language public libraries did not differ in their rates of challenge to materials. Among French-language respondents (as reflected in the choice of language for responding to the questionnaire), 34 per cent reported challenges, while among their English-language counterparts, 35 per cent reported challenges. Statistical analysis confirms the absence of any systematic difference between French- and English-language institutions in their rates of challenge.

Challenge rate was influenced by the presence of institutional access policies (selection policy, policy for handling objections, donations policy, an objections form, and support of the CLA Statement on Intellectual Freedom). Respondents with all five access policies experienced more challenges than did those with no policies, on average almost three challenges each compared to 0.4 challenges over the study period. Those with some but not all five access policies had approximately one challenge each over this period. Statistical analysis shows that challenge rate was significantly influenced by access policy coverage.

Challenge rate was also related to the ownership of titles on the controversial materials checklist. Institutions reporting challenges owned an average of 16 checklist titles, while those reporting no challenges owned 10 titles each. Statistical analysis shows that institutions with more checklist titles experienced significantly more challenges than did those with fewer titles. However, while the correlation between ownership of checklist titles and challenge rate was significant, it explains only 18 per cent of the variation in the number of challenges experienced.

In addition, challenge rate was related to acquisition pressure. Institutions reporting challenges also experienced pressure to accept or acquire material. On average, those reporting acquisition pressure experienced three challenges over the study period, while those reporting no pressure had just under one. Statistical analysis shows that challenge rate and acquisition pressure were significantly related.

Challenge rate was not associated with age-related access restrictions or with differential treatment of potentially controversial or questionable materials. In other words, whether or not an institution had age restrictions made no difference to how many challenges it experienced. Similarly, whether or not an institution treated certain materials differently in selection, classification, shelving, access or circulation made no difference to its rate of challenge.

Because some of these factors may be interrelated, each determinant was analyzed in relationship to all the others that were statistically significant. Analysis of these several factors together shows that challenges to public library collections tended to involve institutions with high circulation and high ownership of checklist titles but serving a slightly smaller municipal population. So, for example, other things being equal, a public library that circulated 1 million items annually, owned 25 checklist titles, and served 100,000 residents would be predicted to experience one challenge to its collection every year, while one with a circulation of 100,000 items, 10 checklist titles, and 10,000 residents would be predicted to experience only one challenge every three years.

Nonetheless, statistical analysis shows that these three determinants together accounted for only 36 per cent of significant influences on the likelihood of a challenge to a respondent collection. Other factors not identified or examined in the present study accounted for two-thirds of the influences on challenge rates among Canadian public libraries.

3. Challenge Rate by Jurisdiction

Over the three-year period from 1985 to 1987, challenges were experienced by public libraries in every territory and province of Canada, but there were wide variations — 30 per cent or fewer of the public libraries in Alberta, Manitoba and Ontario, and all institutions in Saskatchewan, Prince Edward Island, Newfoundland, and the two territories experienced direct challenges.

However, these percentages do not tell the whole story. Two other rates are of interest: challenges per library, and challenges per 100,000 population. While the annual rate across the nation was estimated to be 0.4 challenges per institution between 1985 and 1987, the rate varied from 0.3 challenges per library annually in Alberta, Manitoba, Ontario and Quebec to 3.6 in Saskatchewan.

Challenges per 100,000 population is another way of comparing patterns among political jurisdictions. This method "normalizes" rates of challenge by taking into account total provincial population. While the nationwide normalized rate per year was 1.2 challenges per 100,000 people, normalized rates for other political jurisdictions ranged from less than one challenge annually per 100,000 population in Manitoba, Ontario, Quebec, New Brunswick and Nova Scotia to more than three challenges per 100,000 population in Saskatchewan. (It should be kept in mind that the rates for Yukon and the Northwest Territories are theoretical calculations only, since their respective populations are far less than 100,000.)

Annual rates per library and annual rates per 100,000 population, according to political jurisdiction, are summarized in Table 13:

Table 13. Challenges Annually per Library and per 100,000 Population, by Jurisdiction

Province/Territory	Annual Challenges*	Annual Challenges per Library*	Annual Challenges per 100,000 People*
British Columbia	50.7	1.1	1.9
Alberta	36.0	.3	1.8
Saskatchewan	32.3	3.6	3.3
Manitoba	5.7	.3	.7
Ontario	67.3	.3	.9
Quebec	18.0	.3	.6
New Brunswick	6.0	1.2	.9
Nova Scotia	4.6	.5	.5
Prince Edward Island	1.7	1.7	1.3
Newfoundland	5.6	.7	1.1
Yukon	1.3	1.3	4.9**
Northwest Territories	0.7	.7	1.3**
National	229.0	.4	1.2

* estimated from 3-year data
**theoretical calculations only

It should be kept in mind that Table 13 underestimates the true annual rates of challenge because these rates were obtained by averaging three-year data, in the absence of more accurate and precise information by year from respondents.

Summary

Overall, the present study has revealed that somewhere in Canada at least one direct challenge to public library materials occurred on average every day of the year. As many as four public libraries per week were affected, thus accounting annually for an estimated 21 per cent of all institutions across the country. Nationwide, there were 1.2 challenges annually per 100,000 population; higher than average rates were experienced in British Columbia, Alberta and Saskatchewan.

B. Profile of Challenges

What were these challenges all about? What form did they take? Who were the complainants; what did they object to; what were their reasons; and what did they want done? Among respondents who reported these details, the study found that 583 individuals and groups lodged a total of 649 requests to remove or restrict access to well over 500 titles between 1985 and 1987. Most complainants, 83 per cent, made only one challenge, but as many as 17 per cent made two or more.

To put these patterns into perspective, over a three-year period, fewer than 600 individuals and groups across Canada attempted to intervene in the public library selection process that served to satisfy the needs of more than 13 million Canadian residents.

Table 14 shows the incidence of challenges.

Table 14. Challenges per Complainant, 1985-87

Challenges per Complainant	Complainants Number	Percentage
1	484	83
2 or more	44	8
Not sure how many	55	9
Total	583	100

1. Who Were the Complainants?

Most complainants were registered borrowers — 79 per cent of the 610 whose public library membership status was known at the time the challenge was made. Respondents reported that just under half of the complainants described themselves as parents and a similar proportion as adults. ("Adults" refers to complainants who described their status using this general term.) No young adults or children were among the complainants.

Table 15 shows the breakdown of complainants as described to respondents.

Table 15. Status of Complainants, 1985-87

Complainant Status	Complainants Number	Percentage
Parent	288	45
Adult	286	45
Library staff	20	3
School staff	12	2
Library trustee	12	2
Council member	5	1
Group	8	1
School trustee	3	<1
Other	4	1
Total	638	100

Public library and school staff together accounted for 32 complainants, or 5 per cent. Only 12 complainants, or 2 per cent, were public library trustees, and 1 per cent were members of municipal councils. Groups accounted for 1 per cent. One complainant was a lawyer representing the Aga Khan, alleging that *The Aga Khans* by Mihir Bose was libellous and should be withdrawn from the public library collection.

It is curious that even though so many complainants described themselves as parents, only one in five (57 parents) indicated that their challenge was on behalf of a child.

Table 16 compares the breakdown of complainants, with the group or individual on whose behalf the complaint was lodged.

Table 16. Complainant Representation, 1985-87

Complainant Represented	Adult No.	Adult %	Complainants Parent No.	Parent %	Total No.	Total %
Self	250	90	220	77	470	83
Child	6	2	57	20	63	11
Other	22	8	10	3	32	6
Total	278	100	287	100	565	100

The majority of adults and parents who said that they were acting for themselves, rather than for their children, nonetheless requested the removal or restriction of materials written for children and young adults.

Six of the twelve complainants who were public library trustees said that they were acting for themselves in challenging public library materials; two of the three complainants who were school trustees also said they were acting for themselves; the other complainants acted on behalf of local residents. All five complainants who were members of municipal councils acted for themselves in initiating challenges.

Table 17 shows the intended age level of titles challenged by complainants who said they were acting on their own behalf.

Table 17. Age Level of Material Challenged, by Complainants Representing Themselves, 1985-87

Age Level of Material	Adult No.	Adult %	Complainants Parent No.	Parent %	Total No.	Total %
Pre-school	7	3	21	11	28	7
Elementary	27	13	80	42	107	26
High School	34	16	61	32	95	24
Adult	145	68	30	15	175	43
Total	213	100	192	100	405	100

Overall, the table shows that in fewer than half of the challenges initiated by adults and parents who acted for themselves was the offending material written for adults. Among parents alone, this proportion was much lower still: only 15 per cent of their challenges concerned adult material, while 85 per cent of them presumed to speak for all children and young adults.

While most challenges were initiated by individuals acting on their own behalf or for a child, 33 out of 649, or 5 per cent, were initiated by groups or by individuals representing groups. Respondents named the following groups: Canadian Arab Federation, Canadian Association in Support of Native People, Human Rights Association of Nova Scotia, Muslim Association of New Brunswick, Nova Scotia Human Rights Commission, Real Women of Canada, and Sri Lanka United National Association of Canada.

There were also many different local groups: a committee protesting violence against women and children, a women's group against pornography, a citizens' group ("spiritual fanatics" in the words of the survey respondent), a group of parents, two day-care groups, a Christian Fellowship church, a Christian Reformed church, a church of Scientology, a Mormon church, and several other local religious organizations.

2. Form of Challenge

Requests to remove or restrict material were communicated to library staff almost equally in verbal and written forms, 47 per cent and 53 per cent, respectively. It is almost certain that these findings understate the proportion of verbal requests, which are by nature more elusive and more difficult to keep track of than written challenges. Along these lines, one respondent noted, "Verbal complaints always outnumber written — many are not taken seriously by staff and never reach the branch head for action." And another observed:

> o Our staff throughout our system know that we will not remove books because of pressure from the public to do so. This probably means that a great many complaints do not get beyond a verbal complaint at the desk. No records have been kept of complaints at this level.

In a similar vein, another respondent noted that the reputation of the institution discouraged challenges to materials in the collection:

> o Locally it is a well known fact that attempts at pressure censorship of any kind will be met with strong resistance and public media coverage. So far no one has attempted to "bell the cat." I, personally, as a citizen and librarian, would not allow any citizen or group, legal or otherwise, to remove from the library shelf any book, magazine, video, etc., without a public stand, hue and cry against this kind of censorship. Standing for a principle, and eternal vigilance, is the price and requirement for the preservation of freedom. This type of censorship cannot be allowed in a free nation or society. Censorship in my view is a red flag to most librarians, or should be; it strikes at the very heart of what librarianship is all about.

Another respondent wrote that it was institutional policy to ignore verbal complaints altogether:

> o As we only retain and deal with written requests for reconsideration, the few we have do not reflect the concerns we hear more and more frequently. Sexual content is the number one concern, particularly as it affects the young. Our branch librarians are as concerned as the public, maybe more concerned.

Another respondent observed:

> o Although the library has policies and procedures in place, the whole situation of people expressing concern about a title is hard to deal with. Many people do not bother filling out a form. I suppose that the form to a certain extent turns people away as being too formal. Some people just mention in passing that a particular book was found to have too much bad language, sexual description, but don't wish to object formally as they are aware others may not find the material offensive.

Still another respondent wrote:

> o I am new here as chief librarian. As is commonly the case, the previous chief librarian went out of her way to make sure "official" complaints were not lodged. The request for reconsideration form explicitly stated that it was only to be used if the chief librarian could not be reached. Even when it was used, the situation was resolved without creating any "record." This policy is now changed.

In her nationwide study of challenges to U.S. secondary school library materials, Hopkins found that the ratio of verbal to written challenges was quite different from the mix identified in the present study. In her study, 73 per cent of the challenges were verbal compared to 27 per cent written (Hopkins 1991 4:24).

A few challenges reported in the present study lodged prior to 1985 remained unresolved during part or all of the period under study. One such challenge had been initiated in 1978, and another in 1983. Eight begun in 1984 carried over into 1985.

3. What Was Challenged?

Material challenged was published over a wide range of years, one title as early as 1899, but half had imprints from the 1980s and one-third from the 1970s. The mean date of publication was 1979. Table 18 shows challenged items by publication date.

What material was challenged in terms of publication format, fiction/non-fiction, and age level? Table 19 shows the publication format of items challenged.

Most of the offending items consisted of print formats: 72 per cent were books, 16 per cent were picture books, and 6 per cent were comic books. Very few were non-print media such as records, films, or videos — a not surprising pattern given the relatively small public library that typified the overall survey response.

Fiction was by far the more common category of challenge, three out of four titles, and fiction was even more heavily represented in children's and young adult materials (84 per cent) than in adult materials (61 per cent). By target audience, publications written for adults accounted for 43 per cent of all challenged titles; 7 per cent were intended for preschool children, one-quarter were for children aged 6 to 12, and another quarter were for teenagers aged 13 to 18.

Table 18. Publication Date of Material Challenged, 1985-87

Publication Date	Titles Challenged	
	Number	Percentage
1890s	1	<1
1900s		
1910s		
1920s	2	<1
1930s	4	1
1940s	1	<1
1950s	7	1
1960s	18	3
1970-74	63	12
1975-79	118	23
1980-84	201	39
1985-87	103	20
Total	518	100

Adult materials accounted for 64 per cent of all challenges to non-fiction. For fiction, it was the reverse: adult materials accounted for only 35 per cent of all challenges to fiction. Statistical analysis shows that these differences were significant.

Table 19. Publication Format of Material Challenged, 1985-87

Publication Format	Titles Challenged	
	Number	Percentage
Books	423	72
Picture books	96	16
Comic books	32	6
Periodicals	19	3
Records	6	1
Films and videos	3	1
Other	5	1
Total	584	100

Table 20 compares the age level for which materials were written as well as whether items were fiction or non-fiction.

Table 20. Intended Age Level of Material Challenged, by Fiction/Non-fiction Status, 1985-87

Status	Titles Challenged				
	Pre-school	Elementary	High School	Adult	Total
Fiction	36	102	111	136	385
Non-fiction	4	26	19	86	135
Total	40	128	130	222	520
	(7%)	(25%)	(25%)	(43%)	(100%)

What titles were involved in these challenges? Almost as many different titles were challenged as there were challengers: well over 500 titles by 630 individuals and 8 groups (respondents were able to identify 498 titles specifically). See Appendix E for a complete list of items challenged. There were also 21 complaints against multiple titles in a particular genre or subject area, or by a particular author. Among the multi-title challenges were the following:

- all books by Kevin Major, because a patron argued that "they shouldn't be in the children's section"
- older children's books by Natalie Savage Carlson, because of alleged sexism, cruelty to animals, and spanking
- all books by V.C. Andrews, because of the topic of incest and horror
- all books by Harold Robbins, because a patron did not want her son reading them
- all heavy metal groups such as AC/DC and Twisted Sister, because of references to sin and killing, and because they "destroy respect for life and people — library should not be responsible for supplying such destructive garbage"
- certain books with "daring passages" and certain comics with "daring drawings"
- paperbacks with "lurid covers," not suitable in a school-public library
- various groups of books because of "objectionable swearing," explicit sexual scenes, violence, or a combination of these
- all books on astrology, on the grounds that "truth was not in astrology but in the Catholic religion"
- all books dealing with the occult, because "satanic books damage the minds of the youth and could turn people away from Christianity"
- all books on witchcraft, magic and parapsychology, "the work of the devil"
- all books on witchcraft and homosexuality, which would "lead young people into a life-style that was not normal and damaging"
- general books on drugs, of which a patron felt that the library had too many, "thus making drug information available to teens"
- a series of westerns called *The Gunsmith*, because a parent was concerned that his son was reading explicit sex material before reaching puberty
- various groups of adult western paperbacks, because of explicit sex that was "demoralizing to young minds."

Complaints were lodged only once against almost all of the 498 titles identified by respondents, but 63 titles each received 2 or more challenges. One title was challenged 11 times and another 8 times. Therefore, although it may be possible to identify specific subjects that are vulnerable to censorship pressure, it may not be possible to predict the specific titles that will be challenged. The choice of titles deemed offensive seems to be capricious, if not altogether random.

However, there are a few exceptions. Several titles have been regularly challenged since the early 1980s. These titles can be identified by comparing titles challenged in the present study with titles challenged between 1983 and 1985 in previous surveys, as represented on the controversial materials checklist discussed earlier (see Chapter 5). In total, 6 out of the 30 checklist titles were also challenged frequently between 1985 and 1987. These titles were *Forever, The Haj, Wifey, The Butter Battle Book, In the Night Kitchen,* and *Flowers in the Attic.*

TITLES FREQUENTLY CHALLENGED

Table 21 identifies the 63 titles most frequently challenged.

Table 21. Titles Challenged, 1985-87

11 challenges

Lizzy's Lion

8 challenges

Forever**

6 challenges each

Wifey**
The Haj**
Slugs

4 challenges each

Outside Over There
Where Did I Come From?

3 challenges each

The Butter Battle Book**
Creepshow
Gorky Rises
The Hoax of the Twentieth Century
In the Night Kitchen**
Indian Summer
Mr. and Mrs. Pig's Evening Out
Naomi in the Middle
Out of the Oven
The Tin-Pot Foreign General and the Old Iron Woman
Web of Deceit
The Werewolf Family
What's Happening to Me?

2 challenges each

Angel Dust Blues
Bear
The Beast of Monsieur Racine
Blue Trees, Red Sky
The Body Politic (periodical)

continued

Table 21. Titles Challenged, 1985-87 (*cont.*)

2 challenges each

> *Collection: Livres dont vous êtes le héros*
> *Croc* (periodical)
> *Dancer of Gor*
> *Deenie*
> *The Devil Did It*
> *Don't Hurt Me, Mama*
> *The Enormous Crocodile*
> *Fairy Tales of New York*
> *Father Christmas*
> *The First Deadly Sin*
> *Flowers in the Attic***
> *The Gunsmith*
> *Hag Head*
> *Hands of a Stranger*
> *Happy Lion*
> *Histoires fantastiques*
> *I'll Fix Anthony*
> *Juggling*
> *King of the Cats*
> *King Stork*
> *The Love of Rich Women*
> *Murder in the Family*
> *Now* (periodical)
> *Ordeal*
> *The Penguin Book of Limericks*
> *The Rapist File*
> *Religion Inc.: The Church of Scientology*
> *Scary Stories to Tell in the Dark*
> *Starring Sally J. Freedman as Herself*
> *The Story of Henny Penny* (by Tom Holmes, illustrated by Blonnie [?] Holmes)
> *Tranches de vie*
> *Upchuck Summer*
> *The Vagabond of Limbo: The Ultimate Alchemist*
> *The Vagabond of Limbo: What is Reality, Papa?*
> *Valarie*
> *A Way of Love, A Way of Life: A Young Person's Introduction to What It Means to be Gay*
> *Where Has Deedie Wooster Been All These Years?*
> *Witchery Hill*

1 challenge each

> 435 titles

**also on the controversial materials checklist

This table shows that while a few titles received several objections, most titles received only a few objections. Leading the statistics for most offensive title was *Lizzy's Lion* by Dennis Lee, with eleven challenges over the three years in the study. Published in 1984, this children's picture book tells the story of a little girl and a pet lion she keeps in her bedroom. By the time the lion is finished with the "rotten robber" who is after Lizzy's piggy bank in the middle of the night, Lizzy and the lion have only to stuff the robber's "toes and tum and head" in the garbage, after which "they both went back to bed." This work, incidentally, was awarded the Canada Council Children's Literature Prize for Illustration in 1984.

In second place, with eight challenges, was *Forever* by Judy Blume. This 1975 novel has sometimes been designated by librarians as young adult fiction, but it was originally intended for adults. Writing in the "Adult Books for Young Adults" column of the November 1975 issue of *School Library Journal*, Regina Minudri of the Almeda County (California) Library cautioned, "Librarians buying for junior high schools should be aware that the sexual scenes, while not at all explicit compared to the run of adult novels, may be more than parents of young teens bargain for" (Minudri 1975, 95).

In this novel, Blume tells the story of two teenagers in love who think they will last "forever." During their romance, Katherine, the young woman, finds out about sex, contraceptives, and venereal disease, and eventually realizes that she is maturing in ways that mean her first love can not be forever.

Tied for third were three titles that each received six complaints: *Wifey* by Judy Blume, *The Haj* by Leon Uris, and *Slugs* by David Greenberg. *Wifey*, published in 1978 and definitely intended for an adult audience, is a light romance about a 32-year-old suburban New Jersey housewife's search for personal and sexual identity. Married to a successful, self-centered, obnoxious dry cleaner, Blume's heroine is Sandy Pressman, mother of two and bored country-clubber, who tires one summer of letting other people control her life and starts to find sexual fulfilment with other married men, including an old flame and her brother-in-law.

Published in 1984, *The Haj* is set against Palestinian history between 1922 and 1956, during which time the village of Tabah was headed by the novel's main character, Ibrahim al Soukori al Wahhabi, who, as custom allows, took the name Haj Ibrahim after his hadj (the pilgrimage to Mecca). The novel tells his story as seen through the eyes of his youngest and favourite son, Ishmael.

Slugs is a 1983 children's picture book that enumerates the many dreadful things one can do to slugs, among them to:

> Perch one on a doorknob
> Or on a toilet seat
> Sizzle them on light bulbs
> Squash them with your feet.

But it also warns that even the lowly slug may have its revenge.

Two titles received four challenges each, *Outside Over There* by Maurice Sendak and *Where Did I Come From?* by Peter Mayle. The first is a 1981 children's picture book that tells the story of Ida and her baby sister. Ida plays her wonder horn to keep her sister quiet, only to find in a moment of inattention that goblins have stolen her sister to be a horrid goblin's bride. After an agonizing search, Ida rescues her sister and takes her home.

The 1973 children's picture book *Where Did I Come From? The Facts of Life without Any Nonsense and with Illustrations* describes the reproductive process from intercourse to birth, but first recounts some of the ideas that boys and girls have about where they think they came from.

AUTHORS FREQUENTLY CHALLENGED

The pattern of authors challenged was similar to that of titles challenged: a few authors had several works challenged, while most authors had only a few titles challenged. Four authors and two singing groups had all of their works challenged — V.C. Andrews, Natalie Savage Carlson, Kevin Major, Harold Robbins, AC/DC, and Twisted Sister. In addition, ten works by Judy Blume were challenged, seven works by Norma Klein, and five works each by Raymond Briggs, Roald Dahl, and Maurice Sendak.

The authors who had two or more titles challenged during the study period were as follows:

Table 22. Authors Challenged, 1985-87

Author

all titles challenged

V.C. Andrews
Natalie Savage Carlson
Kevin Major
Harold Robbins
AC/DC
Twisted Sister

10 titles challenged

Judy Blume

7 titles challenged

Norma Klein

5 titles challenged each

Raymond Briggs
Roald Dahl
Maurice Sendak

4 titles challenged each

Peter Mayle
Christian Godard and Julio Ribera

3 titles challenged each

René Durand
Paul Galdone (illustrator)
Lauzier
Graham Oakley
Lawrence Sanders

2 titles challenged each

Frank Asch
Anthony Browne
Sol Gordon
Constance Greene
Wallace Hamilton
Ashida Kim
Milo Manara
Eric Maple
John Norman
Daniel Pinkwater
Jack Prelutsky
Malcolm Ross
Alvin Schwartz
William Steig
Tomi Ungerer
Georges Wolinski

While the large number of offending titles identified in the present study suggests that it may not be possible to predict potentially vulnerable titles, the study shows that there are several authors whose works have been challenged persistently in the recent past. It seems reasonable to predict that as long as they are alive to write and able to resist the chill of sustained minority censure, much of their present and new work will continue to be challenged.

A comparison of frequently challenged works with those identified in the study by Hopkins reveals few titles in common. Ranking first in challenges in Hopkins' study was *Forever*, which received thirteen challenges over a three-year period; this number compares to eight challenges over three years in the present study of Canadian public libraries. It was followed by three titles, which each received ten challenges: *Go Ask Alice*, *The Chocolate War* and *Clan of the Cave Bear*. Only two other titles appeared on both lists of frequently challenged items: *Deenie* and *Angel Dust Blues*, each of which was challenged four times in U.S. secondary schools and two times in Canadian public libraries (Hopkins 1991, 4:21). Differences in targeted titles presumably reflect differences in the client communities served by school libraries and by public libraries. Cultural differences may also be a factor.

4. What Were the Reasons for Challenges?

What were the grounds for challenges? Complainants gave a total of 857 reasons for a total of 687 requests to remove or restrict access to well over 500 titles (respondents were able to identify 498 titles specifically). In 220 challenges, or 32 per cent, they gave 2 or more reasons. These data probably understate the incidence of reasons for challenges, particularly in the case of verbal challenges.

Specific reasons given for objections, by frequency of mention, were as follows:

Table 23. Reasons for Challenges, 1985-87

Complainant Reason	Titles Challenged No.	%
Sexually explicit, nudity	155	18
Unsuitable for age group	121	14
Violence, cruelty	116	14
Promotes unacceptable (negative) moral values	95	11
Coarse language, profanity	64	7
Scary, frightening to child	47	5
Promotes the occult, witchcraft	36	4
Pornographic	35	4
Offensive to religion, blasphemous	28	3
Sexist, demeaning to women	26	3
Promotes homosexuality	24	3
Misinformation, bias	24	3
Racist	22	3
In bad taste	17	2
Badly written	16	2
Anti-semitic	14	2
Promotes drug use	6	1
Other	11	1
Total	857	100

Three clusters of reasons accounted for over half of all challenges. The most common grounds for requests to remove or restrict materials were sexual explicitness, nudity and pornography (22 per cent of all challenges). Second were objections to violence, cruelty, and scary works (19 per cent). Third were objections to titles deemed unsuitable for a particular age group (14 per cent) — often in combination with additional grounds such as sex or violence.

These patterns are somewhat similar to those found in several U.S. studies of public libraries in individual states or regions. The most frequently mentioned reasons reported by respondents to the various surveys were morality, sexual content, obscenity, profanity, immaturity of users, and the occult and witchcraft. Noticeably absent from the upper ranks of this composite list of American complaints, however, were violence, cruelty and scary titles, which figured prominently in the present study.

It is interesting that violence did not figure prominently in the U.S. studies of school library censorship either. In Hopkins' nationwide study of challenges to materials in secondary school libraries, responses showed that violence was at the bottom of the list of concerns, while sexuality, profanity, obscenity and morality ranked highest:

sexuality	242 times
profanity	213 times
obscenity	174 times
morality	143 times
witchcraft	90 times
immaturity of students	77 times
nudity	77 times
family values	77 times
other	77 times
occult	72 times
violence	67 times

(Hopkins 1991, 4:24)

Similarly, the American Civil Liberties Union found that school library materials in Alabama, Georgia, Tennessee and Louisiana were challenged primarily because of obscenity, profanity and morality (American Civil Liberties Union 1986, 18-19). This pattern was echoed in the findings of an earlier survey by the (U.S.) National Council of Teachers of English in which objections to language and sexual references accounted for the majority of challenges to curricular and library materials (Burress 1979, 28-29).

In Canada, a study of Manitoba school libraries showed that the main reasons for challenges were immaturity of readers, profanity and explicit sex. In British Columbia school libraries, sexual references, profanity, violence and inappropriateness were the most frequent reasons for challenges to materials (Poole 1986, 32-34).

The reasons for challenges reveal a fascinating — and at times bewildering — spectrum of community values, social attitudes and ideologies. Although the statistical pattern depicted in Table 23 looks relatively straightforward, the table nonetheless masks a great deal of ideological complexity in the thinking of complainants. It masks their attitudes towards other citizens, especially towards children and young adults. It masks their beliefs about the power of ideas and images to persuade and tempt, and about the power of reading. Above all, it masks their fear of words.

Ideology, attitudes, beliefs and fears are revealed in part through the words of the complainants themselves as they communicate to public library staff the grounds for challenging materials. Many complainants in this study were opposed to the public presentation of certain ideas through fiction written for adults — or, at the least, to the availability of these ideas through the public library. In some cases, complainant concern was motivated by the fear that children might accidentally be exposed to such ideas.

In addition to challenges on the basis of objectionable content, it should be remembered that several of the reasons for complainants' requests to withdraw or relocate materials may well be grounded in legitimate selection policy criteria. Among the reasons public librarians consider legitimate grounds for weeding items from the collection are the following: materials contain factually incorrect information that is potentially harmful; materials are obsolete or irrelevant; materials are little or never used or, conversely, "read out"; materials are in poor physical condition, such as a damaged binding; materials were selected inappropriately in the first place, acquired erroneously as part of bulk orders, or received unsolicited from publishers; materials are being replaced with others of better quality in one way or another, such as those that provide a more balanced perspective.

All of these grounds for weeding apply especially to non-fiction for both adults and children. Although materials considered to fall into one or more of these weeding categories have little claim to public library shelf space, there is still an important element of judgement involved in making these decisions; materials do not present themselves neatly for weeding on the basis of standard selection criteria.

The appropriate treatment of materials on the basis of age suitability is even more difficult. Treatment of materials on the basis of age applies to both fiction and non-fiction, to publication formats, and to the whole span of childhood and young adulthood. The issue involves the misclassification of both adult books in the young adult section of a public library and of young adult books in the children's section. "Picture books for the sophisticated" (as they are sometimes referred to) present special classification and shelving problems for children's librarians.

With children's literature, it is standard practice for book reviewers to indicate appropriate age levels, which generally take into account both reading level and content treatment, and public librarians use this information in making selection and shelving decisions. An intriguing issue raised in this regard is whether or not there are discernible variations across the country in what is acceptable for different age levels; my study did not provide any clear reading on this question.

With literature for young adults, decisions about suitability are more complex because some adult materials are written in a simple style that would be suitable for young adults, but the books deal with adult themes. This problem applies especially to *Forever*, which is described on the original dust jacket of the 1975 hardcover edition as "Judy Blume's first novel for adults." In spite of this note, *Forever* is frequently shelved in the young adult section. Her equally adult novel *Wifey* is frequently shelved in the same way by public librarians. Whether or not these decisions should be treated as genuine misclassifications is not easy to resolve, particularly in light of the wide range of physical and emotional maturity that the category of "young adult" encompasses. Moreover, *Forever* has been republished under a young adult imprint.

Verbatim comments by complainants and summary statements of their views by public library staff reveal the complexity of approaches to offending material. Material in square brackets was supplied by respondents, but I have verified the accuracy of author and title information wherever possible. Audience designations as assigned and reported by respondents have not been altered, and in some cases such designations are missing because they were not supplied by respondents.

ADULT FICTION

Adult fiction was usually challenged on the basis of sexual depictions:

o "Sexually explicit accounts, especially oral sex. This behaviour might become more and more acceptable." (*Romance* by Gwen Davis)

o "Too animalistic. Be careful who takes this book out." (*Clan of the Cave Bear* by Jean Auel)

o "I don't think homosexuality is something to be witty about." (*Buried on Sunday* by Edward Phillips)

o "Book glorified homosexuality, which is against the teachings of God." (*Ice Blues: A Donald Strachey Mystery*, author not given)

o "Disgusting. Author is promoting immoral behaviour." (*Fairy Tales of New York* by J.P. Donleavy)

o "This is a filthy book. Get rid of it!" (*Bear* by Marian Engel)

o "Absolute filth." (*The Mad Woman's Underclothes* by Germaine Greer)

o "Objected to basis of book — rape — lurid and filthy sex habits described and the considerable use of foul language." (*Hands of a Stranger* by Robert Daley)

o "The whole book is an insult to human intellect. Nothing but depravity in human behaviour, narcotics addicts, violence, perversity, etc., etc., with no redeeming features whatsoever — neither in style, language nor artistic endeavour." (*Fear and Loathing in Las Vegas* by Hunter S. Thompson)

o "The book portrays 'lust' from cover to cover... Senior people should be a positive example to the younger generation when immoral degeneracy has crept in, yet this book depicts seniors as an immoral, sexy generation, who are unfaithful to their spouses, men and women alike. I would want to hope that the book does not portray life in our senior citizens complexes." (*Darling I Am Growing Old* by Gene Stone)

o "Suggests that whoring is an acceptable lifestyle." (*Taming a Sea-horse* by Robert Parker)

o "Women used as sexual objects by men. Indicates acceptance of rape, sexual abuse of children." (*Maia* by Richard Adams)

- "Degrading to women ... only happy as sex slaves to men." (*Fighting Slave of Gor* by John Norman)

- "Good plot, well told, why ruin it with pornographic sex scenes?" (*A Pride of Healers* by Richard Clark Hirschhorn)

- "Represented bestiality, verging on pornographic, was in poor taste, and would be offensive to many people." (*Playboar*)

- "I don't believe this book is suitable for a public library. I would not like children to be able to pick up this book and read detailed sexual acts. Many of these are not normal situations; in fact I would suggest pornographic." (*The Storyteller* by Harold Robbins)

- "Violence and sex and bestiality linked together and would not be understood by young users." (*La Terre de la bombe* by Ramïoli and Durand, adult comic book)

- "The painful birth of a child followed by death and flies circling the body; the funeral director masturbating over a dead woman's body; the traumatic death of a prostitute followed by suicide of her husband with details. The reader who innocently reads the inner jacket will not be prepared for the incidents that occur." (*Heart of the Country* by Greg Matthews)

- Objection to portrayal of Roman Catholic Church: "When I think of all the Protestant hands this book has been through." (*The Piercing* by John Coyne)

- "Extreme violence in a prison, shocking treatment." (*The Farm* by Clarence L. Cooper, Jr.)

- Patron objected to the "deranged sex killer." (*Hero and the Terror* by Michael Blodgett)

- "Negative, depressing book with no redeeming features." (*Unlucky Wally* by Raymond Briggs)

- "Language, lack of any kind of purpose in the writing... Burn it!" (*Less Than Zero* by Bret Easton Ellis)

- "This is not poetry." (*The Man with Seven Toes* by Michael Ondaatje)

- "Bad literature. Should be removed." (*Princess Daisy* by Judith Krantz)

ADULT NON-FICTION

In the non-fiction literature for adults, challenges were lodged against ideas not only about sex but also about sexism, religion, racism and politics. At stake were the credibility and veracity of the offending ideas and, in some cases, the appropriateness of depicting reality:

- "Feminist literature undermines the sanctity of family life." (*Ms* magazine)

- "Book comes close to child abuse or neglect; new or confused parents might believe methods." (*The Discipline of Raising Children* by M.A. Treadwell)

- "Everything in this book is contrary to human decency. Every author in it approved of pornography and indecency, the book was biased... This type of book leads to abuse against women, sometimes violence." (*Perspectives on Pornography* compiled by Douglas A. Hughes)

- "Information regarding topic of incest is too voyeuristic. Real danger that this book could encourage incestuous urges." (*Kiss Daddy Goodnight* by Louise Armstrong)

- "Men's fantasies (sexual) — could get the same thing in *Penthouse* — little or no research conducted." (*Men in Love: Male Sexual Fantasies* by Nancy Friday)

- "Promotes homosexuality." (*Gay Parenting: A Complete Guide for Gay Men and Lesbians with Children* by Joy Schulenburg)

- "Pictures of oral sex could turn on homosexuality. Shows injection of the parts of the body; also ejaculation... I think everyone should experience these things in the marriage bed, sanctified and undefiled." (*The Sex Atlas: A New Illustrated Guide* by Erwin J. Haeberle)

- "An explicit account of her sexual activities. Language is foul and uncalled for. Goes into detail — homosexual relations, orgies and bestiality. I feel this book is pure pornography." (*Ordeal* by Linda Lovelace)

- Fourteen-year-old boy borrowed several back issues — parent admitted boy looks over 18 — centrefolds all removed. Said withdraw or else she'd get local alderman after us. (*Playboy*)

- "Book advocates murder." (*Compulsory Parenthood* by Wendell Watters) o "Fear that sex offenders will get their hands on a copy and do what one killer-rapist did — re-enact the brutal acts." (*The Rapist File* by Les Sussman)

o "It has been a known catalyst for a brutal rape-murder and has, in our opinion, the potential for inciting other similar responses." (*The Rapist File* by Les Sussman)

o "Disgusting. Photos depicting an execution." (*Life*)

o "The book illustrates with photographs assassination techniques, stealth, throat-slitting, etc." (*Secrets of the Ninja* by Ashida Kim)

o "How-to-kill fighting techniques could have lethal consequences if acted on by young readers." (*Ninja Death Touch* by Ashida Kim)

o "Author encourages anal sex in a book for family consumption. Anal sex is even frowned upon in an all-male prison. What about the AIDS problem? The rest of the subjects are dealt with in a straightforward and common-sense manner." (*Human Sexuality* by Sharon Goldsmith)

o "The title alone is offensive — who needs *instruction* in adultery?! Zero value — didn't read entire book — it is trash! Can't recommend better book — the person who would read this book needs a marriage counsellor not another 'how-to' book." (*Adultery for Adults* by Joyce Peterson)

o "Chapter 7 p. 174-75 dealing with sexuality ... incest." (*Understanding Your Child from Birth to Three* by Joseph Church)

o "Unnatural and cruel. Group sex." (*Unspeakable Acts* by Simon Bond)

o "Young boys who would be attracted to this book would be affected by the pornography and think, because it was from their library, it would be okay." (*Vans: Customized Vans in Colour* by Alberto Martinez and Jean-Loup Nory)

o "Three-page discussion of historical and current information regarding sexual relations between humans and dogs and section on fighting dogs." (*The Dog Crisis* by Iris Nowell)

o "Chapter titles suggested illegal or immoral occupations — marijuana grower, kept woman/man, etc." (*132 Ways to Earn a Living without Working for Someone Else* by E. Rosenthal and R. Lichtey)

o "Human degradation — contents of this record don't deserve exposure in libraries. What good does that record contribute to society?" (*Bicentennial Nigger* by Richard Pryor, adult LP)

o Patron objected to misinformation in book regarding Mormons. (*Meeting the Mormons* by Jack Roundhill)

o "The book is not the issue — only parts of it. After reading those parts, I was disgusted. I don't think this is literature, not for a public library." (*The Penguin Book of Limericks*)

o "Book encourages women to buy fur coats. Animals should not be killed for this purpose." (*Furs; An Appreciation of Luxury, A Guide to Value* by Edythe Cudlipp)

o "Negative attitude towards handicapped people. Archaic, overblown language and descriptions." (*Your Child's Mind: The Complete Guide to Infant and Child Emotional Well-Being* by Herman Roiphe)

o "The proposition that allegiance to Satan brings wealth, romance, power and happiness." (*A Witches' Grimoire of Ancient Omens, Portents, Talismans, and Charms* by Gavin and Yvonne Frost)

o "I object to the entire book and its author, its original author Satan and all they stand for ... obviously the destruction of Biblical Christianity... Anyone who is interested in anything related to witchcraft or anything else related to the worship of Satan through reading this book will fall from God's grace." (*Buckland's Complete Book of Witchcraft* by Raymond Buckland)

o Patron felt it gave very biased viewpoint with nothing to substantiate it. (*The Word of the Lord Brought to Mankind by an Angel* by W. Draves)

o "Unfair representation of Scientology." (*Religion Inc.* by Stewart Lamont)

o "Eckankar is not a religion. It is mind control pure and simple." (*Eckankar: Compiled Writings*, vol. 1) o "Anti-Catholic and racist." (*Ireland: A Terrible Beauty* by Jill and Leon Uris)

o "Book was racist. Presented the Indian as a savage." (*Indian Summer* by F.N. Monjo)

o Book deemed to be libellous. (*The Aga Khans* by Mihir Bose)

o Patron believed the book had been banned by the Court. (*The Hoax of the Twentieth Century* by Arthur R. Butz)

o "Anti-history, dangerous and insulting — a complex narrative that denies the Holocaust — enough evidence and proof have been given without having to rebut the cold, sociopathic untruth of Butz's propaganda." (*The Hoax of the Twentieth Century* by Arthur R. Butz)

o "Don't promote this man's ideas by having his book here." (*Keegstra; The Trial, The Issues, The Consequences* by Steve Mertl)

o Anti-semitic, denies "Hollywood version" (author's term) of Holocaust. The author's books receive maximum publicity — TV, radio, newspaper, politicians, school boards. Why would the library have hate literature on its shelves? (*Web of Deceit and Spectre of Power* by Malcolm Ross)

o "Deceitful propaganda — putting the Führer in a favourable light." (*Adolf Hitler: Pictures from the Life of the Führer, 1931-35* translated by Carl Underhill Quinn)

o "Implication that Lester B. Pearson was a communist." (*No Sense of Evil: The Espionage Case of Herbert Norman* by James Barros)

o Book concerned political/legal "scandal" involving patron's relative. Patron insisted on buying the book; didn't want it to circulate. [title not given]

o Complainant felt the book constituted U.S. government propaganda. (*The Day We Bombed Utah* by John G. Fuller)

o Patron felt the book had a subtle pro-communist bias and should be removed. (*Preussen, von den Anfängen bis zur Reichsgründung*) [author not given]

o "Leftist. Remove and/or add *The Spotlight*." (*New Internationalist*)

o "It is obscene, degrading and perverted." (*The Maple Laugh Forever* edited by Douglas Barbour)

o "I do not feel this book provides a balanced approach. It is an over-reaction... It concerns me that some woman desperately needing surgery would not go through with it after reading this book." (*The Castrated Woman* by Naomi Stokes)

o Presented only pro-life side of issue. Patron wanted a more balanced representation of the issue. (*Abortion in Canada*, Eleanor Wright Pelrine)

o "Contained information on how to herbally induce spontaneous miscarriage (abortion)." (*Healing the Family* by Joy Gardner)

o "There is no proven cure for arthritis — yet." (*A Doctor's Proven New Home Cure for Arthritis* by Giraud W. Campbell)

o "Erroneous information doing harm to people with epilepsy." (*Nerves in Collision* by Walter Alvarez)

o "Book is classified in medical science — it is dangerous *bunk*... The uninformed might change their habits to more dangerous ones without consulting a doctor or dietitian." (*Diet for a Strong Heart* by Michio Kushi) [emphasis in original]

o Patron is a qualified dietitian and felt this material could be harmful to health if followed closely. (*Fit for Life* by Harvey and Marilyn Diamond)

o "Out-of-date information." (*An Act of Mercy: Euthanasia Today* by Richard Trubo)

o Dog training manual unrevised 30-year-old edition still in print, recommending cruel methods — cattle prods, water, striking, confinement in a dark closet. (*This is the Cocker Spaniel* by Leon F. Whitney)

o "The examples illustrating the rules are insidious and devious." (*Complete Guide to Punctuation*, published by Press Porcépic) o "Carried criticisms by local minister of unnamed people who would be offended." (*United Church Newsletter*)

FICTION FOR CHILDREN AND YOUNG ADULTS

Like the complaints about adult fiction, complaints about fiction for children and young adults usually centered on sex and sexual taboos. But even more pronounced than with adult literature, many challenges to fiction for children and young adults were motivated by the fear that impressionable and younger children might accidentally be exposed to such material. In these instances, parental responsibility was imputed to public library staff. Several complainants commented in this vein:

o "The flap on book did not at all even hint at the abundance of sexual information my child was suddenly confronted with — pg. 15, 20, 45 — I do want my children to be aware of all this, but not at age eight and certainly not by accident." (*Naomi in the Middle* by Norma Klein, fiction for grade 4)

o It would upset her children, who don't know about these things. The patron does realize this occurs in some homes. (*Don't Hurt Me, Mama* by Muriel Stanek, fiction for ages 7 to 8)

o Felt book was too mature for patron's eight-year-old daughter. (*Are You There God? It's Me, Margaret* by Judy Blume, fiction for ages 10 and up)

Other verbatim comments by complainants and summaries by staff were:

o "Suggestions are very explicit. Work is too revealing for young teens and seems to condone sexual freedom." (*Beginner's Love* by Norma Klein, teen fiction)

o "Book promoted acceptance of masturbation." (*Run, Shelley, Run!* by Gertrude Samuels, young adult fiction)

o "Severely lacking morals; advocates abortion, sleeping around." (*It's Not What You'd Expect* by Norma Klein, young adult fiction)

o "Inappropriate classification — YA novel about gay teenage boys. Language and subject too crude for early teens, who gravitate to YA-designated books." (*The Boys on the Rock* by John Fox)

o "Discovering the mother and father had sex and the feelings of girls for girls, etc." (*Flick* by Wendy Kesselman, fiction for age 13)

o "Implied lesbianism and vulgar terms." (*Bouquets for Brimbal* by J.P. Reading, fiction for ages 14 and up)

o "Book dealt with lesbianism." (*Annie on My Mind* by Nancy Garden, fiction for ages 11 to 15)

o Book content had a lesbian relationship in it which apparently gave the child nightmares. [title not given]

o Wrong cataloguing; concern over "changing" Hercules to (female) Heraclea. (*Heraclea* by Bernard Evslin, juvenile fiction)

o "I find the profanity objectionable as well as the explicit description of sexual intercourse on p. 109. It seems to me that both of these make the book unsuitable for young teens, at whom it seems to be aimed." (*Dark but Full of Diamonds* by Katie Letcher Lyle, young adult fiction)

o "Specific description of masturbation made children want to try it." (*Deenie* by Judy Blume, juvenile fiction)

o "Female nudity would corrupt children." (*Tell Me, Grandma, Tell Me, Grandpa*, pre-school) [author not given]

o "Their only relationship is sleeping together — there is no normal relationship." (*Family Secrets* by Norma Klein, young adult fiction)

o "Sex unnecessary to the story-line. Book should be labelled as unsuitable for teens." (*Ariel* by Jack M. Bickham, adult fiction)

o "Incredibly sexually graphic pictures. They were truly pornographic. The breast, the vagina as a source of violence. This is a sexual nightmare come true." (*The Tin-Pot Foreign General and the Old Iron Woman* by Raymond Briggs, picture book fiction for ages 12 and over)

o "Pictures disgusting ... warps the mind ... book discriminates against Margaret Thatcher." (*The Tin-Pot Foreign General and the Old Iron Woman*, juvenile fiction) o "Small children might not get the message about the effects of war and could incorporate these ideas into their play." (*The Tin-Pot Foreign General and the Old Iron Woman*, juvenile fiction)

o "Sexual comments — condoms mentioned — not necessary in collection, not even a good story." (*Where Has Deedie Wooster Been All These Years?* by Anita Jacobs, young adult fiction)

o "Sexual content too specific — use of condoms." (*Angel Dust Blues* by Todd Strasser, young adult fiction)

o "Book described boy's sexual experiences with girl friend." (*Juggling* by Robert Lehrman, young adult fiction)

o "There is an account of Melissa's first sexual experience (16 years) on pages 131-32. There is no hint of this type of content, however, on the jacket description inside cover. Could we have some sort of dot or other system whereby the books in our young adult area could be coded for older and for younger young adult? (*Nothing in Common: A Novel* by Barbara Bottner, young adult fiction)

o Patron had read a critique which claimed book was an allegory of rape. (*The Witches* by Roald Dahl, fiction for ages 8 to 12)

o Graphic representation of birth of puppy offended mother. (*The Last Puppy* by Frank Asch, pre-school picture book)

o "Gives children the wrong impression about sex." (*What's Best for You* by J. Angell, young adult fiction)

o "Nudity, unpleasant story *no* child could enjoy." (*In the Night Kitchen* by Maurice Sendak, pre-school fiction) [emphasis in original]

o "Sexual references re prurient interests of male adolescents." (*Starring Sally J. Freedman as Herself* by Judy Blume, fiction for ages 10 to 13)

o "Book too graphic about genital parts in a *negative* way — making fun of genitals, etc." (*Les Aventures magiques de Corentin au pays de PipiCaca*, juvenile fiction) [author not given] [emphasis in original]

A fascinating cluster of challenges centered on portrayals of less-than-perfect adults and dysfunctional families — portrayals that some individuals apparently found threatening. Specific themes found offensive by complainants were disrespect on the part of children toward parents, unacceptable behaviours such as incest, abuse, violence and suicide, and inappropriate role modelling.

o "Material depicted youths exhibiting disrespect for parents." (*Angel Dust Blues* by Todd Strasser, young adult fiction)

o "Taught children disrespect to relatives and other adults when parents were trying to teach manners." (*Dinner at Auntie Rose's* by Janet Munsil, fiction for pre-school to eight years old)

o "Too violent. Showed parents in a bad light." (*Jim Who Ran Away from His Nurse and Was Eaten by a Lion* by Hilaire Belloc, picture book for ages 3 to 8)

o "I felt the main message to kids to be that violence, abuse, disobedience, disrespect, etc., are not offensive — injurious to kids' minds." (*Hector Protector* by Maurice Sendak, pre-school fiction)

o "Swearing, smoking marijuana, teen attitudes towards adults." (*Wheels for Walking* by Sandra Richmond, young adult fiction)

o "Too scary for children, too violent, seems to condone child abuse." (*Daddy is a Monster...Sometimes* by John Steptoe, picture book for ages 3 to 7)

o "Child abuse." (*Tom Thumb* by Charles Perrault, picture book for ages 6 to 12)

o "Book discussed family cruelty (wife abuse), violence." (*Cracker Jackson* by Betsy Byars, young adult fiction)

o "Book deals with incest, child abuse." (*Abby, My Love* by Hadley Irwin, young adult fiction)

o "Book not suitable for children's library (or indeed any library) because of graphic description of sex, violence, child abuse." (*Barbe-bleue* by Jacques Martin, a comic book for ages 8 to 12)

o "Content and violent pictures show incestuous behaviour." (*Le Petit chaperon rouge* by Bruno de la Salle, fiction for ages 6 to 8) o "The relationship between the brother and sister is simply not a healthy relationship mostly when they are sleeping together, last page and also putting the baby on the mantelpiece. Really." (*My Crazy Sister* by M.B. Goffstein, pre-school fiction)

o Patron felt book was for 10- 12-year-olds, indirectly about suicide. "Not suitable for children at all ... withdraw." (*Le Petit chien* by Jean Prignaud, picture book for ages 4 to 7)

o "Total despair in the conclusion — child commits suicide." (*The Brothers Lionheart* by Astrid Lindgren, fiction for ages 8 to 12)

o At one point in the story, it states the hero's parents "were so worried they were ready to kill themselves." Patron was horrified that such a statement should be in a kids' book. (*Gorky Rises* by William Steig, picture book for pre-school to grade 3)

o When son is lost mother is so distraught she says she will kill herself. (*Gorky Rises*, picture book fiction for pre-school to primary)

o "Talks about people committing suicide. NOT appropriate for small children." (*Gorky Rises*, picture book fiction) [emphasis in original]

o Patron felt boy's response was overly violent — not true to life. Disliked the ending where the mother fantasizes she would be able to watch soap operas while her son fed the baby. (*When the New Baby Comes, I'm Moving Out* by Martha Alexander, pre-school picture book)

o Patron said the book had unfeeling treatment of the subject of death, and disturbed her child, who chose it because of its blue cover in response to our summer reading game. It should be moved to non-fiction. (*Cookies for Luke* by Sheila J. Bleeks, juvenile fiction)

o "Lesson indicates that greed, craftiness and laziness pay off — result of using: a warped sense of values in small children." (*Tom Fox and the Apple Pie* by Clyde Watson, picture book for ages 5 to 7)

o "Gross habit: putting in picture and writing a grandpa blowing his nose without a handkerchief. Disregard just that one particular page." (*My Old Grandad* by Wolf Harranth, picture book)

o Patron found illustrations and poetry offensive and of poor quality, offbeat, e.g., p. 15 "urine" in picture of grandmother. (*High Wire Spider* by George Swede)

o Patron felt the male-female relationship in the book was an extremely negative influence on students: "Burn book (seriously!)." (*One On One* by Jerry Seigel, fiction for grades 9 and up)

o Patron thought book condoned forced marriages, i.e., teen pregnancies. (*Pennington's Heir* by K.M. Peyton, young adult fiction)

o Patron felt the book was showing a bad boy who, although he did misbehave, was never punished. Children reading it would think it was cute to be naughty. (*Bad Thad* by Judy Malloy, pre-school picture book)

o "Stereotyped. Reinforces acceptance of problems rather than encouraging action." (*New Friend* by Charlotte Zolotow, pre-school fiction)

o Patron felt book encouraged children to trust strangers. (*Will You Cross Me* by Marilyn Kaye, fiction for grade 1)

o "The child in the story is wearing a T-shirt with her name on it, which is not recommended practice because of danger from child molesters." (*The Other Emily* by Gibbs Davis, picture book for pre-school/primary)

o "Not proper for a child to read about having to look after a sibling because they are handicapped; children do not understand about people being different." (*Ben* by Victoria Shennon, juvenile fiction)

o "Didn't think it right that an adult could take over from children and didn't like tone of book." (*The Rotten Old Car* by Geraldine Kaye, fiction for pre-school to 7 years old)

o "Book shows Father Christmas (Santa) drinking alcoholic beverages." (*Father Christmas* by Raymond Briggs, picture book for ages 5 to 10)

o Patron said book had no plot or story, sexist, age-discrimination, racist. (*The Just Right Family*, juvenile fiction) [author not given]

o "Did not like children forgetting about dead bird for which they had had a funeral." (*The

Dead Bird by Margaret Wise Brown, fiction for pre-school to grade 2)

o "I was very disappointed to hear the endless stream of insults... I'm trying to teach good vocabulary." (*Two Stupid Dummies* by Mark Thurman, fiction for ages 3 to 7)

o "Picture of dog defecating on floor." (*Some Swell Pup* by Maurice Sendak, picture book for ages 4 to 8)

o "Not tactful in showing need to have possessions." (*Charlie's Pillow* by Haken Jaensson and Arne Worlin, easy fiction)

Several complainants opposed portrayals of the occult, witchcraft, and religion in literature for children and young adults.

o Parent objected to devil being blamed for child's unacceptable behaviour — felt this went against learning to accept responsibility for own actions. (*The Devil Did It* by Susan Jeschke, fiction for pre-school to grade 3)

o "The devil becomes a girl's friend. Becoming a friend of the devil is not good entertainment, especially for kids." (*The Devil Did It*)

o "Dragons are devil figures — shouldn't be in a children's book." (*Firerose* by Susan Jeschke, fiction for ages 3 to 5)

o "Witchcraft is represented as being a real and vital threat to the lives of children... The resolution of the story leaves the witches and underworld figures in the same powerful and threatening position." (*Hag Head* by Susan Musgrave and illustrated by Carol Evans, fiction for ages 6 to 11)

o "Introducing the occult in a matter-of-fact, supposedly innocent way." (*Bumps in the Night* by Harry Allard, picture book for ages 3 to 8)

o "Devils juxtaposed with church, religion." (*Out of the Oven* by Jan Mark, picture book)

o "Ridicules religion by creating an extra-terrestrial being." (*Les Huits jours du diable dans "Super Tintin"* by D. Convard, comic book for ages 9 to 13)

o Patron objected on religious grounds — pastor not portrayed correctly in the story. (*The Church Mice at Bay* by Graham Oakley, picture book for ages 3 to 10)

o Patron said that God was depicted as vengeful, not loving. (*Moses — The Escape from Egypt* by Geoffrey Butcher, board book for pre-school to grade 1)

Many complainants objected to representations of violence and what they considered to be excessive or inappropriate violence.

o "Morbid and contains several senseless murders.... Teaches children to solve their problems by using violence and murder." (*Big Claus and Little Claus* by Hans Christian Andersen, children's fiction)

o "Violence gratuitous and distasteful. Children torture, rape and finally murder babysitter and successfully blame it on a transient farm worker." (*Let's Go Play at Adam's* by Mendal W. Johnson)

o "Encourages children to feel violence will solve problems, encourages revenge — terrible qualities to teach." (*I'll Fix Anthony* by Judith Viorst, picture book for ages 3 to 10)

o "Promotes disunity between brothers. There is no love or forgiveness but only hatred and revenge." (*I'll Fix Anthony*, fiction for ages 4 to 9)

o "Violence condoned. Not a good role model for young children." (*The Beast of Monsieur Racine* by Tomi Ungerer, fiction for ages 5 and up)

o "Makes nuclear war sound like fun." (*The Butter Battle Book* by Dr. Seuss, fiction for ages 3 to 8)

o "Ending is too warlike." (*The Butter Battle Book*, children's fiction)

o "Book condoned war." (*The Butter Battle Book*, picture book fiction for pre-school and over)

o "Fighting, hating and selfishness." (*Mine's the Best* by Crosby Bonsall, easy fiction)

o "Emotional content, rape scene, death and cremation may be too intense for junior YA (ages

11 to 13). Might be more suitable for senior YA (14 to 16)." (*Crabbe* by William Bell)

o "Babysitter wanted to eat kids." (*Mr. and Mrs. Pig's Evening Out* by Mary Rayner, picture book fiction)

o "Story is violent, inappropriate for three-year-old being left with babysitter." (*Mr. and Mrs. Pig's Evening Out*, fiction for ages 4 to 7)

o "Gruesome, inappropriate for young children — since babysitter hired by parents is not to be trusted." (*Mrs. and Mrs. Pig's Evening Out*, picture book fiction for ages 4 to 8)

o "Child was visibly upset by the pictures of eating a live cat and bird and the final basement picture. Upset by wording and torture scene on pages 23 and 24 especially." (*The Werewolf Family* by Jack Gantos and Nicole Rubel, picture book for ages 4 to 10)

o Too violent for patron's child — fox snapped off the heads of his victims. (*The Story of Henny Penny* illustrated by Tom and Blonnie [?] Holmes, easy fiction)

o Patron objected to the second verse of "London Bridge," specifically "chopped off their heads." (*Sally Go Round the Sun* by Edith Fowke, pre-school fiction)

o "This book is gross! It's violent to eat humans — cannibal, and violent to fall apart and split open." (*The Greedy Old Fat Man* illustrated by Paul Galdone, pre-school picture book)

o "Frightening for a child because the vain queen eats the heart of Snow White (she thinks it's her heart, actually a wild boar's heart)." (*Snow White and the Seven Dwarfs* by Wanda Gag, junior fiction)

o "Child was upset by Tittymouse and Tattymouse because Titty was scalded to death." (*Tales to Tell* by Harold Jones, pre-school picture book)

o "Body being beaten, hanging." (*The Punch and Judy Book* by Ron Mann, juvenile/easy fiction)

o Patron was offended by the illustrations in which some faces are grotesque, the giant is scary, and Tom comes out of a cow in a cowpat. (*Adventures of Tom* by Freire Wright, picture book)

o Patron found offensive the part where the tiny woman goes to the graveyard and removes a bone from the top of a grave and then uses it to make soup. (*The Teeny Tiny Woman* by Barbara Seuling, fiction for ages 3 to 8)

o "Story is gory, very unhappy ending, disturbing to young child." (*Big Monster* by Shane Zarowny, easy fiction)

o Dialogue had frightened child when parent read the book to him. Crocodile eats child. Wanted us to warn parents that book would scare children. (*The Enormous Crocodile* by Roald Dahl, easy fiction)

o "Moral dubious, violent, not educational, scary." (*Five Chinese Brothers* by Claire Bishop, picture book)

Sexism and racism were often other grounds for challenges.

o "Sexist, taught rigid sex roles — 1944 publication." (*Let's Play House* by Lois Lenski, picture book for ages 4 to 6)

o Patron thought book was damaging to the image of women, contained violence towards women, women portrayed as sex objects. (*King Stork* by Howard Pyle, picture book for ages 6 to 12)

o "Sexist, anti-male, anti-father, anti-Jewish." (*A Fortunate Catastrophe* by Adela Turin, picture book for ages 5 to 8)

o "Female teddy bear served cocoa to male teddy bear at work in post office — sexist." (*Teddybear Postman* by Phoebe Worthington, pre-school fiction)

o "This was the worst of the lot in its description of Indians, e.g., 'naked wild man' p. 23, 'naked savages' p. 24, 'red devils' p. 28." (*Savage Sam* by Fred Gipson, fiction for ages 8 to 12)

o "Prejudice against native people; violent, causes fear in young children." (*Indian Summer* by F.N. Monjo, fiction for grades 1 to 3)

o "Section on cowboys and Indians is not flattering to the Indians. The girl-boy behaviour is also stereotyped. The girls have a passive role o overall, although it isn't quickly apparent." (*Jump from the Sky*, fiction for grade 2) [author not given]

o Poem "Foreign Children" offensive to Inuit people. (*A Child's Garden of Verses* by Robert Louis Sevenson, picture book for ages 3 to 8)

o "Pejorative in character depiction.... The name Little Black Sambo has been used as degrading nomenclature.... I do not think our public library should be sowing the seeds of disharmony." (*Little Black Sambo* by Helen Bannerman, fiction for ages 3 to 7)

Several complainants objected to the use of profanity in literature, often urging removal or restriction of material on the basis of a single word.

o "Use of word 'fuck'." (*Freddy's Book* by John Neufeld, fiction for ages 8 to 12)

o "The little boys and girls spoke rudely about a penis as a hot dog." (*Blue Trees, Red Sky* by Norma Klein, picture book for ages 3 to 7)

o "It teaches that nudity at play is acceptable — the use of 'slit' instead of 'vagina'." (*Thomas is Different* by Gunilla Wolde, picture book for ages 4 to 8)

o "Pg. 11 word 'slut.' Warn other parents." (*Cinderella* illustrated by Bernadette, juvenile fiction)

o "One part of the text — 'Oh my God'." (*Les Aventures de Benji* by Disney, cassette-book for ages 6 to 8)

o "Encouraged swearing." (*Soap-Box Derby* by the National Film Board, juvenile video)

o Patron objected to language (cat called Fluffybum). (*Badjelly the Witch* by Spike Milligan, junior fiction)

o "Inappropriate language ('fucking,' 'whore's guts') and explicit graphics (couples copulating, naked females). The theme (that God is a depraved old man) is equally offensive." (*The Vagabond of Limbo: The Ultimate Alchemist* by Christian Godard and Julio Ribera, fiction for young adults and adults)

o "Might make coarse language seem acceptable — 'damn,' 'bull,' 'up yours,' 'go to Hell'." (*Alan and Naomi* by Myron Levoy, children's fiction)

o Patron complained about language — "bastard," "pissed," "Hot Damn," and some we could not find. (*Starring Sally J. Freedman as Herself* by Judy Blume, fiction for ages 9 to 12)

o "Coarse language — 'Mrs. Minish is such a bitch' (p. 30). 'Damn that Blubber!' (p. 50). 'Damn!' Mom said (p. 69). Categorize the book so that children under age 11 are less likely to read it." (*Blubber* by Judy Blume, fiction for grades 4 to 6)

Finally, complainants were opposed to a variety of other literary depictions:

o "Children may perceive wolves to be like domesticated animals, which in fact they are not." (*A Wolf Story* by David McPhail, easy fiction)

o "Ecologically unsound (garbage was not recycled)." (*Dear Garbageman* by Gene Zion, picture book for ages 5 to 7)

o "Varied from original story." (*The Frog Prince* by Galdone)

o Written for the "ghetto"—inappropriate here. Had to "translate" the book, which she then enjoyed. (*I Been There* by Carol Hall, pre-school fiction)

o "The author deals with some sensitive subjects in a very insensitive manner." (*I Know You, Al* by Constance Greene, fiction for ages 9 to 15)

o "Distorted view of humour; illustrations in poor taste." (*Won't Somebody Play with Me* by Steven Kellogg, juvenile fiction)

o "Language not suitable for young patrons; made mockery of nursery rhymes." (*Roald Dahl's Revolting Rhymes* by Roald Dahl, juvenile poetry)

NON-FICTION FOR CHILDREN AND YOUNG ADULTS

Challenges to juvenile non-fiction were less common than challenges to adult non-fiction. Some of the grounds given by complainants were as follows:

o "Book contained a picture of a woman removing a bra." [book on rock musical group, title and author not given (non-fiction for ages 10 to 18)

o "Objection to the title — this is not a book for the young, and teenagers are young. Sin is never something to be proud of. I would think this book might result in a very sick society in the future." (*Young, Gay and Proud* edited by Sasha Alyson, young adult non-fiction)

o "Some vulnerable teenager entering puberty might actually believe that homosexuality is okay and give it a try and reap some serious consequences in later years." (*A Way of Love, A Way of Life* by Frances Hanckel and John Cunningham, young adult non-fiction)

o "Mention of masturbation, periods, wet dreams could make children experiment early (pre-puberty)." (*What's Happening to Me: A Guide to Puberty* by Peter Mayle, young adult non-fiction)

o Patron objected strongly to one sentence on masturbation being pleasurable, i.e., okay. (*What's Happening to Me: A Guide to Puberty* by Peter Mayle, non-fiction for ages 11 and over)

o "Material was very explicit and actually encouraging of teenage girls to experiment with pre-marital sex." (*Girls and Sex* by Wardell B. Pomeroy, young adult non-fiction)

o "I object to the tone of the chapter on sex. You as librarian are in a perfect position to set a high moral standard for the community." (*The Teenage Survival Book* by Sol Gordon, teen non-fiction)

o We serve an Iroquois Indian reserve as well as the town of [...]. Tribe member complained book was obscene and spurious. (*Tales from the Smokehouse* by Herbert T. Schwartz, non-fiction for ages 16 and up)

o "Will initiate curiosity, resulting in sexual experimentation by the children." (*Did the Sun Shine Before You Were Born?* by Sol Gordon, non-fiction for ages 3 to 7)

o "My son brought this book to my attention and was upset and embarrassed." (*The Body Book* by Claire Rayner, junior non-fiction)

o "Too detailed for young children." (*Learning About Sex: Contemporary Guide for Young Adults* by Gary F. Kelly)

o As a Catholic parent, patron was concerned that child would have access to such material, especially about birth control. (*Learning about Sex: A Guide for Children and Their Parents* by Jennifer Aho)

o Patron specifically objected to a sentence that used the word "penis" — parent of grade 3 girl felt that she didn't want her daughter to know what a penis was at this early age. (*The Joy of Birth* by Camilla Jessel, described as non-fiction for pre-school to grade 3)

o "Mention of chastity belt." (*A(lexandra) the Great* by Constance C. Greene, non-fiction for ages 10 to 12)

o "Sexist statements regarding appropriate behaviour for boys and girls." (*Girls and Boys Book of Etiquette* by Barbara Hazen, non-fiction for ages 5 to 9)

o Patron believed that if book gets in the hands of the wrong child, a lot of evil could come of it. Felt it is for university level only. (*Out of the Cauldron* by Bernice Kohn Hunt, non-fiction for ages 10 to 13)

o Patron said the book was contrary to the teachings of her fundamentalist church. (*The Big Bang* by Lydia Bailey, children's non-fiction)

o The poster of the rock star Prince was with many others displayed in the YA Listening Centre. The patron found it offensive that his midriff was exposed, and believed he could see pubic hair.

o "Very violent methods used to kill the cat are grossly unacceptable." (*The Cat Came Back* by Dahlov Ipcar, children's poetry) [poetry classified as non-fiction]

o "Prejudicial to the majority community in Sri Lanka." (*A Question of Race* by Beverly Birch, non-fiction for ages 8 to 12)

o Patron felt book contained many inaccuracies. (*Gerbils* by Fiona Henrie, children's non-fiction)

SPECIFIC TITLES

There was not only wide variation in the grounds that complainants offered to justify requests to remove or restrict materials, there were also differences in point of view on the same title. The multiplicity of grounds that have been advanced to justify challenges to library materials is best explained by reference to reading theory. The reader, or viewer or listener, participates in creating the meaning of a text. Indeed, sometimes the reader's interpretation of meaning is so divergent from the author's that it appears the reader has created her or his own text quite independent of whatever the author intended. (I suspect most of us have felt that way about book reviewers and film critics at one time or another!)

Response to a text is based in the reader's personal history, in the reader's reading history, and in the text itself. The reader reacts to a text, consciously or unconsciously, on the basis of several socially constructed criteria. Among these criteria are literary merit, social merit (that is, a text's efficacy as an instrument for socializing individuals into acceptance of certain values and morals), and perceived popularity.

These complex interactions are no better illustrated than in the frequently divergent reasons that people give for disapproving of the same title. For example, although violence was a recurring theme in complaints about *Lizzy's Lion*, there were many different interpretations given to this theme among the 11 complainants who sought its suppression or relocation. The respondent library's classification of the title appears in parentheses.

o "Very violent — may frighten children aged 3 to 6" (fiction for ages 3 to 6)

o "Unnecessary exposure to violence that a young child does not need to be subjected to" (fiction for ages 4 to 9)

o "Lion eating up robber — frightening — inappropriate material for young children" (picture book fiction for pre-school to grade 3)

o "Whole book objectionable — caused children to have nightmares" [no designation given]

o "Too violent — a depressing book" (picture book fiction for pre-school to grade 3)

o "Violence was too graphic" (picture book fiction)

o "Violence — body parts dumped in trash" (non-fiction for ages 4 to 8)

o "Violent and scary" (picture book fiction)

o "Break and enter ideas; insensitive and uncaring about people in general" (juvenile fiction).

Similarly, although sexual explicitness was a recurring theme in objections to *Forever*, several interpretations of this theme were also given by complainants:

o "My daughter's romantic illusions have been shattered. Not suitable for an 11-year-old" (young people's fiction)

o Patron objected to this book being considered a children's book when it had sex scenes (young adult fiction)

o Patron thought subject matter was teaching children to have sex (adult fiction)

o Patron did not want his teenaged daughter reading a sexually explicit book (adult fiction)

o "Too much sex, no remorse on girl's part" (fiction for ages 12 and over)

o "Too sexually explicit" (young adult fiction)

o "Too explicitly sexual" (fiction for ages 12 and over).

The grounds for objections to *Wifey* were also expressed in a variety of ways:

o Unsuitable for children — adult material written by popular children's author (fiction)

o Patron felt that it was inappropriate for YA — cover listed book as adult; too explicit sexually (young adult fiction)

o "Not for children" [no designation given]

o Patron was extremely upset as to sexual nature of book and *very* angry as to placement (fiction for senior high to adult)

o "Unsuitable for young people" (adult fiction)

o "Entire content" (adult fiction).

The reasons for objections to *Slugs* were as follows:

o "Too violent for children" (picture book fiction for ages 4 to 6) o "The book is a bad influence on child-animal relationships and is generally in bad taste" (picture book fiction for ages 6 to 9)

o "Gross content, extreme violence indicated, would promote violence and cruelty in children, etc." (non-fiction for pre-school to grade 3).

With *The Haj*, grounds for challenges ranged from charges that it was anti-Arab to charges that it was pro-Jewish. All institutions catalogued *The Haj* as adult fiction.

o "Unfair treatment of Arabs — openly racist"

o "Statements in this book, e.g., 'women are the chattel of men' (p. 11), are in the opinion of the Muslim Association 'typical traditional insults of Islam and work of mischiefmongers'"

o "Racial slurs, misrepresentation of a particular group"

o "Depiction of Arabian people"

o "Portrayed Arabs in a bad light"

o Patron felt topic was biased in favour of Jewish faith.

Objections to *Where Did I Come From?* were as follows:

o Patron felt book was too explicit and damaging to her 9-year-old son, who was going into the priesthood (non-fiction)

o "Unsuitable for children without parental supervision — writing in poor taste — pictures presented in a poor manner — encourages children to experiment" (non-fiction for ages 10 to 12)

o Patron said chapter "Making Love" was too much of a how-to and inappropriate for age of readers to which it was directed [no designation given]

o Patron felt book should be housed in office because children shouldn't be able to get at it themselves; subject matter should be dealt with by parent. [no designation given]

Objections to *Outside Over There* were as follows:

o "Desensitizes children to accept ugly; shows children expected to take on an adult's responsibility; the magic has an occult flavour; the illustrations make the gnomes look like adults" (picture book fiction)

o "Terrifying pictures" [no designation given]

o "Unnatural, scary story, not educational" (picture book fiction)

o "Simply weird, not suitable for children — doesn't make sense" (picture book fiction for ages 5 to 8).

5. What Did Complainants Want?

Regardless of the varying grounds for challenges, what action did the complainants want carried out? Table 24 shows the pattern of demands made by complainants.

Table 24. Action Requested by Complainants, 1985-87

Action Requested	Titles Challenged	
	Number	Percentage
Remove	481	76
Restrict access	39	6
Relocate from children's to young adult	37	6
Relocate from young adult to adult	23	4
Relocate from children's to adult	11	2
Label	16	2
Reclassify	5	1
Alter content	2	<1
Not specific	20	3
Total	634	100

Three out of four complainants wanted the offending material removed from the public library collection — some even wanted it burned or destroyed as well! And a fringe element also wanted the library staff punished in draconian ways. One-quarter of the complainants wanted some form of restriction imposed on the offending material or action that would have had the effect of restriction.

Internal relocations made up 12 per cent of the requests, usually from children's to young adult or adult sections. While most of these requests were made on the grounds of "unsuitability for a particular age group," many may have been attempts to discourage access by making it harder for certain age groups to find a given item.

Other complainants were more forthright in calling for barriers to access: 6 per cent requested that borrowing privileges or in-house use be explicitly restricted by age. In addition, a small number of complainants wanted a warning label placed on an item, a few wanted materials to be reclassified, and a very small number even wanted content altered.

Some 20 complainants were not specific about what they wanted the library to do, and there is some question whether or not these cases constituted collection challenges *per se*. Nonetheless, since the survey respondents themselves reported these incidents as challenges, I have treated these incidents as challenges in the analysis.

The action requested by a complainant (removal or restriction) depended on several factors: intended audience of the offending title, grounds for the challenge, and whether the challenge was communicated verbally or in writing. Statistical analysis shows that these patterns were significant.

Table 25 shows that complainants were almost five times more likely to request removal rather than restriction of pre-school and adult materials. In comparison, requests to remove elementary and high school materials were only two to three times more likely than requests to restrict them.

Table 25. Intended Age Level of Material Challenged, by Action Requested, 1985-87

Action Requested	Pre-school	Elementary	High School	Adult	Total
Remove	33	95	91	200	419
Restrict*	7	37	45	43	132
Total	40	132	136	243	551

*includes requests to relocate, label, reclassify and/or alter materials

Complainants wanted virtually all of the titles alleged to be pornographic and nine out of ten titles deemed "to promote negative moral values" withdrawn. On the other hand, only half of the titles judged "unsuitable for age group" were targeted for withdrawal.

Medium of communication also made a difference in the kind of action requested by complainants. Of requests for removal, 70 per cent were made verbally, while 81 per cent were in writing.

Action requested by complainants was not associated with the publication format of offending titles, with whether they were fiction or non-fiction, or with the date of their publication. Institutional characteristics — type of governance, dominant language of the community, municipal population, registered borrowers, and library circulation — were also unrelated to the kind of action requested by complainants.

There were many requests that public library staff act *in loco parentis* by removing or restricting materials or by denying a particular child access to certain titles or subjects. One parent told the library staff that she wanted them to remove the teen novel *Queen of What If* by Norma Klein because the language was too frank for her 12-year-old and "she couldn't pre-read everything the child brought home." Another patron wanted the library to withdraw *The Companion* by Scott Siegel, a story for 12-year-olds, because it was a horror story. The patron said to staff: "What do you mean by letting my child read such a book?"

Still another patron wanted her son — but only her son — to be denied access to *Hoodoo Conjuration Witchcraft Rootwork* by Harry Middleton Hyatt. The survey respondent wrote, "Apparently he was bringing it home repeatedly. Complainant did not want general access to be restricted, but threatened to burn the book if her son brought it home again." In yet another instance, a parent reported that his six-year-old daughter had read *Don't Hurt Me, Mama* by Muriel Stanek and was frightened by the content on child abuse. Although he agreed that it was well done, he felt the book should be in the adult section. If he had been aware of the nature of the book, his child would not have read it.

Not only did the reasons expressed by complainants for challenges to materials reveal diversity in their attitudes and values, but their demands also took on a variety of forms. In the case of *Lizzy's Lion*, for example, out of eleven challenges, five complainants wanted the book withdrawn from the collection, two wanted it relocated from the picture book shelf, one patron said to "put it in an upper elementary section or discard it completely," and one wanted it reviewed by the library staff; respondents reported that two complainants were unclear about what action they wanted taken.

Similarly, out of the eight challenges to *Forever*, five complainants wanted it withdrawn, two wanted access restricted to people over a certain age, and one was not specific. Out of six challenges to *Wifey*, three complainants wanted it withdrawn, two wanted it relocated to the adult collection and restricted in access, and one said "do not let my daughter take these books out."

In the case of *Slugs*, the challenges were more uniform: all six complainants wanted it removed from the collection. Challenges to *The Haj* were also uniform: five out of the six complainants wanted it withdrawn, while one did not say. In the case of *Where Did I Come From?*, two complainants wanted the book removed, and two wanted it relocated internally, in one instance to the office so that it would have to be asked for, and in another instance to a parents' shelf. In the case of *Outside Over There*, three complainants wanted it withdrawn, and one wanted children to be warned about it.

One respondent noted the peculiarity of complainant demands that children's material be withdrawn from all patrons rather than just from children:

> o I find it interesting that all of the requests for withdrawal that we receive are made by adults on behalf of children/young adults, and yet the majority of recommendations suggest that the books should be withdrawn from *all* patrons.

Summary

Complaints about titles in public library collections are motivated by individual opinion. Fewer than 600 individuals were so concerned about the words and ideas expressed in public library materials that they attempted to intervene in the institutional process. Nonetheless, the actions of this small group had the potential to affect access to particular materials by more than 13 million other Canadian residents.

Three in four challenges called for the removal of the offending material from the public library collection. Although half of all complainants said they were acting for themselves, the majority of them targeted materials written for children and young adults. Requests to remove or restrict material were communicated to staff almost equally in verbal and written form, although the proportion that were conveyed verbally is probably understated.

Most of the items challenged were published in the 1980s. Fiction was challenged much more frequently than non-fiction, regardless of the age level for which the material was written. More than 500 different titles were challenged, and there were, as well, 21 complaints against multiple titles in a particular genre or subject area or by a particular author.

Respondents recorded 857 reasons for requests to remove or restrict access to the 498 titles specifically identified in the study. The most common grounds were sexual explicitness, nudity and pornography. Second were objections to violence, cruelty and scary works. Third were objections to titles deemed unsuitable for a particular age group, often in combination with additional grounds such as sex or violence. These three clusters of reasons accounted for over half of all challenges between 1985 and 1987. This pattern was similar to the findings of U.S. studies with the exception of complaints about violence, which figured prominently in the present study but ranked very low in U.S. findings (Hopkins 1991).

Most titles were challenged once only, but a few were challenged several times. Similarly, most authors had only one work challenged, while a few had many works challenged. These patterns suggest that, although it may not be possible to predict specific titles that will be vulnerable to censorship pressure in the future, specific subjects can be identified. Highly cited titles and authors may be an exception: a few titles and authors were challenged consistently throughout the 1980s. This finding is corroborated by the findings of previous studies.

C. Outcomes of Challenges

How did public library staff across Canada respond to challenges? In 540, or 86 per cent, of the disputes, challenged titles were retained. However, not all of these titles were retained intact on regular, open library shelves. In 58 instances (13 per cent), materials were either relocated within the library, reclassified, labelled, or restricted by age or grade level. In eight relocations, titles were removed to library storage, a cupboard, "the back room," staff work sections, or an office.

The general effect of most of these relocations, reclassifications, labellings, and age restrictions on challenged materials might have been some limitation on access. If a title was in the catalogue and not on the shelf, the patron would have to ask for it; this situation is no different from trying to find a book that is already in circulation except that the librarian will be able to retrieve and provide it from wherever it is stored. On the other hand, as some patrons rely on serendipitous browsing, their chances of identifying useful titles would be affected. Reduced access might lead to reduced use, but I did not investigate this possibility here.

In six challenges, titles were only temporarily removed and were later returned to the collection, sometimes at the request of other patrons. One respondent said that a title was removed for a few months "until other patrons requested it," and another said that a juvenile title was removed while staff sought the opinions of several parents who recommended putting it back. Another respondent noted that a title was removed until a patron on exchange from another country returned home. While these actions amounted to a denial of patron access for some period of time, they have been viewed in this study somewhat differently from permanent withdrawals.

Table 26 shows the result of challenges over the three years of the study.

Table 26. Outcomes of Challenges, 1985-87

Outcome	Challenges	
	Number	Percentage
Retained without change	448	72
Relocated internally	58	9
Restricted by age/grade	21	3
Reclassified	4	1
Labelled	3	<1
Removed temporarily	6	1
Removed permanently	85	14
Total	625	100

Comparison with other studies shows that the Canada-wide rate of public library withdrawal identified in the present survey is relatively low. In the one-year study mentioned earlier of larger public libraries across the country, respondents reported that 39 per cent of challenges had resulted in the removal of materials (Beta Associates 1982, 90). In the one-year study of Alberta public libraries, it was found that 29 per cent of the challenges resulted in withdrawal of materials (Walker 1984, 20). In Manitoba public libraries, 13 per cent of the challenges over a two-year period resulted in the withdrawal of juvenile materials (Jenkinson 1985, 29). In Hopkins' three-year secondary school library study in the U.S., 26 per cent of the questioned materials were removed (Hopkins 1991 4:27).

Table 27 shows the extent to which public library staff adhered to institutional policy in dealing with challenges.

Table 27. Library Adherence to Policy
in Resolving Challenges, 1985-87

Policy Followed	Challenges	
	Number	Percentage
Yes	495	90
Partially	44	8
No	14	2
Total	553	100

Among institutions that had a policy to deal with challenges, respondents reported that the policy was followed in 90 per cent of the cases resolved between 1985 and 1987. In Hopkins' study of U.S. secondary school libraries, among those institutions with a library materials selection policy of any kind, only two in three respondents indicated that their policy was used during a challenge. Even among this group, there was considerable variation in the extent to which the policy was used (Hopkins 1991, 4:30).

Table 28 shows the pattern of administrative involvement in resolving challenges.

Table 28. Administrative Level in Resolving Challenges, 1985-87

Administrative Level	Challenges	
	Number	Percentage
Chief executive officer	192	32
Branch manager	128	21
Senior management	84	14
Public library board	57	9
Head, children's services	53	9
Supervisor other than management	26	4
Head, public relations	19	3
Review committee	17	3
Municipal council	14	2
Head, youth services	8	1
Head, adult services	6	1
School official	4	1
Total	608	100

Decisions about how to handle challenges were made most frequently by the chief executive officer (32 per cent), by a branch manager (21 per cent), or by a variety of other senior managers such as head of children's services, head of young adult services, head of adult services, or head of public relations (28 per cent). In 9 per cent of the incidents, the decision was made by the public library board, and in 2 per cent by the municipal council. In only 3 per cent of the incidents was a review committee involved in resolving disputes.

Almost half of the challenges were resolved within a month — and, in fact, many were resolved on the same day the complaint was made. While another 28 per cent took up to 2 months to resolve, a total of 96 per cent were resolved within 6 months of initiation. Some 18 challenges took 7 months or longer to resolve, including one that took 34 months. Nine challenges were still unresolved at the end of 1987, including one that had been initiated in 1978.

In only 24 challenges, or 4 per cent of 624 incidents, was there a report in the local media. This reinforces a finding in a report entitled "Silent Censorship; The Sins of Omission, the Sins of Commission," that only 8 accounts of book bannings could be found in Canadian newspapers in 1982 (Bildfell 1984, 4). Almost all of the media coverage in the present study consisted of newspaper articles; in one challenge a radio interview was also involved.

None of the reported challenges was covered by journals or magazines — a noteworthy finding in view of an analysis of Canadian periodical literature for the period 1981-85 by Melody Burton, who, while she was a student in the Master of Library Science program at the University of Alberta, identified 240 periodical articles on freedom of expression and freedom of access (Burton 1986). In Hopkins' study of U.S. secondary school libraries, fewer than 6 per cent of the challenges resulted in media coverage (Hopkins 1991 4:27).

Table 29 shows the reasons given by complainants for those challenges that resulted in permanent withdrawals from public library collections.

Table 29. Reasons for Challenges to Titles Withdrawn, 1985-87

Complainant Reason	Titles Challenged	
	Number	Percentage
Sexually explicitness, nudity	24	19
Violence, cruelty	18	14
Unsuitable for age group	16	13
Pornographic	13	10
Promotes negative moral values	11	9
Misinformation, bias	8	6
Scary, frightening to child	5	4
Offensive to religion, blasphemous	5	4
Sexist, demeaning to women	5	4
Coarse language, profanity	4	3
Promotes homosexuality	4	3
Promotes the occult, witchcraft	4	3
Racist	4	3
Badly written	3	2
Anti-semitic	2	2
Promotes drug use	1	1
Total	127	100

Complainant grounds for withdrawn materials paralleled the grounds that had been given for all challenges: sexual explicitness, nudity, and pornography (29 per cent for withdrawn titles versus 22 per cent for all challenges); violence, cruelty, and scary themes (18 per cent for withdrawn titles versus 19 per cent for all challenges); and unsuitability for a particular age group (13 per cent for withdrawn titles versus 14 per cent for all challenges).

Public library responses to challenged titles were not always consistent across the country. Just as complainants did not always request the same action for a given title, public library staff did not always respond in the same way to challenges to a given title. Some challenges resulted in retention, others in internal relocation, and still others in withdrawal. Among the most frequently challenged titles already identified, the following mixed outcomes were noted:

◆ Of the eleven challenges to *Lizzy's Lion*, eight resulted in retention of the title after discussion with complainants. But in two cases, it was relocated to a juvenile section, and, in another, it was taken out of circulation temporarily.

- Of the eight challenges to *Forever*, five resulted in retention of the title after discussion with complainants. In two cases, it was relocated to a young adult section (one respondent noted, however, that children could still take out YA books if they wished to), and, in another, it was temporarily removed but later returned to the shelves.

- Of the six challenges to *Wifey*, outcomes were equally divided between retention and relocation; in one case, it was relocated to adult fiction, in another to a supervised shelf, and in the third to a restricted adult cart.

- Of the six challenges to *Slugs*, outcomes were more uniform; in all cases it was retained, although in one instance it was recatalogued to poetry in the children's section.

- In all six challenges to *The Haj*, the book was retained.

- Of the four challenges to *Where Did I Come From?*, two resulted in retention and two in relocation.

- Of the four challenges to *Outside Over There*, three resulted in retention and one in a warning label written on the pocket.

1. Factors Influencing Outcomes of Challenges

In analyzing factors that might account for the final outcome of challenges to public library collections, I found that outcome depended on factors that can be clustered into two groupings, challenge characteristics and institutional characteristics. Statistical analysis shows that all of the following factors were significant as determinants of whether offending titles were retained by or withdrawn from the library:

a) Characteristics of the challenge — whether the offending title was fiction or non-fiction, its intended audience, grounds for a challenge, whether library policy was followed in handling a challenge, and whether local media reported the incident.
b) Institutional and demographic characteristics — number of challenges that were experienced, number of titles on the controversial materials checklist that were owned, whether there was an objections policy, an objections form, or a donations policy, existence of a consent requirement for minors, type of governance unit, dominant language of the community, municipal population, number of registered borrowers, and library circulation.

By characteristics of a challenge, 88 per cent of the offending fiction was retained, compared to 79 per cent of the non-fiction. By intended audience, elementary materials accounted for 27 per cent of the titles retained, compared to 12 per cent withdrawn. For adult titles, the reverse was true: they accounted for 41 per cent of the titles retained, in contrast to 59 per cent withdrawn. By grounds for challenges, only 58 per cent of titles alleged to be pornographic were retained compared to 86 per cent overall. In contrast, of items with offensive language, 93 per cent were retained, and of those alleged to be "unsuitable for age group," 91 per cent were retained.

The retention rate was higher in institutions in which library policy was followed in dealing with challenges. In 89 per cent of the disputes where library policy was followed, the offending material was retained. This result contrasts with the rate of retention for disputes in which library policy was not followed or followed only in part, 75 per cent and 49 per cent, respectively.

The retention rate was higher in disputes that did not involve local media coverage; 85 per cent of the items challenged were retained in disputes not reported in the local media, while only half of the items challenged were retained in disputes covered by the media. It should be noted that the total number of cases reported in the media was very small, accounting for only 4 per cent of all incidents.

By characteristics of the institution, retention rates were higher in multi-branch systems and in English-language institutions. Of incidents where material was retained, 77 per cent occurred in single-unit libraries compared to 89 per cent in systems. Of incidents where material was retained, 87 per cent were in English-language institutions, compared to 53 per cent in French-language institutions.

Retention rates were higher in larger municipalities. Institutions that retained offending material served an average 152,000 people, reported 70,000 registered borrowers, and circulated 1.5 million items. By comparison, those that withdrew titles were about half as large. They served 86,000 people, had 38,000 borrowers, and circulated 754,000 items.

Retention rates were higher in institutions that had an objections policy and form as well as a donations policy. Of incidents where material was retained, 88 per cent occurred in institutions that had either an objections policy or form. In cases where there was no policy, the retention rate was only 73 per cent of items challenged; where there was no form, it was 78 per cent. Similarly, of incidents where material was retained, 86 per cent occurred in institutions with a donations policy, compared to 74 per cent in those without one.

Retention rates were higher in institutions that did not require minors to have consent to use the library. Of the incidents where materials were retained, 90 per cent occurred in institutions that had no consent requirement. In contrast, 73 per cent occurred in institutions with a consent requirement.

Institutions that experienced a higher rate of challenges tended to retain the material more than those experiencing a lower rate of challenges. Institutions that retained offending titles reported on average 9 challenges over three years, while those removing them reported fewer than 7.

Retention of challenged material was also more likely in institutions reporting high rates of ownership of the titles on the controversial materials checklist. Institutions that retained offending material owned an average of 21 checklist titles. Among institutions that withdrew material, there were fewer than 17 titles per library.

Retention rates were not associated with any of the following factors: whether the challenged title was a print or non-print format, whether the challenged title was published recently, whether the challenge was communicated verbally or in writing, whether complainants represented themselves or a child, the administrative level at which the dispute was resolved, the length of time taken for resolution, the presence of a selection policy, support for the CLA Statement on Intellectual Freedom, the presence of an age restriction on borrowing privileges, the presence of differential treatment of potentially controversial material, or pressure to acquire or accept material for the collection.

The factors that influence the outcome of a direct challenge are summarized in Figure 4.

Figure 4. Factors Influencing Outcomes of Challenges to Public Library Collections

fiction/non-fiction status
age level of material
grounds for challenge
library policy followed
media coverage
governance
population
number of borrowers
circulation
language of community
objections policy
objections form
donations policy
consent requirement for minors
ownership of titles on the controversial materials checklist
rate of challenges

The pattern of outcomes documented here is somewhat different from the pattern for secondary school libraries that Hopkins found in her nationwide U.S. study covering the three school years 1986-87 through 1988-89. She found that material was more likely to be retained where there was a board-approved selection policy that was followed during the challenge process, the school had a large enrolment, the challenge was in written form, the material challenged was fiction, and the material challenged was in book format (Hopkins 1991, 5:13). I advise using caution in making comparisons, however, because in her statistical analysis Hopkins included "restricted" material with withdrawals, not with retentions, as I did.

D. Titles Withdrawn

The following discussion profiles those challenged titles that were withdrawn from public library collections across the country between 1985 and 1987. Respondents reported that the following titles were withdrawn in accordance with extant policy for dealing with objections:

adult comics (several titles)
a heavy metal magazine
a poster of Prince
An Act of Mercy: Euthanasia Today by Richard Trubo
Algonkians of the Eastern Woodlands by Edward Rogers
Les Aventures magiques de Corentin au pays de PipiCaca
Big Bigger Biggest by Edward Dolch
The Body Politic
Brave Cowboy by Joan Walsh Anglund
The Brothers Lionheart by Astrid Lindgren
Cinderella [edition not specified]
Dancer of Gor by John Norman
The Devil Did It by Susan Jeschke
Dirty Beasts by Roald Dahl
The Discipline of Raising Children by M.A. Treadwell
Fell's Guide to Doubling Performance of Your Car by William Hampton
Lamia by Tristan Travis
Let's Go Play at Adam's by Mendal W. Johnson
Meeting the Mormons by Jack Roundhill
Men in Love: Male Sexual Fantasies by Nancy Friday
Murder in the Family by Marc Brandel (two challenges in different institutions)
National Lampoon
Ninja Death Touch by Ashida Kim
Le Petit chaperon rouge by Bruno de la Salle
Petit et grand Albert
Roald Dahl's Revolting Rhymes by Roald Dahl
The Ultimate Frontier by Eklal Kueshana
The Werewolf Family by Jack Gantos and Nicole Rubel
You Think Just Because You're Big You're Right by Albert Cullum
Where Did I Come From? by Peter Mayle

In the case of some challenges, respondents reported that library policy was not followed or was only partially followed in deciding to withdraw items. The titles were:

adult western paperbacks (several titles)
Annie on My Mind by Nancy Garden
Cathérine saute au paf! by Jean Cabu
Daddy is a Monster... Sometimes by John Steptoe
Did the Sun Shine Before You Were Born? by Sol Gordon
Lizzy's Lion by Dennis Lee
Mon corps est à elles by Georges Wolinski
Nine and a Half Weeks by Elizabeth McNeill
Paulette by Georges Pichard and Georges Wolinski

The Penguin Book of Limericks by E.O. Parrott
Playboar
Les Rockeurs sanctifiés by Lucien Francoeur
Secrets of the Ninja by Ashida Kim
Seven Little Monsters by Maurice Sendak
Uncle Remus: His Songs and His Sayings by Joel Chandler Harris
Zoom

In the case involving *Lizzy's Lion*, the respondent noted that the book was temporarily taken out of circulation even though in this instance the complainant had not requested any specific action. In another challenge to *Lizzy's Lion*, in a joint public-school library, the survey respondent reported that a school trustee "circumvented normal channels, took book to board meeting, and all hell broke loose!!!"

The following items were withdrawn from institutions that reported having no policy for dealing with objections:

Là-bas
The Boys on the Rock by John Fox
Creepshow by Stephen King
Diary of a Drug Fiend by Aleister Crowley
Fungus the Bogeyman by Raymond Briggs
Guide des caresses by Pierre Valinieff
L'Histoire de Kiki Grabouille by Jeanne Willis and Margaret Chamberlain
La Femme piégée
Fit for Life by Harvey and Marilyn Diamond
The Joy of Life by Alan Kingdon
Lampoon
Marmouset et Makumba by Dina-K. Tourneur
Naomi in the Middle by Norma Klein
Poilus, Vélus, Barbus by Babette Cole
Reproduction by Gwynne Vevers
La Vagabond des limbes by Christian Godard and Julio Ribera
Webster's New Collegiate Dictionary
Witchery Hill by Welwyn Wilton Katz
Witches by Peter Usborne

Of the 24 incidents reported in local media, more titles were withdrawn than in the study at large. There were 9 withdrawals, 7 retentions, and 4 internal relocations (the offending material was stolen in 2 other cases, and 2 other cases had not been resolved at the time of the study). The titles involved in media reports are indicated below, together with the outcomes of the challenges:

Removed

adult westerns
Là-bas
The Body Politic
Cathérine saute au paf!
Mon corps est à elles
Murder in the Family
Paulette
Les Rockeurs sanctifiés
Zoom

Retained

Devils and Demons
Father Christmas
The Haj
Paris Match
The Rapist File (two challenges, retained in both cases)
The Vagabond of Limbo: What is Reality, Papa?

Relocated

Forever (relocated to young adult)
Lizzy's Lion (relocated to juvenile non-fiction)
The Vagabond of Limbo: The Ultimate Alchemist (relocated to adult fiction)
When the Wind Blows (relocated to adult)

Stolen

Healing the Family
South African Digest

Unresolved

Spectre of Power
Web of Deceit

Respondents withdrew certain materials from their collections because materials were incorrect, obsolete, irrelevant, little or never used, had been inappropriately selected in the first place, or were being replaced with other materials of better quality.

Some of the withdrawals reported by respondents that appear to have been justifiable in light of such criteria were:

✦ *Dr. Abravanel's Body Type Program for Health, Fitness and Nutrition* by Elliott D. Abravanel. The respondent wrote to the publisher about dangerous misinformation in this book, requesting that a corrected page be sent to replace the incorrect information. The publisher replied that the hardcover edition contained an inadvertent typographical error which had been corrected in the paperback edition and all stocks of the hardcover had been destroyed.

✦ *Nerves in Collision* by Walter Alvarez. In response to a complaint that this book contained erroneous information about epilepsy that could harm people with the disorder, expert opinion was sought by the library staff. It was determined that the information in the book was dated and should be replaced by up-to-date titles, and it was therefore withdrawn.

- *Fell's Guide to Doubling Performance of Your Car* by William Hampton. The complainant alleged that this book contained incorrect information, but it was not clear, from the information provided in the survey response what the nature of the incorrect information was or whether expert opinion was sought before it was withdrawn. Given the lack of information on which to judge, this may be considered a borderline case.

- *This is the Cocker Spaniel* by Leon F. Whitney. The challenge to this 30-year-old book was based on the allegation of "cruel methods" of dog training advocated by the veterinarian author. The staff sought the opinion of the local veterinarian, who considered the methods "pretty draconian." The respondent informed the publisher of the withdrawal of the title from the library and also suggested a revision to it, since there are more "enlightened" dog-training methods available. The publisher disagreed, chastised the respondent for infringing on the right to freedom of expression, and compared the withdrawal to Hitler's book-burning methods.

- *Girls and Boys Book of Etiquette* by Barbara Hazen. The respondent agreed with the complainant that there were better etiquette books for children than this one, published in 1971.

- *An Act of Mercy: Euthanasia Today* by Richard Trubo. Unfortunately, the respondent only indicated that the complainant objected to the "out-of-date" information in this 1973 book. Consequently, it is impossible to judge whether the complainant wished more current material to be substituted, or whether the challenge was on other grounds, such as that the very practice of euthanasia was "out of date." Given the lack of information on which to judge, this may be considered a borderline case.

Several respondents noted that items challenged had been acquired inadvertently or had arrived unsolicited. Some of their comments were as follows:

- *The Word of the Lord Brought to Mankind by an Angel* by W. Draves. The complainant alleged that this book was biased and offered no substantiation for its claims. The respondent noted that the book had been received unsolicited from the publisher. After discussion by the library board, it was returned to the publisher as unsolicited material. As there was no indication by the respondent that the library had a selection policy for dealing with religious material or a donation policy for dealing with unsolicited material, this may be another borderline case.

- *Là-bas*, an adult comic book. The respondent agreed with the complainant that this book should be removed: "After taking a picture-by-picture look at the book, I realized what had slipped through my hands. I destroyed it in the wood stove."

- *Ryder, The Tong Wars* by Cole Weston. The respondent wrote to the complainant explaining that this title had been purchased inadvertently as part of a bulk order and would be withdrawn.

- *Somebody Stole Second* by Louise Munro Foley. The respondent reported that this title was an uncatalogued paperback that had not been chosen by the library's selection committee.

- *Barbe-bleue* by Jacques Martin. The respondent observed that this book must have arrived in the library with a large order of comic books and was obviously not examined by the children's librarian. It was definitely not suitable for a children's library, or even intended by the publisher as a book for young children.

- *Image of the Beast* by P. Jose Farmer. The respondent noted that the library board and staff agreed that this title was unsuitable for the collection.

- *The Nursery* by William W. Johnstone. The respondent noted that paperbacks were normally chosen on the basis of notes on the cover, which in this case inaccurately described the book's contents.

- *Witchcraft and Black Magic* by Peter Haining. The respondent wrote that reviews indicated this book was of poor quality, and, on this basis and its physical condition, it was withdrawn.

- *Tales from the Smokehouse* by Herbert T. Schwarz. The respondent wrote, "We were not concerned about the erotica, but we could not tolerate the inaccuracies."

- *Torture Tomb* by C.D. Andersson. The respondent noted, "Book was removed due to: a) condition, b) no redeeming qualities being evident."

- *The Hoax of the Twentieth Century* by Arthur Butz (two challenges). One respondent wrote: "Please note that provincial Attorney General's office has informed us that RCMP was informed the book is illegal according to Canada Customs and that legal action could ensue if Library circulates. Consequently, the book still sits awaiting someone else to test its status, for the legal fees in such suits are beyond budget!"

- *New Internationalist*. The respondent noted that this magazine did not circulate much.

- *Croc*. The respondent noted that this magazine was removed because of the problem of binding — once borrowed, it had to be mended right away.

- *Creepshow* by Stephen King. The respondent wrote that this title had been due to be weeded shortly anyway, and it was objectionable to many parents for youth to be reading Stephen King (the only volume by him in the youth collection).

- *Naomi in the Middle* and *Creepshow*. The respondent wrote, "I have only removed two books for content. One was called *Naomi in the Middle*. A board member paged through it before it was processed and suggested that I read it before putting it out. I did and decided that it was a 'nothing' sort of book and not worth the effort to process. The other was *Creepshow* by Stephen King — a protean horror. I read it after four kids complained that it was too scary and they had nightmares from it. I thought it was pretty extreme and removed it from circulation. I was not *asked* to remove the book in either case." [emphasis in original]

- [title not given]. The respondent wrote that donations were often accepted and catalogued for the shelves, particularly paperback shelves: "This particular patron was offering his helpful assistance and was suggesting we rid ourselves of a lousy book. Staff person did so; however, this is not the ideal way to handle a complaint."

- [title not given]. The respondent commented that a sex education book for youth had been bought on the strength of a newspaper article, but it did not fit the library's selection criteria.

- [title not given]. The respondent wrote that this paperback was falling apart and would have been discarded without the complaint about teen premarital sex.

The arguments in favour of "justifiable censorship" of the above materials have less to do with censorship than with selection and weeding. The removal of material that is outdated, factually incorrect, or potentially harmful is good collection management and should not be viewed as action that denies patron access — nor should those who inform library staff about the contents of such material be labelled automatically as censors. In this same vein, David Jenkinson observed in his study of Manitoba public and school libraries that, "Some challenges...are going to be completely legitimate, and so the task then becomes one of ensuring that a process is in place which responds consistently and appropriately to valid requests while rejecting those which are not worthy" (Jenkinson 1985, 27).

Hence, if withdrawals deemed justified or "valid" according to library selection and weeding criteria were to be excluded from the analysis of challenge outcomes, the withdrawal rate would be on the order of 10 to 12 per cent of all challenges rather than 14 per cent as indicated in Table 26. I leave it to readers to examine the evidence and decide which rate is more credible.

Summary

The general profile of direct challenges reported in this study for the three-year period from 1985 to 1987 is as follows:

- one challenge occurred every day of the year somewhere in Canada
- 21 per cent of public libraries were involved annually in challenges, 35 per cent over three years
- 600 individuals challenged public library materials
- 188 public libraries reported 687 challenges altogether, averaging 1.2 challenges per year per affected institution
- French- and English-language institutions were equally affected
- one challenge per 100,000 population was initiated every year
- 83 per cent of complainants lodged only one challenge during three years
- 5 per cent of challenges were by or on behalf of groups
- challenges were communicated about equally in writing and verbally
- 94 per cent of challenges were to materials in print format
- 74 per cent of challenges were to fiction
- 57 per cent of challenges were to materials for children and teenagers
- 1979 was the mean publication date of titles challenged
- more than 500 titles were challenged, 87 per cent only once during three years
- 21 challenges were to multiple titles by an author or to a particular genre or subject area
- 22 per cent of challenges were on the grounds of sexual explicitness, nudity and pornography, followed by 19 per cent on the grounds of violence, cruelty, and scary themes
- in 76 per cent of challenges, complainants asked that materials be removed
- 86 per cent of challenges resulted in retention of material
- 90 per cent of challenges were dealt with according to library policy for handling challenges
- 32 per cent of challenges were decided by the chief executive officer and another 21 per cent by a branch manager
- 47 per cent of challenges were resolved within a month of initiation
- 96 per cent of challenges were never reported in local media.

Material challenged was more likely to be retained if:

+ it was fiction rather than non-fiction
+ it was for an elementary age group rather than for adults
+ it was targeted because of offensive language or of unsuitablility for age group rather than because of pornographic content
+ library policy was followed in the challenge process
+ there was no local media coverage
+ the library was a multi-branch system rather than a single unit
+ the library served a large municipality in terms of population, borrowers and circulation
+ the dominant language of the community was English rather than French
+ there was a written objections policy
+ there was a form for dealing with objections
+ there was a donations policy
+ the library did not require minors to have consent
+ the library owned a large number of titles on the controversial materials checklist
+ the library experienced more direct challenges.

E. Effects of Challenges

Public library respondents who experienced challenges were asked to indicate the effects these challenges had on institutional policies and practices. First, respondents were asked to comment on whether, in looking back on the challenges received and the experience of handling them, they would have changed their approach generally or in any particular circumstance. Second, they were asked to indicate the effects, if any, of challenges on library policies and practices in the areas of selection, classification, shelving, access or circulation.

1. Change in Approach to Handling Challenges

Overall, 157 out of 178 respondents (88 per cent) said in retrospect that they would not have changed the way they handled the challenges they experienced. These respondents served municipalities with 12 million residents, or 93 per cent of the population represented in the study. Only 12 per cent of respondents, accounting for 7 per cent of residents served, said that they would have changed in retrospect.

Respondents who reported that they followed library policy in handling a challenge were more likely to say in retrospect that there was no need to change their approach. Of the challenges in which library policy was followed, only 7 per cent of the respondents said that they would have changed their approach in retrospect. In contrast, where library policy was not followed or was only partially followed, 43 per cent of the respondents said that a change in approach was needed. Statistical analysis shows that this difference was significant.

By political jurisdiction, public library respondents in several provinces and territories indicated that, in retrospect, they would have changed their approach to challenges. They were located in British Columbia, Alberta, Saskatchewan, Ontario and Quebec.

Some respondents explained that challenges had led to a decision to act on complaints more quickly and to follow library policies with more confidence in the future. In some cases where titles were removed from the shelves, respondents said that they would not take this action again. Some respondents reported that new policies and forms had been developed, and others said they were being considered. In several cases, respondents indicated that materials were being looked at more carefully at the selection stage. Other respondents stated that patrons were now being asked to put their complaints in writing. Some respondents noted that the library's intellectual freedom position was being publicized to increase patron awareness of the library's role.

Selected comments from respondents indicate the wide range of reactions and views on the impact of challenges on staff perceptions and institutional policies and practices:

o No change in retrospect — every incident requires a creative response. No two are the same.

o I was a tool in the battle against censorship. Our board of directors accepted the requests of this group of spiritual fanatics because they belonged to our community as well as being taxpayers. It's a political question. The result was to yield to this demand.

o In case of paperbacks, condition of book did not warrant time spent. If it had been hardcover, procedure would have been followed.

o The municipal council received a petition aimed at dropping a kind of literature, adult comics, which was judged inadequate regarding public morality; afterwards, the council advised us that the withdrawal of this kind of literature would be appreciated.

o The incident illustrated the need to re-examine periodicals before subscription renewal. It seemed that the nature of *National Lampoon*'s humour — although always risqué — had degenerated to a level unacceptable to both librarians and our public.

o We *did* change because of past problems, and our new policy has worked beautifully over the past two years — no problems at all and we feel we did a good job. [emphasis in original]

o The practices and process for assessment of material are now being codified. A different comment form, for the public's use, is being devised to allow for the receipt of specific details of complaint.

o No change looking back, *but* would like to experiment with written form of complaint. [emphasis in original]

o In one case, I withdrew a book which should have remained.

o Would have put objections to library director's decision in writing and brought to board's attention, or at least insisted on involvement of other branch heads to counter director's arbitrariness.

o No change — although the book was a valuable addition to our joint school-public library's collection and added greatly to the information available to students about their sexual growth. I think the school superintendent's decision was a correct reflection of community standards. The book therefore should have been removed.

o In future, I would be more confident in expressing library policy without going to the board with complaints. However, if the patron insisted I would take the complaint to the board.

o Would have publicized the incidents more, made the public more aware of our anti-censorship stand.

o Yes and no. I personally feel it's the parents who should look out for their children's reading habits. We're not there to censure people. I wouldn't put *Playboy* or material like that but good literature should be read; even if I don't like it. People should have a choice.

o Have incidents dealt with immediately in future. That is now being remedied. The board has appointed a censorship committee and all books will be dealt with in the next couple of months with answers given to respective patrons.

o We should have had the person who complained about *Annie on My Mind* fill out the "Citizen's Request for Reconsideration of Materials" form.

o I would insist — which has already been included in our selection policy — that the complaint must be made in writing in order for it to be considered.

o Yes, for *Le Vagabond des limbes*. No for all the other cases.

o In this case, patron was probably right that the book was lousy. But as administrator, I do not want to remove books on any one patron's request.

o After incident I then took a course in collection development offered by Ontario Library Service (similar to SAIT course) and as a result wrote up a comprehensive selection policy, which was approved unanimously by the board and gives me the backing to respond to complaints with confidence.

o I would not have removed *Fungus the Bogeyman* from circulation. It was not objectionable to me but it was the first complaint I have ever received and I was unsure of how to proceed.

o No, but I would eventually like free access to all library materials and am opposed to hiding books in the office. However, I think such changes have to occur *slowly,* especially in a small town. [emphasis in original]

o I would write up a procedure manual. I would draft complaint forms. I would set up an office to study complaints. But I have neither time nor staff to do so.

Respondent comments highlight the importance of both policy and preparation in responding to collection challenges. While there is no sure recipe for the perfect response to a challenge, there are several basic guidelines that will help to produce the desired resolution, the kind of "win-win" situation for both librarians and complainants that is the goal of all conflict-resolution strategies. At the foundation of these guidelines is the imperative for relevant institutional policies and procedures, namely a board-approved materials selection policy that includes a statement on intellectual freedom, a board-approved procedure and form for handling objections, and board-approved policies relating to other access issues such as age restrictions, parental/guardian responsibility for monitoring children's reading, and confidentiality of library user records. Practical resource guides for developing these policies and procedures are listed at the end of this chapter.

Almost as important as these formal policies and procedures is the ongoing need to know your community and its demographic and political dynamics. Further, you need an active public information program about intellectual freedom and an equally active campaign to promote broad-based community support for intellectual freedom.

But looking outward is only half the picture: staff and board education should also be a regular feature of your long-range strategy to promote intellectual freedom. All of these guidelines are recommended by a variety of practical resources for dealing with collection challenges. If you wait for the censor to come before you begin to prepare, you have waited too long.

2. Effect on Policies and Practices

As to the question of whether or not challenges have had any effect on library selection, classification, shelving, access or circulation, a total of 131 out of 176 respondents, or 74 per cent, reported no effects in any of these areas. Of the 12.9 million Canadians represented by institutions responding to this question, those respondents who said there had been no effects served municipalities with 10.3 million people, or 80 per cent. Only 26 per cent of respondents, accounting for 20 per cent of residents served, said that challenges had affected their policies and practices.

Respondents who said that they followed library policy in handling a challenge were more likely to report no effects of the experience on institutional policies and practices. Of those challenges in which library policy was followed, only 23 per cent of the respondents reported an effect on the institution. In contrast, where library policy was not followed or was followed only in part, approximately half of the respondents reported an effect on the institution. Statistical analysis shows that this difference was significant.

Outcome of challenges also influenced institutional policies and practices. Of those challenges in which items were withdrawn, 40 per cent of the respondents reported that the experience had had an effect on institutional policies and practices, while only 25 per cent reported an effect as a result of challenges in which items were retained. Statistical analysis shows that this difference was significant.

By political jurisdiction, public libraries in 8 out of 12 of Canada's provinces and territories reported that direct challenges had had an effect on their institutions. Only respondent public libraries in New Brunswick, Prince Edward Island and the two territories reported no effects.

Respondents who reported effects were asked to explain them in more detail. Some suggested that subsequent selection was more conservative and cautious and that published reviews had become more important in the selection process. Others mentioned that reviews of controversial books were being kept on hand to help respond to complaints. Some respondents noted that materials such as comics and books for children and young adults were being examined more carefully before purchase and shelving.

Some respondents reported that certain types of books, especially those with violent or sexual content or covers, were not being purchased at all, or that access to them was being restricted to adult patrons. In some libraries, the response to challenges was that young adult books were being classified as adult books to prevent access by younger patrons. Some respondents mentioned that they had started to label controversial items.

Verbatim comments by respondents about effects on library policies and practices were as follows:

o We try to avoid purchasing books with violent or sexual characteristics. For those publications of this nature already in the library, we have not modified their category or classification, hoping they will not be noticed by children.

o We add no more novels with violent covers: battered women, tied up, chained, or too pornographic.

o At present, yes, in the acquisition of materials, especially adult and children's comics; in the access to publications in the adult section for children, who must be accompanied by their parents; all materials which describe violence, horror, esotericism, science, occults, sects with erotic characteristics are indicated with a yellow binding for loan.

o In selection, books are being scanned from one cover to the next before any invoice is paid off, especially in the case of French comic books.

o The specific item was a comic book style for an adult audience and because of that, it didn't fit either adult or juvenile sections. We won't buy that type of material in future — because it was unsuitable in *level* not content or subject. [emphasis in original]

o In regards to witchcraft books — how to's and step-by-step guides are generally avoided, but books on the history of and of general interest are still added to the collection. Books on homosexuality are still added, depending on the quality of subject.

o We have put occult and witchcraft books behind the counter and people have to ask for them. I am not comfortable with this but since we have done this the teenagers have quit coming to look for them (and there were quite a few). I still don't feel comfortable doing this as I feel it is not up to me to censor.

o Became more aware of occult influence on young children.

o Not in the display but in selection. We have eliminated occult literature.

o More careful check that children *do* have permission to borrow adult books before books are signed out. [emphasis in original]

o Very subtly. I would say I have started to buy "younger" young fare.

o One item complained about was what turned out to be a soft-porn western that we agreed had little to recommend it. It had been ordered from a paperback list and we made note of the author and series, so we won't buy any more. That book and others in the series were withdrawn.

o It certainly makes one more aware and accepting of others' viewpoints although one may *not* remove the book from the shelf. [emphasis in original]

o Selection has become more conservative; some of our branches have been given bad PR in their communities which may negatively affect circulation.

o I am more sensitive about offending community standards but am also more determined to ensure that students have access to materials that they see as useful.

o More careful reviewing of picture books with an eye to non-sexist content. Because of our problem with defacing we have shelved *Wanderings* by Chaim Potok, a beautifully illustrated copy, in the back room.

o In a rural area such as this I buy less explicit material than I would if I were a city librarian.

o It has resulted in a closer scrutiny of magazines before subscriptions are renewed.

o I have to admit I pay more attention to book reviews and try to obtain more than one review of a book. Some materials, for example, explicit self-help books on sex, should be shelved separately, where they're not accessible, but available upon request by the patron.

o I feel I tend to be more "cautious," i.e., will the trustee screech about this one?, but only on occasion — mostly things are about the same.

o I'm a little more careful about what books I put up for a teenage display and try to choose those books I am sure would not have adult content in them. At the same time, I cannot refuse a teenager who wishes to read an adult book.

o We now keep reviews of any books that might be in the least way controversial — YA titles only.

o It has a cautionary effect. I had only been in the job about a year and didn't need that kind of trouble. I cannot say, however, that it had a very significant effect on selection.

o In exercising stricter supervision over the illustrations and text of children's books. If there is ambiguity I put it in the adult collection or another section.

o Children's librarian has been instructed to examine all "bandes dessinées" before adding them to collections. These comic-book-format books published in French are often intended for an adult audience — the format can be misleading. The good ones (e.g., *Astérix*) are very much enjoyed by the children, but others are inappropriate.

o Young adult titles which carry the potential of parental complaint are generally classified in the adult collection. A controversial title may be placed in the central library collection only.

o The books were to be classified as "X — controversial literature."

o Pop records were moved into adult collections; guidelines for buying trips are being developed to ensure that unsuitable material is not being purchased without some form of review, series of books (as in the Paul Kropp) will have more attention paid to reviews to ensure appropriateness of individual titles, procedures for receiving and handling complaints on library materials are now being codified.

o We did create young adult sections in the libraries in my region. Books were classified as either adult or juvenile or picture books before. There were books written for YAs which were classified as adult and shelved with the adult books, where teenagers would not think of looking for them, and there were books classified as juvenile which contained more adult themes or language.

o I reorganized and divided the YA collection. I saw this as an "uncensoring" step in a sense because there were several books I felt older teens should have access to — Zindel, Cormier, Hinton, but they had been "hidden" amongst the adult books.

o All teen books were read by staff and a system of labelling introduced to assist parents who are involved in selecting materials for their children. The labelling indicates a title suitable for 12- to 14-year-olds, or 15+ (the latter are more likely to deal with sexual matters).

o Individual cases merited changing the shelving of certain items. Otherwise no effect.

o We will try to be more careful about content when shelving junior books.

o Perhaps in some cases a positive effect. We look more closely at the older "how-to" books seeking evidence of outmoded or antiquated methods.

o We won't buy adult westerns which are described on the cover as being "bawdy and lustful." Apart from that, no effects.

o More careful research so that sensible selection can be made.

o I am more careful in selection and also classification.

o Somewhat with regard to adult fiction dealing with explicit sex scenes. This as a result of occasional complaints prior to 1986 and 1985.

o I think continual staff/public awareness programs are essential — for example, during Freedom to Read Week — to ensure that these complaints don't have a slow "erosion" effect on selection.

o The lesson for the future is not to direct that patron to wartime fiction about Vietnam.

o We became much more selective when book buying.

o Greater care in selecting comics, avoiding works with too much violence or degrading sexual behaviour.

o Greater prudence in selecting publications for children.

o Certain publications could have "daring" passages. Unfortunately, all these publications are not read from beginning to end. Some comics also have "daring" drawings. We are more serious in our selection now and we have thought about an adult comics section.

o I have, following a complaint, suggested that there be a policy requiring the participation of more than one branch head and maybe a board member when library material is challenged. Nothing has happened although the suggestion was well received. Challenges here are fortunately rare.

o More attention in my choice of comics; I consider them more individually from the point of view of the two sexes.

o This is difficult to determine as one does not know how much influence these matters have on the subconscious. On the whole, the library tries to select materials that are requested by the public, at least to a certain degree. Often the materials with potential for controversy are the ones requested by the public.

o As a librarian for 32 years in the same community I can state that there have been occasions, as expected, of concern about certain titles, mainly from well-meaning but misinformed citizens as to the public library's role and the protection of intellectual freedoms and the public's right to read all points of view. When the principle was explained and a firm stand taken against censorship, the matter was resolved. It is my experience that parents and other concerned citizens depend to a remarkable degree on the discretion and judgement of library personnel as far as children's reading is concerned. They expect the use of common sense in regard to minors' access to the stacks and depend on professional staff for guidance as to reading material [appropriate] for age and development.

o The library has received some general complaints from a fundamentalist clergyman that a lot of our magazines are left-wing, socialist-communist, but this was only a comment made when he paid for a magazine subscription (for a religious magazine) for the library.

o A school has removed *A Children's Almanac of Words at Play* from its library here. The subsequent controversy has increased interest in the book and we have two copies for general circulation.

o Since the Keegstra controversy, I have made a point of stocking numerous books on the Holocaust, racism in Canada, etc., and occasionally patrons have argued with me about the validity of the contents of these books — especially Bercuson's *Trust Betrayed*, so we have experienced a lot of reverse discrimination regarding accepted titles. No one, however, has questioned us stocking them or offered us obviously racist material.

A few respondents commented on the difficulties encountered in joint public/school library facilities:

o Since the public library is a guest in the school, the board feels that the school children should not be exposed to blatant sex and violence as described in some books.

o Most complaints are from non-members and non-users, *all* have been from born again or Baptist parishioners, *all* have been *very* upset, angry, disgusted and *not* pleasant in their approach. However, a new policy and guidelines developed two years ago had successfully defused the last three complaints. Problems develop because of the *joint* library setup. In a municipal library separate from school, the policy would make *parents* responsible for what child reads, not the *librarian*. [emphasis in original]

A few respondents commented on problems that may arise from having multilingual collections:

o One of the major objections that is made from time to time is to do with the multilingual collections. We collect some 30 languages and have now in excess of 50,000 volumes as well as videotapes, audiotapes and periodicals, all of which are quite expensive. The major complaints revolve around the concept that people coming to Canada should learn English and that the library board is only encouraging people to hang on to their language and culture. The board, however, has a policy of complementing the culture as reflected in the make-up of the people living in the city.

We have, as well, in the past had objections to some children's books, for example, *Curious George*. The complaints have been lodged from the point of view that the books represent a sexist approach: the doctors are always men, the nurses are always women.

So far the library board has resisted all attempts to withdraw books that have already been purchased through the policies that are laid out in our official document.

o We now have a Japanese high school... which educates students from Japan in English. They use this library, but have very rigid restrictions on what they may read. It is sometimes difficult to find appropriate material.

o Complaints that are the most difficult to deal with in the branch are ones about books and magazines in other languages. Because we cannot read them, we have to forward the complaints to our central selector when a discussion in the branch with the patron might have sufficed, as is the case with most complaints about English-language materials.

Several respondents commented on the unique circumstances of public libraries in small centres:

o In our small community, the public library atmosphere is very relaxed and friendly. We encourage patrons to discuss pros and cons of books, but rarely find major objections. Our verbal policy is "If you don't like the content, put it down. Don't read it."

o This is a very small "recreational readers" library. The librarian has traditionally been a member of the community and has been aware of the fairly conservative nature of the local population. Being on a limited budget, the approach to book buying has been one of buying selections which are likely to be read, rather than those which might serve to "shake up" the user. Therefore, the books which we have on hand reflect the reading habits of our members rather than a specific stance on reading material.

o This library is a one-man operation in every respect. As the "one man," I don't go out of my way to acquire questionable material on our very limited budget. I look for informative, entertaining materials that have a broad appeal. I personally believe adults should be allowed to view whatever they desire but I abhor any aspect of perverted and kiddy porn type material.

o Many of my patrons are older people. If they feel a book is improper (loose morals) they bring it back without reading it and avoid that type of book. They make a comment about the book being unfit to read. We do not have many young readers and the few we have do not read that type of material.

o We really have never had a serious problem with censorship. If a little old lady takes a book that's sexually explicit, we will tell her, and nine times out of ten she agrees that she wouldn't want it and leaves it here.

o Being in a small library and with a limited budget, I've had to be very careful in my selection of both juvenile and adult books ($12,000 for both in 1987). Since I am in a community with more seniors using the library, my book selection is inclined to be conservative.

o Although this board has no written policies as yet, they are supportive of my unwritten ones. This is a small town that I grew up in which makes it much easier to have a "feel" for accepted community standards. I personally feel that censorship is the responsibility of the parent or the individual (if an adult). Many times I've seen parents deny a book only to have the child take it out later unknown to the parent (forbidden fruit is sweet). However, I can see the potential for trouble here as there is a growing "fundamentalist" movement in this area which has created trouble over *The Diviners* by M. Laurence. I make selections with this in mind but I use community standards as a whole. Thankfully I've been able to operate this library for seven years "at my discretion" with no problem.

o I would like to finish with a plea that librarians and trustees, most of whom live and work in urban areas, look for ways to support their colleagues in small communities. In small towns, library staff and board members frequently feel very isolated. Often they do not even have the finances to send anyone to attend provincial conferences where they would have a chance to talk with others dealing with similar problems. We also need the support and encouragement of provincial organizations to make a stand on censorship issues.

While attempts to censor materials in urban areas receive much media attention, I believe that it is the small community libraries across the province and across the country who bear the brunt of attempts to control information available in libraries — both in terms of trying to keep certain materials out and trying to have other materials included in collections. I say this because libraries in small communities are more visible and their staff and board members more accessible. In small communities with limited facilities, libraries become the main resource centre. Because the library plays such a prominent role in the community its collection tends to be examined more critically than might be the case in an urban area where there are many institutions supplying information. And because staff and board members are easily identified and often known in other roles, they are more likely to be approached on book selection issues, both in and outside the library. Libraries in small communities depend on annual grants from their municipalities and donations from the community. With the funding base so precarious it is natural that both library boards and staff in small communities attempt to avoid controversy. This leads to what I consider the most insidious form of censorship — self-censorship. The other problem which may arise is that there is always the potential that members of special interest groups may attempt ... to elect their candidates to the board in the hope that they will be able to influence book selection policy. One only has to look at what has happened with hospital boards to understand the implications this could have for library boards.

o One advantage a small library has over larger ones is that over 75 per cent of patrons are known personally to the staff — particularly in the matter of their reading habits, so complaints can usually be avoided. Also, what is laughingly referred to as my "annual book budget" effectively precludes a spending spree on pornography!

Some respondents commented that, while they had not experienced overt censorship pressure in the past, the possibility seemed imminent.

o I regret to say that the library staff probably exercise a significant degree of caution in selection of materials and avoid materials such as *Playboy* that are overtly objectionable. We do, however, have many titles that appear on the lists of titles being attacked elsewhere in North America. Our community has a significant number of fundamentalist churches, active pro-life groups, and anti-pornography/violence against women in the media groups. To date, they have not attacked us but we can sense the encircling forces just awaiting a favourable opportunity to pounce.

o We feel this survey is a little early! We anticipate some action from pro-life groups, fundamentalists, etc. We have experienced two attempts in the past (1980) to have certain books removed. The policy procedures were followed and, apart from some letters in the local newspaper, nothing happened. These letters evoked a spate of letters supporting the library's intellectual freedom stance.

At the same time, another respondent was more optimistic:

o On the whole I remain surprised when we don't get more complaints. Most people are reasonable when voicing their feelings and are prepared to accept that others have different standards and opinions. Most people are satisfied by being allowed to voice their concerns and having them heard. Many complaints arise because a book is not what it appears to be — people tend to avoid books they think will offend them.

Summary

Among respondent public libraries reporting challenges to their collections, only a very small proportion said that in retrospect they would have changed their approach to the handling of those challenges. Similarly, few respondents reported any effects of previous challenges on institutional policies and practices in the areas of selection, classification, shelving, access or circulation.

Respondents who reported no need to change their approach tended to be those who followed library policy in handling a challenge. Similarly, respondents who reported no effects of the experience on library policies and practices tended to be those who followed institutional policy in handling challenges. In challenges where titles were retained, respondents were more likely to report no effects than in challenges where titles were withdrawn.

Suggested Further Reading

American Library Association. Office for Intellectual Freedom. *Intellectual Freedom Manual.* 4th ed. Chicago, Ill.: Office for Intellectual Freedom, American Library Association, 1992. See subsection 2.14, "Dealing with concerns about library resources," pp 97-103, and part V, "Before the censor comes," pp 205-67.

American Library Association. Young Adult Services Division. Intellectual Freedom Committee. *Hit List: Frequently Challenged Young Adult Titles; References to Defend Them.* Chicago, Ill.: American Library Association, 1989.

Book and Periodical Council. "Freedom to Read Week Kit." Annual. Toronto, Ont.: Book and Periodical Council.

British Columbia Library Association. Intellectual Freedom Committee. *Intellectual Freedom Handbook.* Burnaby, B.C.: British Columbia Library Association, 1991.

Chambers, Aidan. *Introducing Books to Children.* 2d ed. Boston, Mass.: Horn Book, 1983.

Cornog, Martha. "Is Sex Safe in Your Library? How to Fight Censorship." *Library Journal* 118 (August 1993): 43-46. Includes side panel: "Eleven Ways to Answer a Censor."

Foerstel, Herbert N. *Banned in the U.S.A.: A Reference Guide to Book Censorship in Schools and Public Libraries.* Westport, Conn.: Greenwood Press, 1994.

Jones, Frances M. *Defusing Censorship: The Librarian's Guide to Handling Censorship Conflicts.* Phoenix, Ariz.: Oryx Press, 1983.

Karolides, Nicholas J., Lee Burress, and John M. Kean, eds. *Censored Books: Critical Viewpoints.* Metuchen, N.J.: Scarecrow Press, 1993.

Kreamer, Jean Thibodeaux. "Holding the Line: Censorship and Library Trustees." *Wilson Library Bulletin* 68 (May 1994): 36-37.

Marsh, Dave. *Fifty Ways to Fight Censorship and Important Facts to Know about Censors.* New York, N.Y.: Thunder's Mouth Press, 1991.

Morton, Elizabeth. "Picture Books for the Sophisticated." *Feliciter* 38 (July/August 1992): 10-11.

Schexnavdre, Linda and Nancy Burns. *Censorship: A Guide for Successful Workshop Planning.* Phoenix, Ariz.: Oryx Press, 1984.

9 / Covert Censorship

ALTHOUGH COVERT CENSORSHIP OF PUBlic library collections is another part of the picture of patron access, previous research has not taken it into account. Covert or indirect interference with collection access represents a more subtle — and therefore a somewhat more insidious — form of censorial activity than do direct requests to withdraw or restrict materials.

Covert censorship activity consists of incidents of collection loss, theft, defacement, alteration, mutilation or destruction that were, or were thought to have been, attempts to prevent or restrict access. Obviously, the unequivocal identification of such incidents is not always possible; indeed, fully one-quarter of the respondents in the present study said that they were uncertain whether or not various incidents that occurred in their institutions had issued from censorship motives.

Readers, too, may wonder whether some of the circumstances as reported should even be considered attempts to censor. This is particularly true of defacement. Is drawing or writing on materials an act of censorship? In several cases, survey respondents thought so, because they reported such incidents — but there will sometimes be an element of doubt. At the least, these incidents raise the whole issue of the defacement of publicly funded materials.

Altogether, 57 respondent public libraries, or 10 per cent, reported covert incidents of suspected censorship of materials between 1985 and 1987. The annual rate of affected institutions during this period was 3.5 per cent. A total of 99 covert incidents was reported over the three-year period. Extrapolating to the whole population of Canadian public libraries from survey respondents, I estimate that between 1985 and 1987 there was one suspected incident of covert censorship per week. Three different institutions across the country were involved monthly. Among respondents reporting suspected covert censorship, the mean was just under one incident per year. One respondent reported four incidents annually over the three years of the study period.

The present study shows that affected institutions were likely to be multi-branch systems. One-quarter of all systems experienced covert incidents between 1985 and 1987, compared to only 7 per cent of all single libraries. Statistical analysis shows that this difference was significant. While public libraries affected by these incidents represented only one out of ten respondents, they accounted for 30 per cent of all Canadian residents served, and slightly higher proportions of registered borrowers and total circulations. These institutions served 5.4 million people, recorded 2.5 million registered borrowers, and circulated 49.1 million items.

These data reveal a potential denial of access to particular public library materials for three out of ten Canadian residents in the study population between 1985 and 1987. The significant difference in covert incidents between systems and single libraries was also reflected in institutional characteristics. Respondent public libraries serving larger municipalities were more likely to experience this kind of incident than those serving small centres.

The library of the typical respondent reporting covert incidents served a municipality with 95,000 people, 45,000 registered borrowers, and 862,000 library circulations. In contrast, those not affected served an average municipality of 15,000 people, 5,000 borrowers, and 89,000 circulations. Statistical analysis shows that affected institutions served significantly larger municipalities in terms of residents, borrowers, and circulation than did those not affected.

Covert censorship activity affected public libraries in all but three Canadian political jurisdictions — Prince Edward Island and the two territories. Wide variations, ranging from 10 per cent or fewer of the respondents in Alberta, Manitoba, Ontario, Quebec and Nova Scotia, to 25 per cent of the respondents in New Brunswick, 29 per cent in Newfoundland, and 56 per cent in Saskatchewan, were found.

Public library respondents were asked to describe each incident of covert censorship, including year, type of damage, title and author, and the response of the library. The materials most frequently stolen, lost, defaced or destroyed were those on the occult, witchcraft, abortion, creationism, political theory, sex education and human sexuality. Materials with profane language were frequently mutilated, with whole pages torn out or the offending words either blackened or cut out. Remarks were often written in the margins of controversial books. In some cases, materials thought to be controversial were discovered misshelved, apparently hidden to make them more inaccessible. There was no discernible pattern according to year in which incidents occurred.

In most cases, public library staff were unable to identify the offenders. In those cases where the individual was known, action was sometimes taken, but in many cases nothing was done beyond issuing a verbal warning. Often, missing pages or entire volumes were replaced at the institution's — and hence, taxpayers' — expense. Many respondents noted that it was difficult to determine whether some incidents were attempts to prevent or restrict access, or just vandalism prompted by other motives such as a person wanting certain pictures, pages or books for themselves, a youngster stealing "D&D books" (Dungeons and Dragons) to prevent competition, or a student attempting to prevent access by other students to materials for school projects.

One respondent commented, for example, that certain books had been stolen, especially drug books and muscle-building books, but that the thefts had nothing to do with restricting access. Yet another respondent took a very definite view of these kinds of disappearance: "articles in encyclopedias may have been cut out in hopes of stopping classmates' access — which is censorship of another damaging kind — and very frustrating."

Another respondent reported that in only one instance, where a teacher brought in a project which included pictures cut from materials in the library, was there more than just suspicion of the latter motivation.

Other respondents voiced a degree of suspicion about the motivation behind certain activities:

o Does the *Satanic Bible* keep disappearing because people are trying to suppress it or because they want their own copy? Our branch staff tend toward the latter opinion.

o There are so many write-offs from long overdues that I would be surprised if a percentage of such loss (hopefully small) was not attributable to intentional retention to prevent access.

Verbatim comments by respondents indicate the wide range of covert actions suspected to have been attempts to censor public library materials. Several comments related to incidents involving the occult, witchcraft, and other religious issues.

o The book *Les Rockeurs sanctifiés* by Lucien Francoeur has been placed in the adult section. One person wanted to burn the book and not return it to the library. The book was eventually returned but the complaints began.

o *A Witches' Grimoire of Ancient Omens, Portents, Talismans and Charms* disappeared shortly after it was returned to the shelves after reconsideration by the Board.

o When patron lost but paid for *Nostradamus Predictions* and was told if it turned up and was returned within two years the money would be refunded, I was assured the book would *not*!! turn up — although conversation to that point gave the impression it had been misplaced. [emphasis in original]

o Loss of *Book of Predictions* by D. Wallechinsky, *Science and the Supernatural* by T. Taylor, *Learning to Read Music* by Lilienfeld, *Measurement of Melody* by G. Millar, assortment of craft books, *This is South Africa*.

o Parent tore Shirley Jackson book in half and garbaged it — devil worship and work of the devil, she said. Parent was billed and paid for the book and was told she was destroying public property, etc., etc.

o One Portuguese book questioning authenticity of the Virgin of Fatima was suspected stolen by someone who found it offensive. Several books on occult, witchcraft have been mutilated, possibly for the same reason.

o Section on Mormons in the book *Cults* cut out. Didn't replace as we had other material on this subject which was more current. Hard to say if other material has "walked" — we are not on computer yet and don't have time to keep a check on every book.

o In the past anti-Scientology books have had a short life span but I am unaware of any specifics recently.

o One patron has systematically gone through our collection of Dutch books and obliterated any profanity/obscenity.

o Latter part of 1987, longtime patron — avid reader — suddenly decided he was fed up with blasphemy, deleted all references to "God," "Christ," "Jesus Christ," etc.; about one dozen mysteries and war stories "treated" before we caught up with him. No further problems since it was gently pointed out that library privileges did not include editing!

Several incidents involved materials of a more directly political nature:

o Defacement of socialist-oriented magazine, *Canadian Dimensions* — comments were added to the magazine and sections were blacked out.

o I do not have any dates or specific incidents I can cite but there has been an increase in the numbers of books being defaced, comments being written in the margins, and the majority of these books are of a controversial nature, e.g., Palestinian question, Israel, Iran, Zundel trial.

o One patron borrowed several books dealing with Jewish-Nazi relations and wartime experiences. He covered the margins with editorial comments and crossed out some lines in the books with which he disagreed. Some of the material had to be discarded. Patron was phoned and warned that further destruction would result in having to pay for the damaged books.

o *Nuremberg and Other War Crimes Trials* was stolen. *101 Uses for a Cabbage Head Doll* was taken out and then reported missing. *The Holocaust — 120 Questions and Answers* is missing from our collection.

o *Web of Deceit* — this title, because of publicity, was heavily requested. While on loan to another library, the book was reported lost. We *suspected* that this was an attempt to remove title; however, after some weeks, the book was returned. [emphasis in original]

o *Keegstra* by Steve Mertl and John Ward and *Holy Terror* by Flo Conway and Jim Siegelman — writing throughout, on margins, stapled in articles and booklist from the Canadian Intelligence Service. *Missile Envy* by Helen Caldicott, *With Enough Shovels* by Robert Scheer, and *Starmageddon* by Richard Rohmer — all of these books are defaced with the same handwriting by a person with fascist views; the comments are cross-referenced and systematic. No action yet taken or solution found; unable to discover who's doing it.

o *The Sexual Life of Savages in North-Western Melanesia* by Bronislaw Malinowski — defacement throughout, written comments which were abusive in nature, rude illustrations. *Let's Visit Pakistan* — written racial slurs, rude illustrations throughout, cover of book defaced. Various other books — all defacement appears to have been committed by one person who exercises two types of censorship: 1) any swearing involving the word "Christ" is heavily inked out (four-letter words are allowed to pass without comment), and 2) running commentary placed in book, some of which is very strange and involves novel's character statements, especially as they relate to class. Staff at this particular branch attempt to check material after return by the particular borrower to determine any defacement. They hope to have a conversation with the borrower regarding this treatment of materials.

o European magazines are sometimes turned back out or tucked behind other periodicals. Books are sometimes tucked away in unusual locations within the library.

o One branch experienced repeated borrowing of a phonorecord of North Vietnamese songs purposefully removed in this manner by the South Vietnamese community.

Abortion as politics was also a source of covert activity:

o A group of pro-life borrowers requested the purchase of more such materials and we suspect have taken some abortion information from our files.

o Photographic sections of anti-abortion books have been defaced — whether or not this was politically motivated is unclear.

o Right-wing anti-abortion group has offered donations, requested titles, removed pamphlets and books that are pro-choice or informative.

o Our copy of *Morgentaler* by Pelrine was slashed, back and front cover and inside, with a razor blade. We mended and put back in circulation.

o We suspect that our collections of books discussing abortion might be being depleted by those campaigners on both sides of the issue. Pro-choice supporters are removing the "right-to-life" titles and the right-to-lifers are removing the pro-choice books.

Incidents involving popular novels were also mentioned.

o A section of Harold Robbins' book was cut out — we did not know whether it was an attempt to restrict material or whether some patron wanted to duplicate a particularly nasty torture-rape type scene.

o Ken Follett's *Lie Down with Lions*, pages 211-14 cut out. Other patrons annoyed to find pages missing.

o Someone removed all traces of romance from the paperback westerns. They did not touch the hardcovers!! I find most annoying people who cut out pieces from books and magazines for their own use, rather than copying them.

o We have not kept track of specific incidents, but on several occasions pages have been ripped out from popular novels, e.g., Jackie Collins' *Hollywood Husbands, Girls in High Places*, Sydney Sheldon's *Rage of Angels*. In each case, the library has replaced the missing pages with photocopies. No verbal or written complaints have been received about the content of the material.

o *Kane and Abel* by Jeffrey Archer — pages were torn (the "dirty" parts). We traced it to the patron, a young 16-year-old. Either her mother (a Jehovah's Witness) ripped them or the young girl kept them. Our response was not to get involved in a family matter; we simply discarded it and bought another one. We also get children's books damaged — a variety of them.

A number of incidents involved materials about sexuality, and in particular sexuality and children. Several incidents involving *The Joy of Sex* were suspected by respondents to have been covert attempts to censor it, but doubt lingers that theft for personal use may also have been the motive for at least some of the disappearances.

o A lot of our anatomy books and human sexuality/ reproduction materials get drawn on.

o A sex education book (LC 612) illustrated was put in the toilet.

o *Joy of Sex* and *More Joy of Sex* disappeared form shelves — replacements also vanish. Have finally given up replacing them.

o *Joy of Sex* repeatedly goes missing — is replaced every year. We don't know what the reason for the theft is — to censor or to own a copy.

o It is possible that *Joy of Sex, More Joy of Sex*, and *Show Me* were taken by people wishing to censor. It is hard to be sure of reason.

o The only book that we know was actually taken from the collection for censorship reasons was *The Rapist File*. This occurred some years ago and was a city-wide incident that hit the newspapers and then the newspapers in their indubitable way located all the copies and, as you may well imagine, all of the copies went missing.

o Two copies of *The Castrated Family* lost. Purchased new copy (still in catalogue). *Ordeal* by Linda Lovelace stolen, and returned anonymously with pages 30-40 ripped out, others destroyed. *Dancers of Arun* by Elizabeth Lynn lost from collection some time after a verbal request by patron to remove it from collection was not complied with.

o Certain pages (two) describing homosexual acts. Another book about black magic had three pages removed. Certain novels had one or two pages removed. I am unaware of the reason for this or of the content of these pages.

o M. Foster's *Not So Gay World* — had text altered, notations that we had to erase. V. Newall's *Encyclopedia of Witchcraft and Magic* had pages destroyed and removed — had to replace with photocopies. William J. Whalen's *Handbook of Secret Organizations* — circulating copy defaced — had to withdraw.

o Mother destroyed young adult paperback, *Beginner's Love* by Norma Klein. Library charged mother for book. Fine paid.

o Hutterite children put beards on adult males in children's picture book.

o Pre-1983 comic books were introduced to our libraries. A gentleman ripped up several comic books and asked the library to bill him. As an Orthodox Jew, he objected to having such material available to children. The library reminded him of their policy of open access to a variety of materials to various communities. There have not been any problems with the comic books since.

o A parent tore one page from the magazine *Comics Notebook* which showed a naked man.

o *The Body Book,* pre-schooler's to grades 1-2 level book on the human body, borrowed by born again Christian family — page with four small cartoons depicting Cro-Magnon man evolving into modern man and statement underneath "Some people believe man evolved from monkeys" — crossed out and in LARGE BLACK letters: "WRONG! BLASPHEMY! *GOD CREATED MAN!*" No way to prove it — no response except inner anger! [emphasis in original]

o *In the Night Kitchen* M. Sendak — naked little boy got felt marker diapers — couldn't finger the culprit. Also, I have suspected pro-choice material stolen out of my vertical file (the file contains both views) on abortion.

o *Doctors of Death* stolen — replaced, and stolen again. All our books on AIDS defaced.

Summary

Overall, the study has revealed that covert censorship activity in Canadian public libraries is not nearly as pervasive as are direct challenges to the presence of certain materials. It is estimated that there was one covert incident of suspected censorship per week between 1985 and 1987. While this involved only one out of ten public libraries across the country, they served municipalities with 30 per cent of the people represented in the study. These figures imply a potential biasing of public library collections for three out of ten Canadian residents in the study population.

Those few incidents that were reported by respondents occurred about equally often in French- and English-language institutions. Multi-branch systems everywhere were more likely targets of this kind of censorial activity than single-unit libraries, as were larger municipalities.

Nonetheless, caution is warranted in interpreting the study data, because fully one-quarter of the respondents said that they were undecided about whether or not various incidents that had occurred in their institutions were in fact motivated by a desire to prevent access by other residents of the community: the problem of diagnosis remains in large part beyond the grasp of empirical observation and measurement, intractable if not altogether unsolvable. What is especially lacking is the percentage of covert censorship of the adult collection compared to the young adult and children's collections. Based on respondent comments, it might be conjectured that it is the latter materials that are affected rather than those intended for adults, but this cannot be verified.

10 / Acquisition Pressure

ANOTHER KIND OF COMMUNITY ACTIVITY that has been neglected in the research literature is "undue" pressure on public library staff to acquire certain materials. Such pressure would go beyond the level of suggestion, recommendation, request or even "strong encouragement," as one respondent put it, for acceptance or acquisition of items. The survey questionnaire asked respondents to indicate whether or not they had been pressured to accept or acquire certain individual titles or certain types of materials for their collections.

While some readers will have difficulty thinking of undue acquisition pressure as a censorship problem rather than as an attempt to influence book selection policy, it is included here for two reasons. One is that such pressure can be viewed as a strategy for influencing the make-up and balance of a collection, and the other is that such pressure sheds light on the overall climate of intellectual freedom in public libraries. If a challenge to remove or restrict material in a collection is unsuccessful, a complainant may attempt to have materials with a certain viewpoint added to it.

I would argue that undue pressure to add rather than subtract materials has a similar effect on the collection: criteria outside those found in approved policy are invoked to move the content of the collection in a partisan direction, thereby compromising traditional goals of balance and representativeness. Hence, I think that an adequate conception of censorship includes all forms of strategy to alter collection composition, whether the strategy is direct challenge, covert action, or pressure to acquire materials.

Overall, 121 respondent public libraries (22 per cent) said that they had experienced acquisition pressure. Based on these data, I estimate that among the whole population of Canadian public libraries, one institution was pressured to acquire or accept materials every week during the study period, somewhere in Canada. The typical institution reporting acquisition pressure was more likely to be a multi-branch system than a single library. Almost half of all systems experienced acquisition pressure, compared to only 16 per cent of all single libraries.

Public libraries reporting acquisition pressure accounted for one out of five institutions, but they represented 54 per cent of all Canadian residents in the study and slightly higher proportions of registered borrowers and library circulations. They served municipalities with a total of 9.8 million residents, 4.2 million borrowers, and 80.7 million circulations. These data reveal a potential biasing of public library collections for more than half of all Canadian residents in the study population.

The significant difference in acquisition pressure between systems and single libraries was also reflected in institutional characteristics. Respondent public libraries serving larger municipalities were more likely to be pressured to acquire or accept certain materials than those serving small centres. The typical respondent affected by acquisition pressure served a municipality with 81,000 people and had 35,000 registered borrowers and 680,000 circulations. In contrast, those not affected served an average municipality of 20,000 people and had 7,000 borrowers and 139,000 circulations. Statistical analysis shows that affected institutions served significantly larger municipalities in terms of residents, borrowers, and circulation than those not affected.

Acquisition pressure was associated with the presence of institutional access policies (selection policy, policy for handling objections, donations policy, an objections form, and support of the CLA Statement on Intellectual Freedom). Respondents with all five access policies experienced more pressure to acquire or accept materials for their collections than did those with either some policies or none at all. Among respondents with all five policies, 37 per cent experienced acquisition pressure. Among those with some but not all five policies, it was 22 per cent, and among those with none, it was 10 per cent. Statistical analysis confirms a significant relationship between acquisition pressure and access policy coverage.

While acquisition pressure was not associated with age-related borrowing restrictions, it was related to the requirement for minors to have consent to use certain materials. Among respondents whose libraries have a consent requirement, 35 per cent experienced acquisition pressure. In contrast, only 19 per cent of those not requiring consent said that they experienced acquisition pressure. Statistical analysis confirms a significant relationship between acquisition pressure and consent requirements.

Similarly, whether or not an institution treated certain materials differently in selection, classification, shelving, access or circulation made a difference in rates of acquisition pressure experienced by respondents. Among those reporting differential treatment, one-third also reported acquisition pressure, while only 18 per cent of those that did not treat potentially controversial materials differently said that they experienced acquisition pressure. Statistical analysis confirms a significant relationship between acquisition pressure and differential treatment of certain materials.

Acquisition pressure was also related to ownership of titles on the potentially controversial checklist instrument developed for the questionnaire survey and to direct challenges to withdraw or restrict materials. Institutions experiencing acquisition pressure owned an average of 17 checklist titles, while those not reporting acquisition pressure owned 11 titles each. Statistical analysis shows that institutions affected by acquisition pressure owned significantly more checklist titles than did those not reporting this pressure.

Similarly, pressure to acquire or accept material went hand in hand with requests to remove or restrict material. Institutions experiencing acquisition pressure reported 2.9 challenges per respondent over the study period compared to 0.8 challenges for those not experiencing such pressure. Statistical analysis shows that institutions affected by acquisition pressure experienced significantly more direct challenges than did those not reporting this pressure.

Respondents in all but two Canadian political jurisdictions, New Brunswick and Prince Edward Island, reported acquisition pressure. Forty per cent or more of the respondents in British Columbia, Saskatchewan and the two territories were affected.

Respondents were asked to elaborate on the pressures they had experienced. One wrote, "Our biggest problem is pressure to buy, or accept donated material, not demands for the withdrawal of controversial books." While several respondents noted that "pressured" was too strong a word, they said they were constantly being "urged" to accept donations or purchase materials on a wide variety of subjects. Overall, the most common source of these pressures and requests was religious groups and political interest groups that wanted literature supporting their beliefs to be placed on the shelves of the public library. One of the most frequently mentioned topics of pressure-group interest was abortion.

Respondents did not, however, mention any trend, such as an increase or decrease in these kinds of pressures. Respondents noted that, after evaluation, much of the material intended for donation was rejected, with a tactful explanation of the library's selection policy. In some cases, materials were accepted but not processed and were merely made available on tables or on racks for in-house use.

Verbatim comments by other respondents indicate the wide range of acquisition pressures experienced by public libraries across Canada. The following selected comments illustrate this diversity of pressures and the materials involved:

o Every church/religious organization in town tries to put their materials on the shelf. "Thank heaven" for the existence of our policy on donated material.

o Every now and then certain religious groups try and sneak in their material (J.W.s and *The Plain Truth*, Pentecostals, Rosicrucians, etc.).

o Organizations such as Scientology, Rajnee, TM press to have multiple copies of their titles in library. Similarly, small religious groups who want high-profile display of their material. Policy is to select a few representative titles from each group.

o Interest groups, Freemasonry, fundamentalist religions.

o Jehovah's Witness pressured to have J.W. material included to inform public. I explained it was inappropriate and that the library did not disseminate official points of view.

o We have been asked occasionally to buy more wholesome "Christian" books (especially in the YA field). We feel we buy a balance now. We have not changed our buying, though we are producing a booklist of "family/happy" type YA books.

o Bible stories — have plenty, did not buy. Responded by buying more Islamic stuff.

o Other than pressure for different formats (videos) and donations, the library has been specifically campaigned to acquire: 1) *The Christian Socratic*, a periodical published by local citizen; 2) *Compleat Mother*, magazine about pregnancy, birth, and breast feeding; 3) *Children's Own*. These were accepted for free distribution to the public — not added to the periodical collection of the library.

o A bookseller is very insistent that I purchase her "Christian" storybooks so that readers can see how to live a "good life." She is a born again fundamentalist and her books reflect her philosophy in a very heavy-handed manner.

o Pressure by pro-life groups; by persons wanting certain religious materials in the library; by business firms wanting their catalogues in the library; and some persistence by such groups as Alcoholics Anonymous.

o The local pro-life chapter has donated a subscription to their periodical and a selection of anti-abortion permabound paperbacks. We invoked the library policy of allowing *them* to choose the two most important works from their donation to be placed on the shelves and promised to examine the remaining group for possible inclusion under our normal criteria. (We added one additional title.) [emphasis in original]

o A pro-life group wanted to give the library some abortion/fetal models in plastic to be displayed. The library board turned down the request. When pro-life person was contacted about the decision, she was annoyed.

o A local pro-life organization donated six books promoted by their organization. These books have not been incorporated into our collection but an effort was made to elaborate information in our vertical file on both pro-life and pro-choice abortion issues.

o Anti-choice abortion groups have "donated" material they expect me to put directly on the shelves.

o We were pressed to accept several pro-life titles. Some we did and others we rejected. We have from time to time been approached by, or offered gift books by, the Jehovah's Witnesses, Baha'i faith and a gentleman promoting a list of right-wing fundamentalist titles called the "Must Book List."

o Baptist preacher wanted 26 pro-life, anti-abortion books purchased for library. Born again Christian faction urged large purchase of Christian literature — fiction. Same faction wanted preachings of Oral Roberts, Jimmy Swaggart, etc., on shelves.

o Pro-life and religious groups are particularly interested in having their materials in our collections. We have several approaches: 1) accept material, process it as "Pamphlet" with note indicating "Placed in library by...."; 2) refuse material as not meeting selection policy, 3) let organization know we will refer requests (if any) for this type of material to them.

o Right-to-life, Eckankar.

One respondent told in great detail of the persistence of a local special-interest group in having its literature made available through the public library.

o Local pro-life group donated a package of books to the library. With a couple of exceptions the books were very sensational in style and poorly written. I felt it was important that some of the Society's material be added, as the group is an active organization with many supporters in the community. I decided to keep two of the books and, anticipating the potential for controversy, I discussed my decision with the board, which concurred with my decision. Two years later, a member of the Pro-Life Society asked why the books were not in the collection. I explained my decision and pointed out that we had a number of books which dealt with the abortion controversy, presenting both sides of the issue. The reply I received was, "There is no other side."

Shortly afterwards I received a phone call and later a visit from the mayor, who had been receiving phone calls from members of the Society saying that the library had ten "pro-abortion" books but none representing the pro-life position. I found out later that some board members had received similar phone calls. I explained the type of material we had and followed up our discussion with a memo to the mayor and the library board, listing the books we had on the subject of abortion and giving a short outline of their contents. With the exception of the Pro-Life donations, all the books in our collection attempted to deal with the issue as a controversy, discussing both perspectives.

About a month later the Pro-Life Society asked to make a presentation to the library board. At that time they stated that although most of the library's books on abortion purported to deal with both sides of the issue, they were really pro-abortion. They presented excerpts from each book to support this position. I suggested to them that it was possible that they could go through the same books and find excerpts that supported the pro-life position. After a great deal of discussion with the board we agreed that on this subject it appeared to be impossible to deal with both sides of the issue in one book to everyone's satisfaction. I indicated that I had already ordered a couple of titles representing a pro-life position and would order others, while also ordering books that promoted a pro-choice position. The board conveyed this policy to the Pro-Life Society and we have not had any complaints from them since.

I have to say that we now have an unbalanced collection on the subject of abortion, as, while I had no trouble finding pro-life titles, books presenting the pro-choice position have been difficult to locate — most books deal with both sides of this difficult issue and do not present a strong advocacy position.

Several respondents mentioned the pressure brought to bear by particular religious groups to have their literature made available through the public library:

o Apart from individual authors selling their books, the Church of Scientology and supporters of "creationism" have made a concerted effort to make sure that we have sympathetic titles in stock.

o I notice a repeated insistence from the Scientology church to give or deliver us their bible.

o Not *great* pressure but Scientologists occasionally check to make sure Ron Hubbard's *Dianetics* is available. Patrons have commented that the collection does not reflect right-wing points of view as well as perceived left-wing views. [emphasis in original]

o The Baha'i faith local organization was persistent in giving us their video, which was very acceptable. A local "author" made sure we got her vanity press autobiography (quite racy!).

o A member of the Baha'i faith was concerned that materials about his religion were not in the library's collection. He donated materials, which he insisted should be added to the library. The librarian at that time did not feel the materials were suitable and did not add them.

o A member of the Baha'i faith wanted to donate five books on the religion to the library. After going through them per policy only two were accepted and the others (one in the German language) returned. Materials on comparative religions are welcome but it was felt that, considering demand, space, and content, these two were sufficient. The person was upset.

o Religious groups such as the Baha'i and "creationist" Baptists attempt to force us to accept their material.

o Mormon bible and other Mormon literature.

o Material representing certain religions such as Hare Krishna, material in subject areas (usually represented by a club or association), material by a particular author (usually represented by that author). Books for children prepared by specific religious groups; adult Christian fiction.

o Several church groups have donated their books to us. One lady, a Jehovah's Witness, was determined we should add to our collection one of their publications on creationism to represent "the other side." We did add it to the collection.

o Fundamentalist periodicals. Accepted two, *Plain Truth* and *Watchtower*, in "free pile" — not retained.

o A leader of a local religious offshoot complained we would not shelve all the books he wanted pertaining to his religious sect. Even wrote a letter to city council. Explained we had two books on shelf and could not show overbalance to any one viewpoint. Man took back his books and left threatening never to darken our door again.

o *Schools on Trial: A Positive Alternative* and various other materials with a religious bias.

o Children's and adult material on creationism, to "balance" the paleontology collection. Pro-life material to balance the pro-choice collection.

o Metaphysical books and books dealing with the occult.

Several other respondents noted pressure to acquire or accept material in a variety of subject areas:

o We are often pressured into buying fad diet books not recommended by Public Health, as well as "hype" books on AIDS, Masters and Johnson's new book, *And the Band Played On*, etc.

o Besides some suggestions for ordering, some people exerted pressure on the library to buy books dealing with subjects that are non-conventional, agnostic, esoteric, etc.

o One patron insisted we buy books on UFOs, inventions, and other life forces.

o No real pressure, although some donors can be quite persistent, e.g., Alcoholics Anonymous.

o Some groups wanted us to distribute the magazine *La ... Verité* but we refused.

o One user strongly insisted that the library should acquire *J'accuse ma... de victorian Theoret* [?]. This sensationalism does not fit into the library's policy for collection development.

o We were pressured to increase our French content — which is not applicable to this area.

Several respondents mentioned pressure by political groups to have materials added to the public library collection, Holocaust "revisionist" publications in particular.

o The library welcomes patron suggestions, but a few patrons become rather insistent. Most pressure in recent years has usually been in connection with periodicals, e.g., *Natural Motherhood*, a militant/radical/back-to-basics periodical published in Ontario. Some other titles were turned down as too specialized or too esoteric for our community.

o One member is pressuring on a regular basis to purchase material published by the Institute for Historical Review in California. We did purchase *The Hoax of the Twentieth Century* as an example of this particular school of thought. As a result of his complaints that our collection was heavily "Pro-Zionist" (our population is 20 per cent Jewish) we did an evaluation of our books on the Middle East and have since purchased books (from reviews) explaining the Palestinian perspective so that our collection is now better balanced.

o Arthur Butz's *Hoax of the Twentieth Century* and other publications of this type.

o Revisionist material concerning the Holocaust.

o Right-wing group asked to have material distributed and after reading I complied.

o *Western Guard* newspaper.

o Documents sent by embassies (U.S.S.R., South Africa) and by propaganda organizations (movements of GRAAL, etc.).

o By book donations, above all regarding philosophy or new and doctrinal beliefs. Also about certain countries like Albania and South Africa.

o Mostly foreign embassies.

o Ethnic publications — often costly periodicals — without substantial population to support their use, and publications which focus on one regional group.

o Some Sikhs insisted we subscribe to a Sikh newspaper. We decided that it was more a political broadside than newspaper and did not subscribe. No further pressure was applied.

One respondent told in detail of the extremes to which a local member of the community had gone to have a certain periodical accessible through the public library:

o I am sure all librarians deal with huge amounts of unsolicited mail and I suspect much of yours goes the same place mine does — straight into the garbage. About a year and a half ago we started receiving an unsolicited publication called *The Spotlight*. This is an American paper purporting to tell the true news suppressed by leftwing publications like *Time* and *Newsweek*. The content is almost entirely American, although there are occasional articles dealing with international issues such as the conspiracy to suppress the Philippines election results. *The Spotlight* claimed that Marcos won by a landslide and not President Aquino, as had been reported in the international press. Needless to say, I put this paper into the circular bin along with many other unsolicited publications. A couple of months later I received a letter from a man saying that he had donated a subscription of *The Spotlight* to our library and asking why it was not on display in the library alongside the other magazines.

I replied saying that I had no idea the publication had been donated, explained our donation policy, and declined to add the publication to our periodical collection because it dealt almost entirely with American politics, for which there is little demand in our library. I also pointed out that I had been unable to find any reviews of the paper and it was not listed in Katz's *Magazines for Libraries*. I concluded by suggesting that in future if he wished to make a donation, he discuss it with me in advance so that he could choose an appropriate publication for our library. In reply I received a long abusive letter, which was also copied to library board members and the newspaper. In the letter the donor accused me of suppressing information I did not agree with and filling the library with material presenting my views.

The library board discussed *The Spotlight* at length and after all members had read issues of the paper, decided to uphold my initial decision, citing three criteria in the book selection policy: a) poorly written or badly presented material, b) unreliable information, c) little or no demand.

While the newspaper did not print the donor's letter, it did print several articles about the issue. It also printed an editorial in which the editor accused the library of stifling freedom of expression by refusing to put *The Spotlight* on its shelves.

Summary

Overall, it is estimated that approximately one institution per week was pressured to acquire or accept materials between 1985 and 1987. While this involved only one out of five public libraries across the country, they served municipalities with 54 per cent of the population represented in the study. In general terms, what these figures imply is a potential biasing of public library collections for more than half of all Canadian residents in the study population.

Acquisition pressure tended to involve multi-branch systems serving large municipalities; French- and English-language institutions were similar in the rates of pressure that they experienced to acquire or accept materials.

The study has also shown that acquisition pressure was associated with the presence of institutional access policies, the requirement for minors to have consent to use certain materials and treatment of certain materials differently in selection, classification, shelving, access or circulation, and ownership of titles on the controversial materials checklist. It also went hand in hand with a high rate of direct challenges.

Part 3

THE FUTURE

OF ACCESS

11 / Summary of Findings

CANADIAN PUBLIC LIBRARIES ARE ORGANized administratively either as single-unit libraries or as multi-branch systems, and the systems are either urban or regional (though there are also cooperative regional systems that do not function as administrative organizations, such as those in Alberta and Ontario). There are many more single libraries than multi-branch systems across the country, but single libraries serve a much smaller percentage of the population than the multi-branch systems.

In spite of the difference in populations served, the two types of institutions are alike in terms of major characteristics: circulation per capita is about the same, circulation per borrower is about the same, and borrowers constitute about the same percentage of their municipal populations.

Respondents to the study represented 56 per cent of all institutions and 76 per cent of the Canadian population in 1987.

Access Policies and Practices

Overall, 70 per cent of the public libraries had some or all of the basic institutional access policies relating to intellectual freedom — selection policy, policy for handlng objections, donations policy, an objections form, and support of the CLA Statement on Intellectual Freedom. Fewer single-unit libraries had all or some of them than did multi-branch systems, 65 per cent compared to 92 per cent. English-language institutions were more likely to have them than their French-language counterparts.

Access Restrictions on Children and Young Adults

Age-related access restrictions were identified in the study as either restricted borrowing privileges for children and young adults or the requirement that minors have parental or guardian consent to borrow or consult materials. A major finding is that 60 per cent of all public libraries placed no restrictions on children and young adults.

Multi-branch systems were more likely than single-unit libraries to restrict access based on age. English- and French-language institutions did not differ in the extent to which they restricted access by age. Institutions that endorsed the CLA Statement on Intellectual Freedom were just as likely to have age restrictions as those that did not.

Institutional treatment of children and young adults may be related to the concept of *in loco parentis*: in small towns where people are apt to know each other, there may be less need to devise formal policy restrictions, while in larger, more diverse communities, these restrictions play a role for which individual library staff members do not have the time. Also, because in recent years the class of young adult literature has matured, public libraries now have three general age-group collections to manage (children's, young adult, and adult).

While there are materials in each of these classes that spark controversy, some public library staff have used age restrictions as a solution to the problem of dealing with juvenile titles. The most common concerns behind the restrictions on children and young adults are the same as for television and music videos — sex and violence.

Differential Treatment of Materials

Institutions with age-related restrictions also tended to treat potentially controversial or questionable materials differently from others in the collection in one way or another — selection, classification, shelving, access or circulation. Reported differential treatment was the same in both single-unit and multi-branch libraries, in both English- and French-language communities, and in both large and small centres. Overall, however, a major finding is that 79 per cent of the public libraries treated such materials similarly to other materials.

Collection Vulnerability

A measure of the susceptibility of a collection to censorship pressure was constructed for the study in the form of a checklist of potentially controversial materials. It consisted of 30 titles that had been reported challenged in previous Canadian censorship studies; for this reason, some of the titles were not of very recent publication date.

Half of the public libraries owned 11 or more of the checklist titles. Multi-branch systems owned twice as many of these titles as did single-unit libraries. Since the titles were all published originally in English, French-language public libraries owned fewer than their English-language counterparts, but what was surprising was that they owned as many of the titles as they did.

Ownership of materials on the checklist was related to the presence of institutional access policies: the more checklist titles the public library owned, the more likely that it also had such policies, particularly a selection policy. Ownership of titles on the checklist titles was also related to the rate of collection challenges: the more checklist titles that the public library owned, the more challenges it was apt to experience.

Direct Challenges

The most important finding is that 65 per cent of the public libraries experienced no direct challenges to their collections over the three years studied; one in five was challenged annually. Almost as important is the finding that there were fewer than 700 challenges to collections. Extrapolating to all public libraries, I estimate that there was one challenge every day somewhere in the country.

Institutions reporting challenges were much more likely to serve larger municipal populations, circulate more materials, and own more titles on the controversial materials checklist. Language did not play a significant role in the incidence of challenges. Neither age-related restrictions nor differential treatment of certain materials played a role in the incidence of challenges.

Almost all of the challenges were made by unaffiliated adults acting on their own behalf. One might have thought that library trustees, council members, and school trustees and staff (several units were housed in public schools) would initiate challenges in fairly large numbers. This was not the case, however. Together they accounted for only 8 per cent of all challenges, often acting for themselves rather than on behalf of members of the community. Even when adults objected to materials for children and young adults, they rarely claimed to be representing a child.

Regardless of any factor considered in the three years studied, I can confidently state that complaints about titles in public library collections during this period were motivated by individual opinion. There was no ground swell of censorship by the population of public library users of Canada, no concerted attack by organized groups on public librarians and their book selection policies.

Fewer than 600 individuals over three years were sufficiently concerned about the words and ideas expressed in public library materials to attempt to intervene in the collection management process. They objected to well over 500 different titles. Only 5 per cent of all challenges were initiated by groups or individuals acting on a group's behalf.

These data suggest that censorship pressure on Canadian public libraries is almost entirely an individual affair. The fact that three out of four challenges were to fiction, and particularly to fiction for children and young adults, indicates the general tenor of complaints. The topics that bothered the majority of individuals were sex and violence.

A major finding is that challenges were handled primarily by public library staff themselves, and with considerable dispatch. Only 11 per cent of the challenges were decided by public library boards or municipal councils. Challenges were resolved speedily — almost half within a month. They were also resolved without the involvement of the local media.

Another major finding is that 86 per cent of all challenged titles were retained; in a minority of cases, the complainant was satisfied when the offending item was relocated internally, reclassified, or labelled. Only 14 per cent of all challenged titles were permanently withdrawn from public library collections. Not unexpectedly, the rate of retention was higher in multi-branch systems than in single-unit libraries, and in larger municipalities.

English-language institutions retained more of the challenged titles than their French-language counterparts. Retention rates were also higher in those institutions that owned more of the titles on the controversial materials checklist and in those that experienced more challenges. Retention rates were higher in institutions with an objections policy and form and a donations policy and where minors were not required to have consent to borrow materials.

Retention was higher for fiction than non-fiction and for elementary age materials than adult materials. Retention was higher for materials with offensive language or materials considered unsuitable for age group than for materials with pornographic content. Retention rates were also higher when library policy was followed and when local media did not cover the incident.

Public librarians were, overall, fairly confident in their professional stance towards collection challenges: 88 per cent said that with hindsight they would not have handled these cases differently. And almost as many were satisfied with the way that they conducted their ongoing professional activities: 74 per cent reported that the challenges they experienced had had no effect on the selection, classification, shelving, access or circulation of materials. These findings were as true of the staff of single-unit libraries as of multi-branch systems, and of the staff in French- as in English-language institutions.

Covert Censorship

This concept was more difficult to measure than direct actions, but the best data gathered in this study indicate that at least one in ten public libraries experienced incidents of covert censorship — theft, defacement, alteration, mutilation, or destruction of materials. Multi-branch systems reported more of this kind of activity than single-unit libraries. French- and English-language institutions did not differ in covert censorship.

One tentative finding about this activity differs from the findings related to direct challenges: the range of subjects is somewhat wider when censorship is done on the sly than when the individual must speak face to face with a member of the staff. Here subjects included the occult, witchcraft, "D&D books" (Dungeons and Dragons), drugs, muscle building, nazism, the Holocaust, religion, anthropology, popular novels, romances, westerns, creationism, politics, sex education, and, of course, sex in general.

Since this kind of activity is secret, one cannot know if it is primarily done by children, young adults, or adults. Many of the titles reported suggest the handiwork of young adults; one might conjecture that it is the result of age-related access restrictions, but there is no evidence to verify this conclusion. The problem of diagnosis of covert incidents of suspected censorship remains intractable, in large part beyond the grasp of empirical observation and measurement.

Acquisition Pressure

This concept was not only difficult to measure but also difficult to reconcile with the concept of censorship; nonetheless, "undue" pressure on public library staff to acquire or accept certain materials for the collection suggests another strategy for achieving censorial ends — to control the content and orientation of the collection.

One in five public libraries reported this kind of activity. Again, multi-branch systems reported more activity than single-unit libraries. As well, French- and English-language institutions did not differ in the extent to which such pressure was reported. Tentative evidence suggests that acquisition pressure was exerted by single interest groups with political and social agendas: anti-abortion and religious groups were frequently mentioned.

Summary

Censorship activity in Canadian public libraries will continue — the fear of words will not be overcome any time soon. Some readers will see in the evidence of this study a considerable amount of censorship pressure taking a variety of forms to alter the composition of public library collections across Canada, but it is important to keep this activity in perspective. Of the tens of millions of items that were borrowed and consulted in-house by many millions of library users during the period studied, only a few hundred individuals felt so strongly about their negative reactions to particular library materials that they complained. Nonetheless, the actions of this small group of people had the potential to affect access to particular materials by more than 13 million other Canadian residents.

Presumably, the millions of uncontested items are evidence that public library staff are successfully meeting patron demands. From respondent comments, I do not perceive a notion that the staff are trying to "change" their clientele with provocative literature. Rather, staff are familiar with the interests of members of the community and are trying to satisfy those interests.

This situation may be especially true in smaller communities, where it might be conjectured that there are more shared values because people know each other; respondents there frequently reported knowing personally many members of the community. This familiarity with the community could account for librarians' knowledge of which books to select in order to match users and their interests. In larger communities, the goal is the same but staff rely more on formal policies and social patterns to assist them in satisfying the interests of their users.

In conclusion, this study has revealed, via the responses of public library staff to censorial challenges, a pattern of creative tension between institutional expertise and community advocacy. In most instances, public library staff used collection challenges as opportunities for fruitful dialogue with members of the community. Individuals communicated their concerns and values and attitudes, and staff communicated the public library's role in a democracy and the need for tolerance in communities of cultural diversity.

In this interaction between staff and citizen can be found a public education process: the staff learn more about the community; the citizen learns more about the public library. Many of the written comments by respondents showed this educational dialogue in action. In one letter explaining the thinking behind the selection of an item, a staff member wrote to a patron who had requested reconsideration of *Lizzy's Lion*.

> o Prior to purchasing any book for our collections, we consult reviews of the book by noted critics and librarians. The reviews for *Lizzy's Lion* were excellent. Dennis Lee, the author, is a former recipient of the Canadian Association of Children's Librarians' medal awarded to the author of the most outstanding children's book of the year in Canada. The illustrator, Marie-Louise Gay, was awarded the Canada Council Children's Literature Prize for her work on *Lizzy's Lion*.
>
> *Lizzy's Lion* is written in the form of nonsense verse. Children's literature has had many famous practitioners of this form from Edward Lear and Hilaire Belloc through to modern authors such as Jack Prelutsky and, of course, Dennis Lee, who has written the Canadian classics *Alligator Pie* and *Garbage Delight*. Nonsense verse, besides verging on the ridiculous, will often include some grotesque scenes which are meant to add to the nonsense. It is all meant as fantasy, but there are often moral overtones as well, with good overcoming evil as is the case in *Lizzy's Lion* when the little girl overcomes the robber.
>
> *Lizzy's Lion* is not meant to be taken seriously, but because it is a picture book, we recommend that parents preview all such books before they are read to children. Indeed, we request parental responsibility for a child's reading by asking parents to countersign their child's library card.
>
> Because *Lizzy's Lion* has been judged as an outstanding Canadian children's book, it will not be withdrawn from our collection. I would like to thank you, however, for taking the time to make your concerns known to me.

I think we can say from the evidence of this study that the Canadian public library is functioning effectively in the arena of censorial pressure. While public librarians are open to challenges and challenges are indeed initiated, the materials in dispute for the most part remain accessible. Vocal members of the community are not silenced, but, in the vast majority of cases, the staff uphold the public mandate of their institutions to safeguard freedom of expression for all members of the community, not just for those segments of it that are so clear and firm in their convictions that they take the time to press them openly.

I have suggested that public librarians are functioning effectively in safeguarding intellectual freedom — however, they do not function perfectly. Perfect achievement of goals is a utopian ideal that can never fully be realized, as Martin Duberman, acclaimed U.S. historian, has written in another context, but only utopian goals will allow us partly to succeed (Duberman 1991, 297).

12 / Conclusions

THIS STUDY, THE FIRST NATIONAL PROJECT of its kind in the world, has attempted to identify the scope and nature of community pressures to censor materials housed in the nation's public libraries, and to document the ways in which public librarians across the country have responded to these pressures.

Several respondents mentioned that they were pleased to see a study in the area of censorship problems and had been influenced by it to reconsider the issues involved. Many noted that they and their boards were against any kind of external censorship and strongly condemned it as an infringement on the rights of patrons. Some respondents, however, admitted that their staff probably do engage in self-censorship during the selection process. Many respondents commented that their small book budgets did not allow them to purchase a lot of questionable material.

There are at least three areas which merit further examination and discussion by Canadian public librarians. The first is the matter of formal written policies relating to intellectual freedom and access. The second is the public library community's treatment of one of its largest constituencies, children and young adults. And the third is the public library community's public defence and promotion of freedom of expression.

Many public libraries still do not have adequate access policies for selecting materials and for handling objections. And yet, comments by numerous respondents indicated that the key to dealing successfully with challenges to public library collections was the implementation of a collection development policy. Further, patrons should be made aware of these policies to help them better understand the role and responsibility of the public library in facilitating freedom of expression and in promoting each person's right to choose.

A concern for due process is not new. In a compilation of media reports of English-language book censorship in Canada between 1935 and 1978, Peter Birdsall and Delores Broten argued that public librarians as a group had not been "outstanding champions of the library's responsibility to the whole community" and that it was easier for them to "withstand pressure from minorities outside of mainstream beliefs, such as the Scientologists, than from the more vociferous local Christian sects." They urged public librarians to adopt formal procedures for dealing with challenges to their collections, noting that they should "insist that the library board must not act against the collection before public complaints are received and evaluated" (Birdsall and Broten 1978, 60).

Until formal access policies are worked out and adopted by a public library, its commitment to intellectual freedom is somewhat qualified. The absence of formal policy initiatives may be viewed as another manifestation of a phenomenon observed by Michael Pope in his doctoral study of librarians' opinions about sexually oriented literature, *Sex and the Undecided Librarian*: "Research indicates that librarians give strong support to the concepts of intellectual freedom and open access to information but do not necessarily implement these concepts in their libraries" (Pope 1974, 184).

Principles divorced from practice are trivial and irrelevant at best, and at worst they breed cynicism about the integrity of the public library as a social institution. Principles not transformed into institutional mechanisms send mixed messages to both staff and clientele, leading to inconsistency in policy and practice.

But having a policy is one thing; having a defensible policy is another. Public library treatment of children and young adults brings this distinction into sharp focus. The evidence from the present study shows that public librarians as a professional community do not have a defensible national policy on intellectual freedom for minors. Among respondent public libraries, there appears to be a fairly common qualification to the principle of unrestricted choice for children. Moreover, there are wide variations across Canada in the age at which these restrictions apply.

What is the philosophical foundation for restricting access to patrons aged 13 and over in some public libraries, while in others the age is set at 14, or 15, or 16, or 17, or 18? Why do some public libraries classify and shelve sex education books written specifically for children as though they were adult books? And even when a public library does not restrict access to print materials, what is the philosophical foundation for age restrictions on access to film and video in quiet obedience to the inconsistent policies imposed by provincial regulatory and censorship agencies across the country?

The Canadian Library Association Statement on Intellectual Freedom makes no mention of age-related access restrictions. On the contrary, it states that "all persons" in Canada have the fundamental right of access to "all expressions of knowledge, creativity and intellectual activity." Age-related restrictions therefore violate the CLA policy. Incidentally, they also violate the American Library Association Library Bill of Rights which has prohibited discrimination on the basis of age since 1967. Nevertheless, neither endorsement of the CLA Statement nor the adoption of the other formal access policies by public libraries automatically rules out the imposition of age restrictions on access. The present study shows that institutions were just as likely to have age restrictions if they endorsed the CLA Statement on Intellectual Freedom as if they did not endorse it, and just as likely to have age restrictions whether or not they had other patron access policies.

When public library staff with age-related access restrictions see the words "all persons" in the CLA Statement, do they make a mental translation to "all adults"? One suspects that a certain amount of self-delusion plays a role in this kind of discrimination. Comments by some respondents showed that they saw no barriers to access in age restrictions:

o Children's books dealing with sex education/abuse are housed in the office but are freely accessible if asked for.

o In the children's section, books on childbirth are kept behind the counter. But any children can take them out (staff uses their judgement).

o Our library is very distinctly divided and until children go into grade 7 their nook is the children's room. They are not "banned" from the adult room but unless parents are with them it's rare they venture into the adult section.

There is yet another dimension to the assumption of institutional *in loco parentis*: blanket age restrictions on all children deny to parents and guardians their freedom — and right — to determine their own child's reading, viewing and listening. If a parent or guardian wishes her or his child to have access to certain material that the institution has restricted on the basis of age, is parental autonomy thereby infringed? (Presumably, a parent or guardian could borrow materials on his or her card, but that might inconvenience both adult and child.)

In addition, many public libraries require minors to have parental or guardian consent for borrowing or using library materials on site. While staff may argue that a consent requirement is merely an affirmation of the legal responsibility of parents and guardians for minors, the effect may be to discriminate against children and young adults and to constrain their access to public library materials.

Other major barriers to access by minors that many public libraries need to reconsider are a variety of policies and practices identified in "Free Access to Libraries for Minors; An Interpretation of the Library Bill of Rights," found in the *Intellectual Freedom Manual* published by the American Library Association.

Among others, these barriers include restricted reading rooms for adult use only, library cards limiting circulation of some materials to adults only, closed collections for adult use only, collections limited to teacher use or restricted according to a student's grade level, and interlibrary loan service for adult use only (American Library Association. Office for Intellectual Freedom 1992, 24).

There is also the issue of client confidentiality. While respondent comments suggest a caring service philosophy in their treatment of minors, some respondents said that they occasionally telephone parents to discuss a child's intended borrowing. This action appears to be an invasion of privacy and a breach of client confidentiality.

The most unsettling ramifications of these restrictive policies and practices, however, have been identified in a 1986 report by the American Association of University Professors entitled *Liberty and Learning in the Schools: Higher Education's Concerns*. Their concerns are twofold: first, that restrictive policies and practices are self-reinforcing, and second, that young people will come to see suppression, by the example of their authoritarian elders, as an acceptable way of responding to controversial ideas (American Association of University Professors 1986).

By limiting access so as to appease a few vocal parents and unaffiliated adult patrons, public libraries with restrictive policies condition the community and its children to believe that the institution has the right and duty to act for parents — and even in their place. This message may have a chilling effect on intellectual freedom, and for some young people the by-product is surely distrust or resentment of public librarians. It may also promote the ideology of state control, an ideology in which the state and its institutions decide everything of importance for the citizenry, and assume both the right and the obligation to protect citizens and their children from themselves.

The evidence from this study suggests that public librarians as a community should become more consistent champions of the rights of children and young adults to have unqualified access to library materials. It is rather ironic that recent amendments to the Criminal Code reduce the age of consent for sexual relations to 14 (*Martin's Annual Criminal Code*, 1993), but some public libraries still restrict access to sexuality materials to those 18 and over — young people may have sex but not read about it.

While it is true that books and other materials are published for specific age groups, age-related restrictions and other institutional barriers to access violate the "social contract" for intellectual freedom that public library staff unofficially, if not officially, endorse. The point here, I would argue, is that public librarians ought to recognize that a Canadian kid is a Canadian kid is a Canadian kid.... How a balance can be achieved between social ideology that expects public librarians to protect children and the larger moral imperative to respect the rights of minors, is and remains an unresolved — and difficult — issue.

At the same time, it would be incorrect to leave the impression that the ideas to which children are exposed have no power. As Alison Lurie, author and critic of children's literature and a professor of English at Cornell University, has observed in *Don't Tell the Grown-Ups; Subversive Children's Literature,*

> Most of the great works of juvenile literature are subversive in one way or another: they express ideas and emotions not generally approved of or even recognized at the time; they make fun of honored figures and piously held beliefs; and they view social pretenses with clear-eyed directness, remarking — as in Andersen's famous tale — that the emperor has no clothes.
>
> ...
>
> The great subversive works of children's literature suggest that there are other views of human life besides those of the shopping mall and the corporation. They mock current assumptions and express the imaginative, unconventional, noncommercial view of the world in its simplest and purest form. (Lurie 1990, 4, xi)

Nonetheless, as Susan Madden, literacy and young adult services librarian in Washington state and long-time advocate of young people's right to intellectual freedom, pointed out in 1989 to the Intellectual Freedom Interest Group of the Library Association of Alberta, the public should not fear reading but rather the inability to read:

> I was a juvenile court librarian for 7 years. During that time I saw literally thousands of kids, but I never saw one who was in lock-up because of something they had viewed or read. In fact, I would say that over 80% of them were there because they could not read ... wouldst that we could devote as much time to the literacy of our patrons as we do to their protection. (Madden 1990, 21)

Another concern that arises from the present study is the need for more vigorous and sustained campaigns by the public library community to defend and promote freedom of expression in Canada. With the major exception of the concerted reaction to Bill C-54, public librarians have not taken a national leadership role on intellectual freedom issues. They have been slow to support Freedom to Read Week, an event that is run by the Book and Periodical Council.

Intellectual freedom has a relatively low priority for the Canadian Library Association, if one can judge by its 1992 Strategic Plan, which does not mention intellectual freedom (Canadian Library Association 1992), and by its annual conferences, which have not regularly included programs on intellectual freedom in recent years. To give the Association its due, the February issue of the *Canadian Library Journal* and now the January issue of *Feliciter* have been devoted to freedom of expression.

The Association has come a long way, however, from the days of its Committee on Undesirable Literature, established in 1958 to "consider the various types of undesirable literature which are being published or distributed in Canada." This committee metamorphosed three years later into the present Intellectual Freedom Committee (Horn 1978).

There are, however, exceptions to the low priority that many public libraries give to the promotion of intellectual freedom in their communities:

- Halifax City Regional Library has an ongoing public program of support for intellectual freedom. See, for example, their booklets "Canadian Books and Challenges to Intellectual Freedom" and "Censored Imagination: Banned or Challenged Fiction and the Freedom to Read."

- Thunder Bay Public Library responded to the controversy sparked by the library's purchase of Madonna's *Sex* in 1992-93 by forming a community-based Freedom to Read committee and by producing a broadcast-quality video on intellectual freedom for local and national use (*Freedom to Read: Don't Take It for Granted!*).

- The City of Edmonton Public Library has produced a brochure, "Freedom to Read, to View, to Listen."

- The Intellectual Freedom Committee of the Library Association of Alberta initiated requests for municipal proclamations in 1992 in support of Freedom to Read Week. The cities of Edmonton and Calgary issued formal proclamations of support for Freedom to Read Week 1992, the first major metropolitan centres in Canada to do so. As well, Edmonton supported Freedom to Read Week 1993 and 1994. The proclamation in 1993 in Edmonton was sponsored by the Writers Guild of Alberta and in 1994 by the Edmonton Public Library.

- CANSCAIP Minus-30, the Northern Alberta Chapter of the Canadian Society of Children's Authors, Illustrators and Performers, has launched an active program to promote public awareness of censorship activity in Alberta schools and libraries and to provide support for librarians involved in challenges. CANSCAIP Minus-30 is developing a database of books challenged in Alberta school libraries; the 1992 list is appended to my article "Eternal Vigilance within Canadian Libraries" (Schrader 1993). They have also produced a brochure, "Don't Throw the Book Away."

The value to public librarians of a more active public awareness strategy was revealed in the comments of several respondents to the study:

> o We had a prominent display during Freedom to Read Week which aroused a lot of interest in the community. In general, it seems that proxim-

ity to the city has resulted in more tolerant attitudes to different types of material than I have experienced in many rural areas. The general feeling about Freedom to Read Week was that censorship can't/doesn't happen here.

o Displays, posters in branches during Freedom to Read Week resulted in good media coverage in larger centres and a lot of interest/questions from patrons.

o I think our regional library has a good attitude towards censorship. We have been encouraged to participate in "Freedom to Read Week" and have displays up and activities to make patrons aware of the facts.

Future Research

It is obvious that other factors not studied here also play an important role in the public library censorship phenomenon. Some of these concern the governance of the institution — trustee leadership, municipal council support, the leadership of the chief librarian, and the relations among these constituencies. Other factors concern the cultural mix of the local community — religious and political affiliation, education, and other socio-demographic characteristics. Future research might address these concerns.

Still other factors awaiting investigation relate to the institutional culture of the local public library and staff — their attitudes toward selection and self-censorship, their attitudes toward censorship and intellectual freedom, their philosophy of client service, their perception of community and political support, overall institutional effectiveness in the community, and other socio-demographic characteristics. Finally, there are broad social, political and economic factors associated with the culture of the mass media and the publishing industry that merit further — and sustained inquiry.

At the level of the individual psyche, there are other factors at work that deserve attention. Reader response theory, for example, helps to explain why there were so many different reasons given by complainants to justify their objections to particular library materials. As Aidan Chambers, children's author and critic, explains in *Introducing Books to Children*, response to a text is based in a coming together of the reader's personal history, the reader's reading history, and the text itself. The reader inevitably participates in creating the meaning of a text, a meaning that for each reader may differ either somewhat or substantially from the author's original concept. A reader's personal history includes the formation of cultural, moral and aesthetic values (Chambers 1983).

These values play a part in determining a reader's response to a text and are among the criteria that a reader uses, consciously or unconsciously, to decide whether a text is good or bad. If a text is judged on its literary merit, aesthetic values should be the dominant criteria. But literature has always been understood to be a force for socializing individuals, and the moral and cultural values that a reader brings to and finds in a text will influence the reader's judgement of it. These dynamic interactions are nowhere better illustrated than in the frequently divergent reasons that people give for disapproving of the same title. A similar line of inquiry might be centered in cultural studies theory.

But reader response theory does not explain why some people want to prevent or restrict access to public library material, and little if any empirical research has been done to answer this question. One promising anecdotal account is provided by Norman Poppel, professor of psychology, and Edwin Ashley, director of the library (both at Middlesex County College in Edison, New Jersey), in their article "Toward an Understanding of the Censor." Among supporters of censorship, there appears to a pervasive fear of the power of words and ideas.

Individuals who want to censor appear to hold the view that images have fixed meanings — exactly the opposite of what reader response theory says. They appear to hold the view that the human mind — especially the mind of the child and the adolescent — is like a sponge, absorbing everything in its path without discrimination, seduced by and imitating every idea without reflection, incapable of distinguishing between imagery and reality, equally influenced by vicarious experience and actual experience. They seem to believe that we are what we read last, that environment, schools, peers and extended family leave no permanent mark on our values and belief systems.

It is unfortunate that this "sponge theory" of the effects of reading on attitudes and behaviour has not been adequately examined in the literature. One fruitful avenue for further study is the perspective of general systems theory, originally enunciated by Ludwig von Bertalanffy, noted biologist and philosopher. In this perspective, for example, the human mind is regarded as a system with both biological and cultural dimensions that interact with other systems, both human and non-human.

Information in one form or another is constantly being presented to the human mind *qua* system from its surroundings, and the function of the system is to select that which it wants and to reject that which it does not want. Hence, not everything offered to a system is taken in by it — just as not everything that it offers to its surroundings is accepted by them (Bertalanffy 1968).

In such a general systems view of the human condition, fear of exposure to ideas would be replaced by respect for the autonomous individual's capacity for evaluating ideas and for acting in accordance with the moral and ethical responsibilities that issue from the social contract.

Another fruitful avenue for further study is the perspective of social learning theory, in which one important element is the affective filter: people affirm what fits into their value system and concomitantly have strong emotional reactions that tend to confirm rather than change their beliefs (Beach 1979). Still another is the perspective of anthropological theory, in which perceptions, meanings, and values are constituted through continuous social struggles in a world made up of multiple discourses (Lacombe 1994).

While it is true that we are shaped by what we read, see and hear, I believe we are nonetheless safe as long as we are exposed to a diversity of views. The real danger is in having access to only one view. This is my fear — not of too many words, but rather of too few.

All of these problems, from theoretical perspectives to empirical patterns, await more complex research designs than the one constructed for the present descriptive investigation. Other areas for research may also be suggested. Of course the most obvious is a replication of the present study so that trends could be determined in rates of censorship pressure and kinds of institutional response. Studies could also be undertaken of English and social studies teachers, school administrators, school consultants, and school librarians. At a more focused level, a broader and more representative checklist of potentially controversial titles could be developed for periodic testing of the censorship susceptibility of Canadian public libraries. Qualitative case studies of complainants and their motivation could also be undertaken.

Another major area that is ripe for further research is self-censorship. Although Marjorie Fiske and Charles Busha made important contributions, their landmark studies have not led to the development of a research tradition in this area. As Richard McKee noted in a review of censorship research to 1977, studies matching the rigour of the work by Fiske and Busha are uncommon (McKee 1977).

Self-censorship can take a variety of forms — avoiding controversial topics and titles, citing the absence of reviews to justify the exclusion of controversial titles, resorting to budget constraints, and ignoring alternative press publications. For example, according to a letter to the editor in the summer 1992 issue of the *IFRT Report* by Charles Willett, founder and president of CRISES Press (a non-profit company that markets alternative publications to libraries), *Alternative Press Index* is unavailable in "vast regions" of the U.S., and even those libraries that have it subscribe to "a mere smattering" of its titles (Willett 1992). The situation in Canada is unknown.

Carolyn Caywood, a librarian with the Virginia Beach Public Library and regular "Teens & Libraries" columnist for *School Library Journal*, commented recently on the allure of self-censorship to avoid the controversial topic of gay-positive materials:

> ... I do not assume that the fear of censorship accounts for all libraries that lack materials on gays and lesbians. No doubt, there are librarians who think that none of the teens who use their library could possibly be interested in these materials, or that reading about gays will contaminate young minds. It will not be easy for all librarians to reconcile the need to provide such materials with their personal beliefs, but the consequences of self-censored collections can be devastating. (Caywood 1993, 50)

Cal Gough and Ellen Greenblatt, who jointly edited *Gay and Lesbian Library Service*, enumerated ten myths that many librarians cling to about gay and lesbian patrons, in defence of self-censorship of materials and services to them:

1. "No gays and lesbians live around here ..."
2. "Well, if there are any lesbians or gay people living near me, they don't seem to use my library ..."
3. "Gay/lesbian materials are too technical/too academic/too clinical/too esoteric for the people who use my library."
4. "But it's so difficult to find reviews of these materials ..."
5. "Library vendors don't handle those books, do they?"
6. "We don't/shouldn't cater to specialized needs ..."
7. "We simply haven't yet found the time to devote attention to covering this particular subject area ..."
8. "I'm not qualified to order those books ..."
9. "Can't people just use interlibrary loan to get these things?"
10. "My library can't afford these materials ..."

(Gough and Greenblatt 1991, 4-5)

In particular, further research should be conducted into the relationship between public librarian self-esteem, self-censorship, and response to challenges (Blake 1987). And when one hears stories about a staff member who accidentally spills something on any library book thought to be offensive so that it can be discarded (thus, presumably, in good conscience), or about catalogers who never quite get around to processing certain titles, or about others who simply "disappear" items that they personally dislike, we should not be complacent about the need for further investigation into the many forms that self-censorship can take.

Still, the tentative evidence from the present study suggests that the great majority of Canadian public librarians do not knowingly and deliberately treat potentially controversial or questionable materials differently from others in their collections in any way, whether it be in selection, classification, shelving, access or circulation.

Finally, although it is of a different order than the empirical and bibliographic studies suggested above, the twin concepts of the balanced collection and public library impartiality bear further research, particularly with respect to such issues as sexism, racism, homosexuality, and other sexual values. In this context, the words of Bernard Berelson, written in 1938, still merit attention.

Sociologist, communications researcher, educator, and at the end of the 1940s dean of the Graduate Library School at the University of Chicago, Berelson argued that the balanced collection concept, in which the public library provides material on all sides of a question but takes no side, was a convenient barrier behind which the profession could retreat "from the responsibility of serving a more useful social purpose." Although he made it clear that the public library must provide material on all sides of a question, he suggested that this was only the beginning of its social function, not the end. He wrote:

> I say that the library should not be impartial, for instance, between democracy and dictatorship, or between intelligence and stupidity or prejudice, or between the general public welfare and special interests, or between peace and war, or between reason and force. If the library wishes to be considered as seriously devoted to the best interests of society, then it must realistically recognize that impartiality is not always compatible with such devotion and it must be prepared to take its place in defense of those interests. (Berelson 1938, 88)

Conclusions

The national profile that emerges within these pages is an unfinished story: every day, new twists are added to the ongoing narrative. I hope that this study will shed light on the prevailing climate of intellectual freedom in Canadian public libraries and help to promote discussion about the limits on freedom of expression that are appropriate in the Canadian body politic.

It is true that words and ideas are powerful, but they are not supernatural. Their magic is the magic of imagination and enchantment, not the magic of the occult. As long as words convey ideas, public librarians will be needed to help us give voice to the human instincts for naming and sharing.

One of the most important and one of the most intractable problems for democratic institutions is the role of the expert in the service of the lay community: who decides, ultimately, which ideas will find their way onto public library shelves? In the fine balance between institutional prerogative and the citizen's right to dissent, the public library should strive to serve all of its potential clientele. Unless public librarians live the principles of intellectual freedom and access as agents for all of the body politic, through policies, procedures and integrity, they abdicate their claim to institutional prerogative and institutional autonomy.

As Lester Asheim commented in his reappraisal in 1983 of the issues of censorship and selection, the defence of ideas is the librarian's concern, and "the best solution to the problem of access is to add positively to the store of ideas, not negatively to reduce it" (Asheim 1983, 184).

Freedom of expression is the very foundation of political life; without it, there is no choice of liberal or conservative philosophy, of right or left. The instincts for freedom and individual responsibility are the keystones to social organization and to democratic government. In the last resort, it is not the force of law but only the force of free intelligence that can save a people from its own folly.

In this light, I believe that it is better to err on the side of more access rather than on the side of less, and that those who advocate reduced access must prove beyond a reasonable doubt that it will do more good than harm. Convincing evidence must be produced that a less free society will be a safer one, but also one that will respect differences and provide equality for all. Nothing less than democracy itself hangs in the balance.

As one respondent commented,

> o I feel censorship, in any form, is the worst crime against libraries and the public in general. I always felt, and still do, that our country's freedoms and rights are what make life here so enjoyable. Freedom of choice is what separates us from countries where the government is the ultimate power.

I believe that the dubious prospects for the emergence of evidence that would justify censorship explains why the framers of the Universal Declaration of Human Rights, adopted by the United Nations General Assembly on December 10, 1948, included Article 19:

> Everyone has the right to freedom of opinion and expression; this right includes freedom to hold opinions without interference and to seek, receive and impart information and ideas through any media and regardless of frontiers. (Article 19 International Center on Censorship 1991, 409)

For public librarians, as for all Canadians who respect the civil rights of their fellow citizens, the price of continuing liberty is indeed eternal vigilance. For one prediction can be made that needs no comprehensive study to back it up: the fear of words will never cease and the desire to censor them will never die. And while public librarians should acknowledge that members of the community have a right to complain as well as to inquire about materials, a right to due process in the consideration of their complaints, and a right to be treated with dignity in that consideration, members of the community should likewise acknowledge that the institution has a right to serve all of the community, a right to promote freedom of expression, and a right to defend the freedom to read, to view and to listen. The concept of "community rights" must refer to the civil rights of every resident of whatever age and of whatever taxpayer status — the concept is not a slogan for marginalizing and silencing certain minorities that other vocal minorities find distasteful or offensive.

Our sense of community is vital, but it is a sense firmly rooted in the practice of freedom and resonsibility that is the keystone to democracy.

Given this perspective, the onus is on public librarians to develop innovative and credible methods for coming to know their communities and for helping their communities come to know the meaning of intellectual freedom. In the latter regard I would like to suggest that public libraries publish annually a list of titles in their collections that are formally challenged in writing — a sort of annual report on the climate of intellectual freedom — together with the names and affiliations of complainants, the actions that have been requested, and the disposition of each challenge. In this way, "community rights" will be fully honoured and preserved. In addition, every library should review its various access policies with all staff and trustees on an annual basis.

But commitment to intellectual freedom means more than mere affirmation. It means an understanding of the value of information in a democratic society, and it means society must invest the resources necessary to turn affirmation into community service. Only in this way will the public library's ethical task of stewardship of democratic values be fulfilled.

I hope that the research reported here will be of value to public librarians everywhere in their continuing efforts to evaluate the adequacy and effectiveness of their own responses to censorship pressure.

As this is a book about what public library staff say and do on a day-to-day basis in their service to the community, it is fitting that they should have the last word. Among the many frank and insightful and humorous comments that I received, one respondent reminded us:

> o Since book selection can not be a science, we can only hope to guard against our biases warping our collections. Changing staff doing the selection is probably the most palatable solution. Diversity of selectors should help provide balance. Please note that not only are there controversial and/or questionable books we do not buy, but also non-controversial, non-questionable books that we do not buy.

And finally, this respondent reminds us that all research findings are permanently conjectural and tentative by nature:

> o Questionnaires do not always tell the whole story. This community may be ripe for a challenge. We do not know.

Suggested Further Reading

Boast, Laura. "Library Defends Reading Freedom." *Chronicle-Journal / Times-News* (November 21, 1993): A3.

Buckingham, David, ed. *Reading Audiences: Young People and the Media.* Manchester, Eng.: Manchester University Press, 1993.

Burstyn, Varda, ed. *Women against Censorship.* Vancouver, B.C.: Douglas & McIntyre, 1985.

Cornog, Martha. "Is Sex Safe in Your Library? How to Fight Censorship." *Library Journal* 118 (August 1993): 43-46.

Cornog, Martha, ed. *Libraries, Erotica, Pornography.* Phoenix, Ariz.: Oryx Press, 1991.

Dasenbrock, Reed Way. "Do We Write the Text We Read?" In *Literary Theory After Davidson*, edited by Reed Way Dasenbrock. University Park, Penn.: The Pennsylvania State University Press, 1993.

Easthope, Antony and Kate McGowan, eds. *A Critical and Cultural Theory Reader.* Toronto: University of Toronto Press, 1992.

Ericson, Richard V., Patricia Baranek, and Janet B.L. Chan. *Representing Order: Crime, Law, and Justice in the News Media.* Toronto, Ont.: University of Toronto Press, 1991.

Hentoff, Nat. *Free Speech for Me — But Not for Thee; How the American Left and Right Relentlessly Censor Each Other.* New York, N.Y.: HarperCollins, 1992.

Herman, Edward S. and Noam Chomsky. *Manufacturing Consent; The Political Economy of the Mass Media.* New York, N.Y.: Pantheon Books, 1988.

Hicks, Robert. "The Devil in the Library." *School Library Journal* 37 (April 1991): 53.

—. *In Pursuit of Satan: The Police and the Occult.* Buffalo, N.Y.: Prometheus Books, 1991.

Jansen, Sue Curry. *Censorship: The Knot That Binds Power and Knowledge.* New York, N.Y.: Oxford University Press, 1991.

Jensen, Carl and Project Censored. *Censored: The News That Didn't Make the News — and Why.* The 1994 Project Censored Yearbook. New York, N.Y.: Four Walls Eight Windows, 1994.

Johnson, Richard. "Cultural Studies in a Strong State." *The English Magazine* 22 (Summer 1989): 1014.

Kiss and Tell. *Her Tongue on My Theory: Images, Essays and Fantasies.* Vancouver, B.C.: Press Gang Publishers, 1994.

Lacombe, Dany. *Blue Politics: Pornography in the Age of Feminism.* Toronto, Ont.: University of Toronto Press, 1994.

McCook, Kathleen de la Pena. "The First Virtual Reality." *American Libraries* 24 (July-August 1993): 626-28.

McDonnell, Kathleen. *Kid Culture: Children & Adults & Popular Culture.* Toronto, Ont.: Second Story Press, 1994.

MacLean, Eleanor. *Between the Lines: How to Detect Bias and Propaganda in the News and Everyday Life.* Montreal, Que.: Black Rose Books, 1981.

Montgomery, Kathryn C. *Target: Prime Time; Advocacy Groups and the Struggle over Entertainment Television.* New York, N.Y.: Oxford University Press, 1989.

Neill, S.D. "A Clash of Values: Censorship." *Canadian Library Journal* 45 (February 1988): 35-39.

Oboler, Eli M. *The Fear of the Word: Censorship and Sex.* Metuchen, N.J.: Scarecrow Press, 1974.

Parenti, Michael. *Inventing Reality: The Politics of Mass Media.* New York, N.Y.: Saint Martin's Press, 1986.

Salutin, Rick. *Living in a Dark Age.* Toronto, Ont.: HarperCollins Publishers, 1991.

Strossen, Nadine. *Defending Pornography: Free Speech, Sex, and the Fight for Women's Rights.* New York, N.Y.: Scribner, 1995.

Swan, John and Noel Pettie. *The Freedom to Lie: A Debate about Democracy.* Jefferson, N.C.: McFarland, 1989.

Thunder Bay Public Library. *Freedom to Read: Don't Take It for Granted!* Thunder Bay, Ont.: Northern Insights, 1994.

Williams, Linda. *Hard Core: Power, Pleasure, and the "Frenzy of the Visible."* Berkeley, Calif.: University of California Press, 1989.

References

Alberta. Culture and Multiculturalism. 1988. *Libraries Act.* Chapter L-12.1, 1983. "The Libraries Regulation, 1984. With amendments up to and including September, 1988." Edmonton: Alberta Culture and Multiculturalism.

American Association of University Professors. 1986. *Liberty and Learning in the Schools: Higher Education's Concerns.* Washington, D.C.: American Association of University Professors. Also reported in "University Professors Warn Against School Censorship," *Newsletter on Intellectual Freedom* 36 (January 1987): 7, 35.

American Civil Liberties Union. 1986. *Censorship in the South: A Report of Four States, 1980-85.* Atlanta, Ga.: American Civil Liberties Union.

American Library Association. Office for Intellectual Freedom. 1992. *Intellectual Freedom Manual.* 4th ed. Chicago, Ill.: Office for Intellectual Freedom, American Library Association.

Article 19 International Center on Censorship. 1991. *Information Freedom and Censorship: World Report 1991.* London, Eng.: Library Association Publishing.

Asheim, Lester E. 1953. "Not Censorship But Selection." *Wilson Library Bulletin* 28 (September): 63-67. (Also published as "The Librarian's Responsibility: Not Censorship, but Selection." In *Freedom of Book Selection* (Proceedings of the Second Conference on Intellectual Freedom, Whittier, California, June 20-21, 1953), edited by Fredric J. Mosher, 90-99. Chicago, Ill.: American Library Association, 1954.)

Asheim, Lester E. 1983. "Selection and Censorship: A Reappraisal." *Wilson Library Bulletin* 58 (November): 180-84.

Beach, Richard. 1979. "Issues of Censorship and Research on Effects of and Response to Reading." In *Dealing with Censorship*, ed. James E. Davis. Urbana, Ill.: National Council of Teachers of English.

Berelson, Bernard. 1938. "The Myth of Library Impartiality; An Interpretation for Democracy." *Wilson Bulletin for Librarians* 13 (October): 87-90.

Bertalanffy, Ludwig von. 1968. *General System Theory Foundations, Development, Applications.* New York, N.Y.: George Braziller.

Beta Associates. 1982. *Public Libraries in Canada; A Study Commissioned by the Canadian Book Publishers' Council.* Toronto, Ont.: Beta Associates.

Bildfell, Laurie. 1984. "Silent Censorship; The Sins of Omission, the Sins of Commission." *Quill and Quire* 50 (September): 4-6.

Birdsall, Peter and Delores Broten. 1978. *Mind War: Book Censorship in English Canada.* Victoria, B.C.: CANLIT.

Blake, Virgil L.P. 1987. "Self-Esteem, Self-Censorship, and Censorship: Librarians as Censors." *Urban Academic Librarian* 5 (Fall): 8-19.

Book and Periodical Council. 1988. Minutes, Meeting of the Freedom of Expression Committee, held in Toronto, Ontario, June 28, 1988.

Book and Periodical Development Council. 1984. "BPDC Sponsors Freedom to Read." *Feliciter* 30 (July/August): 19.

Book and Periodical Development Council. 1986. "Books Challenged or Banned in the Last Eleven Years — 1974 to 1985." In Freedom to Read Week Kit. Toronto, Ont.: Book and Periodical Development Council.

Burress, Lee. 1979. "A Brief Report of the 1977 NCTE Censorship Survey." In *Dealing with Censorship*, edited by James E. Davis, 14-47. Urbana, Ill.: National Council of Teachers of English.

Burton, Melody C. 1986. "Freedom of Access and Freedom of Expression: An Annotated Bibliography of Recent Canadian Periodical Literature." Unpublished M.L.S. project, University of Alberta.

Busha, Charles H. 1972a. *Freedom Versus Suppression and Censorship: With a Study of the Attitudes of Midwestern Public Librarians and a Bibliography of Censorship.* Littleton, Colo.: Libraries Unlimited.

Busha, Charles H. 1972b. "Intellectual Freedom and Censorship: The Climate of Opinion in Midwestern Public Libraries." *Library Quarterly* 42 (July): 283-301.

Canadian Library Association. 1987. "Response to Bill C-54." *Feliciter* 33 (July-August): 1. (Letter to the Minister of Justice and Attorney General of Canada from the Executive Director, June 29, 1987.)

Canadian Library Association. 1992. "President's Update on the Strategic Plan." Ottawa, Ont.: Canadian Library Association.

Carnovsky, Leon. 1950. "The Obligations and Responsibilities of the Librarian Concerning Censorship." *Library Quarterly* 20 (January): 21-32.

Caywood, Carolyn. 1993. "Reaching Out to Gay Teens." *School Library Journal* 39 (April): 50.

Chambers, Aidan. 1983. *Introducing Books to Children*. 2d ed. Boston, Mass.: Horn Book.

Delaware Library Association. 1985. "IFOA Committee Announces Survey Results." *Delaware Library Association Bulletin* (Fall-Winter): 5. Also available as an unpublished report by Brenda Ferris, Wilmington, Delaware.

Dochniak, Jim. 1986. "When Silence is not Golden: Reviewing the Censorship Issue." In *Alternative Library Literature, 1984/1985: A Biennial Anthology*, edited by Sanford Berman and James P. Danky, 71-73. Jefferson, N.C.: McFarland and Co. (Reprinted from *Minnesota Reviews* August/September 1985.)

Duberman, Martin. 1991. *Cures: A Gay Man's Odyssey*. New York, N.Y.: Plume.

Engelbert, Alan. 1982. "Censorship in Missouri: A Survey." *Show-Me Libraries* 34 (December): 5-10.

England, Claire St. Clere. 1974. "The Climate of Censorship in Ontario: An Investigation into Attitudes Toward Intellectual Freedom and the Perceptual Factors Affecting the Practice of Censorship in Public Libraries Serving Medium-Sized Populations." Unpublished Ph.D. dissertation, University of Toronto.

Fiske, Marjorie. 1959. *Book Selection and Censorship: A Study of School and Public Libraries in California*. Berkeley, Cal.: University of California Press.

Flavelle, Dana. 1987. "28 Libraries Close as Staff Protests Federal Porn Bill." *Toronto Star* (December 11): A5.

Fowlie, Les. 1988. "Bill C-54 — A Bogus Prescription." (Editorial) *Canadian Library Journal* 45 (February): 5-6.

Ginnane, Mary. 1988. "Annual Report, May 1987-June 30, 1988." Oregon Intellectual Freedom Clearinghouse, Oregon State Library, Salem, Oregon.

Gough, Cal and Ellen Greenblatt. 1991. "Ten Myths of Gay and Lesbian Library Service." *GLTF Newsletter* 3 (Fall): 4-5. Reprinted from *Gay and Lesbian Library Service*, edited by Cal Gough and Ellen Greenblatt. Jefferson, N.C.: McFarland, 1990.

Heuertz, Linda. 1993. "Library Challenges in Washington State: A Statewide Survey of Challenges to Materials in Public Libraries, 1989-1992." Unpublished Master's project, University of Washington.

Hopkins, Dianne McAfee. 1989. "Toward a Conceptual Model of Factors Influencing the Outcome of Challenges to Library Materials in School Settings." *Library and Information Science Research* 11 (July-September): 247-71.

Hopkins, Diane McAfee. 1991. *Factors Influencing the Outcome of Challenges to Materials in Secondary School Libraries: Report of a National Study*. Washington, D.C.: U.S. Department of Education, Office of Educational Research and Improvement, Library Programs.

Horn, Steven. 1978. "Intellectual Freedom and the Canadian Library Association." *Canadian Library Journal* 35 (June): 209-15.

Jenkinson, David. 1985. "The Censorship Iceberg: The Results of a Survey of Challenges in School and Public Libraries." *School Libraries in Canada* 6 (Fall): 19-29.

Jenkinson, David. 1986. "Censorship Iceberg: Results of a Survey of Challenges in Public and School Libraries." *Canadian Library Journal* 43 (February): 7-21.

Jones, Frances M. 1983. *Defusing Censorship: The Librarian's Guide to Handling Censorship Conflicts*. Phoenix, Ariz.: Oryx Press.

Krug, Judith F. and James A. Harvey. 1992. "ALA and Intellectual Freedom: A Historical Overview." In *Intellectual Freedom Manual*, xiii-xxxvi. *See* American Library Association. Office for Intellectual Freedom.

Lacombe, Dany. 1994. *Blue Politics: Pornography and the Law in the Age of Feminism*. Toronto, Ont.: University of Toronto Press.

Lurie, Alison. 1990. *Don't Tell the Grown-Ups: Subversive Children's Literature*. Boston, Mass.: Little, Brown.

McKee, Richard E. 1977. "Censorship Research: Its Strengths, Weaknesses, Uses, and Misuses." In *An Intellectual Freedom Primer,* edited by Charles H. Busha, 192-220. Littleton, Colo.: Libraries Unlimited.

Madden, Susan. 1990. "The Librarian — A Quiet Censor?" In *Letter of the L.A.A.* issue 73 (March/April): 20-21. (From a presentation to the Library Association of Alberta Intellectual Freedom Interest Group, Edmonton and Calgary, May 25-26, 1989.)

Martin's Annual Criminal Code. 1993. Aurora, Ont.: Canada Law Book Inc.

Merritt, LeRoy Charles. 1970. *Book Selection and Intellectual Freedom.* New York, N.Y.: H.W. Wilson.

Minudri, Regina U., ed. 1975. "SLJ/Adult Books for Young Adults." *School Library Journal* 22 (November): 95.

National Commission on Libraries and Information Science. 1986. *Censorship Activities in Public and Public School Libraries, 1975-1985. A Report to the Senate Subcommittee on Appropriations for the Departments of Labor, Health and Human Services, and Education and Related Agencies.* Washington, D.C.: NCLIS.

Poole, Diana. 1986. "Veiled Knowledge: Censorship in the Public Schools of British Columbia." Unpublished M.Ed. major paper, University of British Columbia.

Pope, Michael. 1974. *Sex and the Undecided Librarian: A Study of Librarians' Opinions on Sexually Oriented Literature.* Metuchen, N.J.: Scarecrow Press.

Poppel, Norman and Edwin M. Ashley. 1986. "Toward an Understanding of the Censor." *Library Journal* 111 (July): 39-43.

Schmidt, C. James. 1987. Letter from the Chair of the American Library Association Intellectual Freedom Committee to the Chairperson of the Canadian Library Association Intellectual Freedom Committee, January 13, 1987. (unpublished)

Schrader, Alvin M. 1983. "Toward a Theory of Library and Information Science." Unpublished Ph.D. dissertation, Indiana University, Bloomington, Indiana.

Schrader, Alvin M. 1993. "Eternal Vigilance within Canadian Libraries: Price of Continuing Liberty." *PNLA Quarterly* 57 (Spring): 14-15.

Schrader, Alvin M. and Keith Walker. 1986. "Censorship Iceberg: Results of an Alberta Public Library Survey." *Canadian Library Journal* 43 (April): 91-95.

Serebnick, Judith. 1979. "A Review of Research Related to Censorship in Libraries." *Library Research* 1 (Summer): 95-118.

Serebnick, Judith. 1982. "Self-Censorship by Librarians: An Analysis of Checklist-Based Research." *Drexel Library Quarterly* 18 (Winter): 35-56.

Swan, John. 1986. "Challenges Increase but Most Libraries Resist." *Focus on Indiana Libraries* (May): 3-4.

Walker, Keith. 1984. "Censorship in Alberta Public Libraries: A Survey of Requests for Removal of Library Materials." Unpublished M.L.S. project, University of Alberta.

Willett, Charles. 1992. Letter to the Editor. *IFRT Report* no. 34 (Summer): np.

Appendix A

SURVEY QUESTIONNAIRES
& COVERING LETTERS

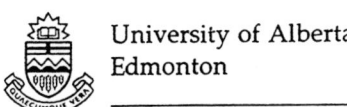 **University of Alberta**   **Faculty of Library Science**
Edmonton

Canada T6G 2J4   3-20 Rutherford South, Telephone (403) 432-4578/4140

February 16, 1988

Dear Chief Librarian:

I would be most grateful for your cooperation in completing the attached survey form.

The objective of the survey is to gather information about pressures to remove or restrict materials in public library collections across Canada, over the past three years. It is the first national survey of its kind.

The project is funded in part by generous grants from the Alberta Foundation for the Literary Arts and the University of Alberta's Small Faculties Endowment Fund.

The project consists of two parts, a survey questionnaire and a checklist of selected holdings. The checklist is something of an experimental idea for a project like this, consisting of items that have drawn public criticism during the past 4 or 5 years, as reported in other studies.

Information from the survey should provide a comprehensive picture of how public librarians throughout the country have handled objections and concerns of various kinds. The results of the project should be useful to public librarians, trustees, other policy-makers, students, and educators.

Please be assured that no person, library, or library system will be identified in any report, whether verbal or written, of this project.

Would you please complete the attached form, and return it in the postage-paid envelope by *March 11, 1988*. If you have any questions about the survey, please call me collect at (403) 432-4578.

Thank you for your cooperation.

Sincerely yours,

Alvin M. Schrader, PhD
Associate Professor

QUESTIONNAIRE SURVEY:

REQUESTS TO REMOVE OR RESTRICT LIBRARY MATERIALS, 1985-1987

Please be assured that no person, library, or library system will be identified in any report, whether verbal or written, of this survey.

LIBRARY _____

BRANCH _____ POSTAL CODE _____

1. Does your library have a written selection policy? Yes __ No __

2. Does your library have a written procedure or written policy for handling objections to materials in the collection? Yes __ No __

    If YES, does the policy endorse the Canadian Library Association's Statement on Intellectual Freedom? Yes __ No __

3. Does your library have a written form for registering objections to or requesting reconsideration of materials in the collection? Yes __ No __

4. Does your library restrict borrowing privileges by age/grade level? Yes __ No __

    If YES, please elaborate: _____
    _____
    _____

5. Does your library require minors to have written parental/guardian consent to consult in-house or to borrow certain individual titles or certain types of materials? Yes __ No __

    If YES, please elaborate: _____
    _____
    _____

6. Other than by age/grade level, does your library restrict in-house access or borrowing privileges to certain individual titles or to certain types of materials? Yes __ No __

    If YES, please elaborate: _____
    _____
    _____

7. During 1985, 1986 or 1987, was your library requested to remove from its collection, or otherwise to restrict access to any book, magazine, or other material? Yes __ No __

    If NO, please go to question #10. If YES, to next page, "History Sheet."

HISTORY SHEET
(Use one sheet per title per objection—photocopy if more are needed)

For <u>each</u> request to remove or restrict materials during 1985, 1986 or 1987 (and earlier if you wish), please provide the following background information.

a) Title: _____

   Author/creator: _____

   Date of publication: _____ Type of format: _____
   Fiction __ Non-fiction __   Age level: _____

b) Date of initial objection (month/year): _____

c) Who was the objector? Adult patron __ Parent __ School trustee __
   Library staff __ Council member __ Library trustee __
   Other (specify) _____

d) Was this person representing: self __ other (specify) _____

e) Was this person a registered borrower? Yes __ No __ Don't know __

f) Was this the only objection received during 1985, 1986 and 1987 from this person?
   Yes __ No __ Not sure __   If NO, note on other History Sheets.

g) Was the objection: Verbal __ Written __ Verbal, then written __

h) Specific reason(s) given for the objection (please quote if possible):
   _____
   _____

i) Action requested by complainant: _____
   _____

j) Final result of the objection:
   • discussion with complainant, no further action __
   • material removed from library __
   • material relocated __ to where? _____

   • other (please elaborate) _____
   _____

k) Was library policy followed in dealing with the objection?
   Yes __ No __ Partially __ No policy __

   If NO or PARTIALLY, please explain the circumstances: _____
   _____

l) At what administrative level was this objection resolved? _____
   _____

m) Date of final resolution (month/year): _____

n) Was this incident reported in the local media (newspaper, radio or
   television)? Yes __ No __   If YES, please enclose clippings, etc.

8. Looking back on the objection(s) received, and your experience in handling them, would you have changed your approach generally or in any particular circumstances? Yes __ No __

    If YES, please elaborate: _____
    _____
    _____
    _____
    _____

9. Would you say that the objection(s) received have had any effect on your library's selection, classification, shelving, access, or circulation? Yes __ No __

    If YES, please elaborate: _____
    _____
    _____
    _____
    _____

10. During 1985, 1986 or 1987, did your library experience loss, theft, defacement, alteration, mutilation, or destruction of any book, magazine or other material which you suspected was an attempt to prevent or restrict access by others? Yes __ No __ Hard to say __

    If YES, please describe each incident, including year, type of damage, title and author, library response, etc. (use additional sheets if necessary):
    _____
    _____
    _____
    _____
    _____
    _____
    _____
    _____

11. Has your library been pressured to accept or acquire certain individual titles or certain types of materials, during 1985, 1986 or 1987?
    Yes __ No __

    If YES, please elaborate: _____
    _____
    _____
    _____
    _____
    _____

12. Does your library have a written policy on donation of materials for the collection? Yes __ No __

13. Does your library treat potentially controversial or questionable materials differently from other materials in selection, classification, shelving, access, or circulation? Yes __ No __

    If YES, please describe the special treatment and identify the types of materials or specific titles:

    _____
    _____
    _____
    _____
    _____
    _____
    _____
    _____
    _____

14. Background information on your library:

    - municipal population in 1987: _____

    - service area population (if different) in 1987: _____

    - registered borrowers in 1987: _____

    - circulation in 1987: _____

    - hours per week open to the public in 1987: _____

    - Check here if your library is school-housed: __
      If YES, school enrollment in 1987: _____

15. Does your library collect materials in:
    English __ French __ Other languages __

16. Please indicate whether or not your library owns or has ordered the materials listed below—in any edition or language. (Not all French translations of English-language titles have been verified.)

ADULT FICTION   YES   NO

Andrews, V.C.	Flowers in the attic / Fleurs captives	___	___
Auel, Jean	Valley of the horses / La Vallée des chevaux	___	___
Blume, Judy	Forever	___	___
	Wifey	___	___
Doerkson, Margaret	Jazzy	___	___
Jong, Erica	Fear of flying / Le Complexe d'Icare	___	___
Kosinski, Jerzy	The Painted bird	___	___
Robbins, Harold	Goodbye Janette	___	___
Smedley, Agnes	Chinese destiny	___	___
Uris, Leon	The Haj / Le Hadj	___	___

ADULT NON-FICTION

Baigent, Michael	Holy Blood Holy Grail / L'Enigme sacrée	___	___
Ferry, J. and D. Inwood	The Olson murders	___	___
Lovelace, Linda and Mike McGrady	Ordeal	___	___
McCoy, Kathy and Charles Wibbelsman	The Teenage body book	___	___

JUVENILE FICTION

Bellairs, John	Figure in the shadows	___	___
Blume, Judy	Then again, maybe I won't / Et puis, j'en sais rien	___	___
Klein, Norma	It's okay if you don't love me	___	___
Major, Kevin	Hold fast / Tiens bon	___	___
Neufeld, John	Freddy's book	___	___
Rockwell, Thomas	The Thief	___	___
Suddon, A.	Cinderella [Cendrillon]	___	___

JUVENILE NON-FICTION

Cohen, Barbara	I am Joseph	___	___
Dayee, Frances, S.	Private zone	___	___
Dickinson, Peter	City of Gold and other stories from the Old Testament	___	___
Johnson, Corinne and Eric Johnson	Love and sex and growing up	___	___

PICTURE BOOKS AND EASY

Lareuse, Jean	Devils in the castle	___	___
Maestro, Betsy	Lambs for dinner	___	___
Sendak, Maurice	In the night kitchen / Cuisine de nuit	___	___
Seuss, Dr.	Butter battle book	___	___
Wildsmith, Brian	The True cross / La Légende de la vraie croix	___	___

17. Do you have any other comments?

_____
_____
_____
_____
_____
_____
_____
_____

18. Has your Library Board written to the Minister of Justice about Bill C-54, or otherwise taken a public stand on it?
Yes __ No __ Don't know __

If YES, what was the Board's position?
- support the Bill __
- withdraw the Bill __
- other (please specify) _____
_____

19. Survey results will be published, but if you would like to receive a summary of findings, please enclose a self-addressed envelope with this form.

Thank you for contributing to this project. Please return this form, in the envelope provided, by __March 11, 1988__, to:

Canadian Intellectual Freedom Study
Etude sur la liberté intellectuelle au Canada
Room 3-20 Rutherford South
Faculty of Library Science
University of Alberta
Edmonton, Alberta
T6G 9Z9

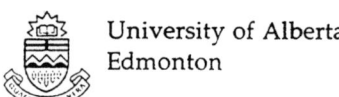 University of Alberta Faculty of Library Science
Edmonton

Canada T6G 2J4   3-20 Rutherford South, Telephone (403) 432-4578/4140

le 16 février, 1988

Madame la bibliothécaire en chef,
Monsieur le bibliothécaire en chef,

Je vous saurais gré de remplir le questionnaire ci-joint.

L'objectif de la présente enquête est de recueillir des données sur les pressions exercées dans les bibliothèques publiques du pays au cours des trois dernières années pour enlever diverses ressources ou en restreindre l'accès. Il s'agit de la première enquête de ce genre à l'échelle nationale.

Ce projet est rendu possible, en partie, grâce à des subventions considérables de l'Alberta Foundation for the Literary Arts et du Fonds de dotation des petites facultés de l'université de l'Alberta.

Le projet comprend deux parties : un questionnaire et une liste de certains titres de ressources. Cette liste constitue une idée expérimentale pour un projet de ce genre étant donné qu'elle comprend des titres de ressources qui ont soulevé des plaintes du public au cours des 4 ou 5 dernières années, selon ce qu'ont constaté d'autres études.

Les données tirées de cette enquête nous permettront de mieux connaître la réaction des bibliothécaires des bibliothèques publiques face à des plaintes et à des préoccupations de diverses sortes. Les résultats de cette enquête seront certainement utiles aux bibliothécaires du secteur public, aux membres des conseils d'administration de bibliothèques, aux autres décideurs, aux étudiants et aux éducateurs.

Personne, ni aucune bibliothèque ni aucun réseau de bibliothèques, ne sera identifié, oralement ou par écrit, dans tout rapport qui paraîtra sur cette enquête.

Je vous serais reconnaissant de remplir le questionnaire ci-joint et de nous le retourner dans l'enveloppe pré-affranchie prévue à cette fin d'ici le 11 mars, 1988. Si vous avez des questions, n'hésitez pas à me téléphoner, à frais virés, au (403) 432-4578.

En vous remerciant de votre collaboration, je vous prie d'agréer, Madame la bibliothécaire en chef, Monsieur le bibliothécaire en chef, l'expression de mes sentiments distingués.

Alvin M. Schrader
Professeur agrégé

QUESTIONNAIRE:

DEMANDES VISANT A ENLEVER DES RESSOURCES DE LA BIBLIOTHEQUE OU A EN RESTREINDRE L'ACCES (1985-1987)

Personne, ni aucune bibliothèque ni aucun réseau de bibliothèques, ne sera identifié, oralement ou par écrit, dans tout rapport sur cette enquête.

BIBLIOTHEQUE _____

SUCCURSALE _____ CODE POSTAL _____

1. Votre bibliothèque possède-t-elle des lignes de conduite écrites concernant le choix des ressources? Oui __ Non __

2. Votre bibliothèque possède-t-elle des directives écrites ou des lignes de conduite écrites concernant la façon de traiter les plaintes soulevées à l'égard des ressources qui font partie de votre collection? Oui __ Non __

    Si OUI, ces lignes de conduite appuient-elles l'Enoncé de la <u>Canadian Library Association</u> sur la liberté intellectuelle? Oui __ Non __

3. Votre bibliothèque a-t-elle mis au point une formule que doivent remplir les personnes qui soulèvent une plainte ou qui désirent que l'à-propos de certaines ressources soit étudié à nouveau? Oui __ Non __

4. Votre bibliothèque restreint-elle les privilèges de prêt en fonction de l'âge/l'année d'études? Oui __ Non __

    Si OUI, donner plus de détails. _____
    _____
    _____

5. Votre bibliothèque oblige-t-elle les mineurs à fournir le consentement écrit de leurs parents ou de leur tuteur pour consulter, à la bibliothèque même, ou emprunter certaines ressources ou certains genres de ressources? Oui __ Non __

    Si OUI, donner plus de détails. _____
    _____
    _____

6. Votre bibliothèque restreint-elle l'accès, à la bibliothèque même, à certaines ressources ou à certains genres de ressources, ou en limite-t-elle le prêt à certaines personnes en fonction d'un autre facteur que l'âge/l'année d'études? Oui __ Non __

7. En 1985, 1986 ou 1987, a-t-on demandé à votre bibliothèque d'enlever des livres, des revues ou d'autres ressources, ou d'en restreindre l'accès d'une autre façon? Oui __ Non __

    Si NON, passer directement à la question no 10. Si OUI, remplir la page "Historique".

HISTORIQUE
(Une feuille par titre par plainte—faire des photocopies si besoin est)

Prière de donner les renseignements suivants sur <u>chaque</u> ressource qu'on vous a demandé d'enlever en 1985, 1986 ou 1987 (et avant si vous voulez) ou dont on a souhaité que l'accès en soit restreint.

a) Titre : _____

   Auteur/Créateur : _____
   Date de publication : _____ Format : _____
   Groupe d'âge : _____ Romans, nouvelles, etc. __ Etudes, essais, etc. __

b) Date de la première plainte (mois/année) : _____

c) Personne à l'origine de la plainte : Client adulte __ Parent __
   Counseiller scolaire __ Personnel de la bibliothèque __ Counseiller municipal __
   Membre du conseil d'administration __ Autre personne (préciser) _____

d) Cette personne agissait-elle : en son propre nom __ au nom d'une autre personne ou d'un organisme (préciser) _____

e) Cette personne était-elle un abonné inscrit? Oui __ Non __ Je ne sais pas __

f) Est-ce la seule plainte qu'a portée cette personne en 1985, 1986 ou 1987?
   Oui __ Non __ Incertain __   Si NON, identifier les autres Historiques connexes.

g) Cette plainte a-t-elle été faite : oralement __ par écrit __ oralement puis par écrit __

h) Quelle(s) raison(s) précise(s) motivait/motivaient cette plainte? (citer textuellement si possible) _____
   _____

i) Quelles mesures préconisait cette personne? _____
   _____

j) Résultat final :
   o conversation avec la personne - aucune autre mesure prise __
   o ressource enlevée de la bibliothèque __
   o ressource déplacée __ où? _____
   o autre mesure (donner plus de détails) _____
   _____

k) Les lignes directrices de la bibliothèques ont-elles été suivies en ce qui concerne la plainte? Oui __ Non __ En partie __ Aucune ligne directrice __

   Si NON ou EN PARTIE, expliquer les circonstances. _____
   _____

l) A quel niveau administratif la plainte a-t-elle été réglée? _____
   _____

m) Date à laquelle la plainte a été réglée (mois/année) : _____

n) Cet incident a-t-il été signalé dans les médias locaux (journal, radio ou télévision)? Oui __ Non __   Si OUI, inclure les coupures de presse, etc.

8. Quand vous repensez aux plaintes reçues et à la façon dont vous les avez traitées, changeriez-vous votre approche d'une façon générale ou particulière? Oui __ Non __

   Si OUI, donner plus de détails. _____
   _____
   _____
   _____
   _____

9. Diriez-vous que les plaintes reçues ont influé sur vos lignes de conduite en matière de choix, de classification, de classement sur les étagères, d'accès ou de prêt?
   Oui __ Non __

   Si OUI, donner plus de détails. _____
   _____
   _____
   _____
   _____

10. En 1985, 1986 ou 1987, des livres, des revues ou d'autres ressources ont-ils été abîmés, endommagés, volés, barbouillés ou détruits en raison, selon vous, d'une tentative d'en interdire ou d'en restreindre l'accès à d'autres personnes?
    Oui __ Non __ Difficile à dire __

    Si OUI, décrire chaque incident et donner l'année, la nature du dommage, le titre, l'auteur, la réaction de la bibliothèque, etc. (annexer d'autres feuilles en cas de besoin).
    _____
    _____
    _____
    _____
    _____
    _____
    _____
    _____

11. A-t-on exercé, en 1985, 1986 ou 1987, des pressions sur votre bibliothèque pour qu'elle accepte ou acquiert certaines ressources ou certains genres de ressources? Oui __ Non __

    Si OUI, donner plus de détails. _____
    _____
    _____
    _____
    _____
    _____

12. Votre bibliothèque possède-t-elle des lignes de conduite écrites concernant le don de ressources à la collection? Oui __ Non __

13. Votre bibliothèque traite-t-elle les ressources controversables ou susceptibles de faire l'objet de plaintes d'une façon différente des autres ressources en ce qui concerne le choix, la classification, le classement sur les étagères, l'accès ou le prêt? Oui __ Non __

    Si OUI, décrire les mesures spéciales prises et identifier les sortes de ressources ou les titres.

    _____
    _____
    _____
    _____
    _____
    _____

14. Renseignements d'arrière-plan sur votre bibliothèque :

    - Population de la municipalité en 1987 : _____
    - Population de la zone desservie en 1987 (si elle est différente) : _____
    - Nombre d'abonnés inscrits en 1987 : _____
    - Nombre de prêts en 1987 : _____
    - Nombre d'heures d'ouverture par semaine de la bibliothèque au public en 1987 : _____
    - Cocher si votre bibliothèque est située dans une école : __
      Si OUI, effectif scolaire en 1987 : _____

15. Votre bibliothèque collectionne-t-elle des ressources en : anglais __ français __ d'autres langues __

16. *Indiquer si votre bibliothèque possède ou a commandé les ressources énumérées ci-dessous - sous n'importe quel format ou dans n'importe quelle langue. (Les traductions françaises des ouvrages anglais n'ont pas toutes été vérifiées.)*

ROMANS, NOUVELLES, ETC. POUR ADULTES

		OUI	NON
Andrews, V.C.	Fleurs captives / Flowers in the attic	__	__
Auel, Jean	La Vallée des chevaux / Valley of the horses	__	__
Blume, Judy	Forever	__	__
	Wifey	__	__
Doerkson, Margaret	Jazzy	__	__
Jong, Erica	Le Complexe d'Icare / Fear of flying	__	__
Kosinski, Jerzy	The Painted bird	__	__
Robbins, Harold	Goodbye Janette	__	__
Smedley, Agnes	Chinese destiny	__	__
Uris, Leon	Le Hadj / The Haj	__	__

ETUDES, ESSAIS, ETC. POUR ADULTES

Baigent, Michael	L'Enigme sacrée / Holy Blood Holy Grail	__	__
Ferry, J. et D. Inwood	The Olson murders		
Lovelace, Linda et Mike McGrady	Ordeal	__	__
McCoy, Kathy et Charles Wibbelsman	The Teenage body book	__	__

ROMANS, NOUVELLES, ETC. POUR LA JEUNESSE

Bellairs, John	Figure in the shadows	__	__
Blume, Judy	Then again, maybe I won't	__	__
Klein, Norma	It's okay if you don't love me	__	__
Major, Kevin	Tiens bon / Hold fast	__	__
Neufeld, John	Freddy's book	__	__
Rockwell, Thomas	The Thief	__	__
Suddon, A.	Cendrillon [Cinderella]	__	__

ETUDES, ESSAIS, ETC. POUR LA JEUNESSE

Cohen, Barbara	I am Joseph	__	__
Dayee, Frances, S.	Private zone	__	__
Dickinson, Peter	City of Gold and other stories from the Old Testament	__	__
Johnson, Corinne et Eric Johnson	Love and sex and growing up	__	__

LIVRES IMAGES ET FACILES A LIRE

Lareuse, Jean	Devils in the castle	__	__
Maestro, Betsy	Lambs for dinner	__	__
Sendak, Maurice	Cuisine de nuit / In the night kitchen	__	__
Seuss, Dr.	Butter battle book	__	__
Wildsmith, Brian	La Légende de la vraie croix / The True cross	__	__

17. Avez-vous d'autres commentaires? _____
    _____
    _____
    _____
    _____
    _____
    _____

18. Est-ce que le conseil d'administration de votre bibliothèque a écrit au ministre de la Justice au sujet du projet de loi C-54, ou pris publiquement position d'une autre façon? Oui __ Non __ Je ne sais pas __

    Si OUI, quelle était la position du conseil d'administration?
    - appui du projet de loi __
    - retrait du projet de loi __
    - autre (préciser) _____
    _____
    _____
    _____
    _____

19. Les resultats de l'enquête seront publiés; toutefois, si vous désirez reçevoir un résumé sur les conclusions, inclure une enveloppe pré-adressée.

> Nous vous remercions d'avoir collaboré à ce projet. Prière de retourner le présent questionnaire, dans l'enveloppe prévue à cet effet, d'ici le 11 Mars, 1988, à :
>
> *Etude sur la liberté intellectuelle au Canada*
> *Canadian Intellectual Freedom Study*
> *Room 3-20 Rutherford South*
> *Faculty of Library Science*
> *University of Alberta*
> *Edmonton, Alberta*
> *T6G 9Z9*

Appendix B

Statements on Intellectual Freedom

Canadian Library Association Statement on Intellectual Freedom

All persons in Canada have the fundamental right, as embodied in the nation's Bill of Rights and the Canadian Charter of Rights and Freedoms, to have access to all expressions of knowledge, creativity and intellectual activity, and to express their thoughts publicly. This right to intellectual freedom, under the law, is essential to the health and development of Canadian society.

Libraries have a basic responsibility for the development and maintenance of intellectual freedom.

It is the responsibility of libraries to guarantee and facilitate access to all expressions of knowledge and intellectual activity, including those which some elements of society may consider to be unconventional, unpopular or unacceptable. To this end, libraries shall acquire and make available the widest variety of materials.

It is the responsibility of libraries to guarantee the right of free expression by making available all the library's public facilities and services to all individuals and groups who need them.

Libraries should resist all efforts to limit the exercise of these responsibilities while recognizing the right of criticism by individuals and groups.

Both employees and employers in libraries have a duty, in addition to their institutional responsibilities, to uphold these principles.

(Ratified by the Board of Directors and Council at the 29th Annual Conference in Winnipeg, June 1974 and amended November 17, 1983 and November 18, 1985)

Canadian Library Association Information and Telecommunication Access Principles

Preamble

The convergence of computers and high-speed telecommunication networks provides increased opportunity for public access to information and participation in the democratic processes of society. Conversely, access and participation could be reduced through the imposition of user fees and centralized control.

Librarians, libraries, and library organizations will work to assure the "public good" is represented in all government and corporate initiatives for information dissemination and telecommunications policy. Co-operation with other organizations and public interest groups to protect social interests will strengthen the efforts of the library community.

All people have the right to:

1. Literacy

The opportunity to learn to read and write is fundamental for all people. Basic literacy includes numeracy and information literacy. Literacy is an important requirement for participation in the economic, social, cultural, and political life of the country.

Everyone should have the opportunity to acquire the necessary skills to find and use information.

2. Universal, Equitable, and Affordable Access

Access to information and telecommunication network services should be available and affordable to all regardless of factors such as age, religion, ability, gender, sexual orientation, social and political views, national origin, economic status, location, and information literacy.

Diverse sources of information should be developed through encouraging non-profit organizations and community groups to provide information and opinions and by preventing information monopolies.

Opportunities should be created for broad public participation in the determination of information and telecommunication policy.

3. Communicate

Individuals have the right to create, exchange, access, and receive the widest range of ideas, information, and images.

Individuals should have the right to choose what information to receive and what not to receive and what information to give and not give including that which others may find objectionable.

4. Public Space on the Telecommunications Networks

Government information is fundamental to participation in the democratic process and should therefore be accessible in a current, timely, accurate, and comprehensive manner.

Access to government information should be guaranteed through active programs of dissemination.

Opportunities to communicate electronically with elected and appointed government representatives is a vital extension of democracy.

Government policy should encourage and support archiving of information in support of the collective human memory.

Government policies should encourage and support the development of community information networks, such as FreeNets.

Government should provide resources for libraries and other community organizations to make electronic access to information available and to provide training to the public in the use of such technology.

Individuals have the right to know the positive and negative personal and social consequences of the introduction of information technology.

Individuals have the right to a safe, ergonomically sound environment and appropriate training or retraining when new technologies are introduced.

Social policies accompanying the introduction of new and more efficient information technologies must emphasize benefits to the whole population, such as greater leisure time and shorter work weeks, rather than narrow economic interests.

5. Privacy

Privacy of personal information should be carefully protected and extended.

Personal data collected should be limited to the minimum necessary and only after the prior written approval of the individual affected.

Personal information collected for one purpose cannot be traded or sold without the express written permission of the individual affected.

Individuals should have the right to examine personal information collected by government and corporations and have mistakes corrected at no charge.

Approved by CLA Executive Council June 18, 1994

Charte des Droits du Lecteur

Toute personne a le droit à la liberté intellectuelle, c'est-à-dire le droit fondamental d'accéder à toutes les formes d'expression du savoir et d'exprimer ses pensées en public.

Le droit à la liberté intellectuelle est essentiel et vital à une saine démocratie et au développement de la société québécoise.

En vertu de cette déclaration, les administrateurs et le personnel des bibliothèques ont, envers le lecteur, l'obligation:

— d'assurer et de maintenir ce droit fondamental à la liberté intellectuelle;

— de garantir et de faciliter l'accès à toute forme et à tout moyen d'expression du savoir;

— de garantir ce droit d'expression en offrant les services usuels, physiques et intellectuels, de la bibliothèque;

— de s'opposer à toute tentative visant à limiter ce droit à l'information et à la libre expression de la pensée tout en reconnaissant aux individus ou aux groupes le droit à la critique.

Les bibliothécaires doivent promouvoir et défendre les principes de cette déclaration.

Adoptée par le Conseil d'administration de l'Association des bibliothécaires du Québec/Québec Library Association, lors de sa réunion, le 31 mars 1976.

Adoptée par le Bureau de l'ASTED (Association pour l'avancement des sciences et des techniques de la documentation), lors de sa 21e réunion, le 27 octobre 1976.

Adoptée par le Bureau de la Corporation des bibliothécaires professionnels du Québec, lors de sa 76e réunion, le 13 mai 1976.

Reproduced with permission

Ontario Library Association Statement on the Intellectual Rights of the Individual

In affirming its support of the fundamental rights of intellectual freedom, the freedom to read and the freedom of the press, as embodied in the Canadian Charter of Rights and Freedoms, the Ontario Library Association declares its acceptance of the following propositions: -

(i) That the provision of library service to the Canadian public is based upon the right of the citizen, under the protection of the law, to judge individually on questions of politics, religion and morality.

(ii) That it is the responsibility of librarians to maintain this right and to implement it in their selection of books, periodicals, films, recordings and other materials.

(iii) That intellectual freedom requires freedom to examine other ideas and other interpretations of life than those currently approved by the local community or by society in general, including those ideas and interpretations which may be unconventional or unpopular.

(iv) That freedom of expression requires freedom of the writer to depict what is ugly, shocking and unedifying in life when such depiction is made with serious intent.

(v) That free traffic in ideas and opinions is essential to the health and growth of a free society and that the freedom to read, listen and view is fundamental to such free traffic.

(vi) That it is therefore part of the library's service to its public to resist any attempt by any individual or group within the community it serves to abrogate or curtail the freedom to read, view and listen by demanding the removal of any book, periodical, film, recording or other material from the library.

(vii) That it is equally part of the library's responsibility to its public to ensure that its selection of material is not unduly influenced by the personal opinions of the selectors, but determined by the application of generally accepted standards of accuracy, style and presentation.

Ontario Library Association
Toronto, November 23, 1990
Reproduced with permission

Saskatchewan Library Association — Intellectual Freedom

The Saskatchewan Library Association endorses the Canadian Library Association's Statement on Intellectual Freedom as ratified by the CLA Board of Directors and Council at its 29th Annual Conference in Winnipeg, June, 1974.

The Saskatchewan Library Association has also adopted the following policy statement on open ACCESS:

1. All library materials and services will be available to everyone in the community regardless of age. Children and young adults will be given equal rights with adults and may borrow all circulating materials.

2. The library recognizes the fact that people — young and old — vary as to individual intellectual ability, reading skill, and level of maturity; and it cannot, therefore, place arbitrary age restrictions on the use of materials.

3. The library will provide qualified staff to acquire materials and to assist anyone wishing to use those materials.

4. The library will not prevent patrons from using any materials that they require.

5. The library will issue to all patrons a uniform borrower's card which will carry no implicit or explicit restrictions on access to materials or services.

6. The library may require that parents or guardians sign the application cards of their children up to a certain age before a borrower's card will be issued.

Adopted by the Saskatchewan Library Association, ca. 1975
Reproduced with permission

British Columbia Library Association Statement on Intellectual Freedom

1. It is in the public interest for libraries and librarians to make available the widest diversity of views and expression, including those which are unorthodox or unpopular with the majority.

2. It would conflict with the public interest for libraries to establish their own political moral or aesthetic views as the sole standard for determining what books and other materials should be published or circulated.

3. It is contrary to the public interest for libraries or librarians to determine the acceptability of a book solely on the basis of the personal history or political affiliation of the author.

4. There is no place in British Columbia for extra-legal efforts to coerce the taste of others, to confine adults to the reading matter deemed suitable for adolescents, or to inhibit the efforts of the writers to achieve artistic expression.

5. It is not in the public interest to force a reader to accept with any book the prejudgment of a label characterizing the book or author as subversive or dangerous.

6. It is the responsibility of library administrators and librarians, as guardians of the people's freedom to read, to contest encroachments upon that freedom by individuals or groups seeking to impose their own standards or tastes upon the community at large.

7. It is the responsibility of libraries and librarians to give full meaning to intellectual freedom by providing books and other materials that enrich the quality of thought and expression. By the exercise of this affirmative responsibility, librarians can demonstrate that the answer to a bad book is a good one, the answer to a bad idea is a good one.

8. Non-book materials should be judged by the same criteria as books.

Adopted in the mid-1980s
Reproduced with permission

Book and Periodical Council — The Freedom of Expression and the Freedom to Read

A statement of the basic tenets of the Committee for Freedom of Expression of the Book and Periodical Council.

The freedom to read is essential to the democratic way of life. It is essential to the democratic process. Today the freedom to read is under attack. Private groups and public authorities in various parts of our country are working to remove both books and periodicals from sale, to exclude certain books from our public schools, to censor and silence magazines and newspapers, to label "controversial" books and periodicals, to distribute lists of "objectional" books and authors, to limit the granting powers of arts councils in relation to certain authors and publishers and to purge libraries. These actions apparently arise from a view that censorship and suppression are needed to protect society. We, as Canadian citizens devoted to the use of books and periodicals, and as writers, publishers, distributors and librarians responsible for the creation and dissemination of books and periodicals, wish to assert the public interest in the preservation of the freedom to read.

The suppression of reading materials is suppression of creative thought. Further, without creative thought democracy will become extinct and people will fall prey to the dictatorship of the few. Those who dictate what we may not read are in fact dictating what we shall read.

Books and periodicals are not alone in being subjected to suppression. We are aware that these efforts are related to a larger pattern of pressures, both political and social, being brought against the educational system, against films, radio and television and against the graphic and theatre arts. These pressures are at work in the world of communications and in the administration of justice. We are best equipped to counter these pressures by exercising our expertise in the areas of our professional concerns. We oppose suppression of the written word. To that end, we have struck this Committee for Freedom of Expression. Without such freedom of expression, no responsible debate of controversial issues can take place.

Books, newspapers and magazines are the instruments of freedom. We abhor the expurgation and barring of literature on the false grounds of obscenity. We are particularly concerned with the threat to Canadian literature which is a unique voice of our culture. There is no obscenity in truth. What is obscene is the suppression of truth and the suppression of any part of literature that seeks to create a compassionate understanding of the human condition.

Free communication is essential to the preservation of a free society and a creative culture. Current pressure to impose uniformity limits the range and variety of inquiry and expression on which our nation and culture depend. Every Canadian community must jealously safeguard the freedom to publish, to circulate, and to sell in order to protect freedom itself. We believe that writers, publishers, distributors and librarians have a profound responsibility to maintain the freedom by making it possible for readers to choose freely.

Freedom to read is a precious heritage. It is a part of a much larger heritage common to the human spirit which we call freedom of expression. As professional organizations and associations already congregated under the auspices of the Book and Periodical Council, we seek through this statement to express our absolute commitment to combating, in whatever form it takes, the suppression of books and periodicals because we believe that the written word is the ultimate mode of free expression.

Adopted by the Council
October 17, 1978
Reproduced with permission

American Library Association Library Bill of Rights

The American Library Association affirms that all libraries are forums for information and ideas, and that the following basic policies should guide their services.

1. Books and other library resources should be provided for the interest, information, and enlightenment of all people of the community the library serves. Materials should not be excluded because of the origin, background, or views of those contributing to their creation.

2. Libraries should provide materials and information presenting all points of view on current and historical issues. Materials should not be proscribed or removed because of partisan or doctrinal disapproval.

3. Libraries should challenge censorship in the fulfillment of their responsibility to provide information and enlightenment.

4. Libraries should cooperate with all persons and groups concerned with resisting abridgment of free expression and free access to ideas.

5. A person's right to use a library should not be denied or abridged because of origin, age, background, or views.

6. Libraries which make exhibit spaces and meeting rooms available to the public they serve should make such facilities available on an equitable basis, regardless of the beliefs or affiliations of individuals or groups requesting their use.

Adopted June 18, 1948.
Amended February 2, 1961, June 27, 1967,
and January 23, 1980, by the ALA Council.
Reproduced with permission

Appendix C

Main

Questionnaire

Item Responses

	Yes	No	Valid Responses Number	Rate
1. Does your library have a written selection policy?	54%	46%	545	97%
2. Does your library have a written procedure or policy for handling objections to materials?	51%	49%	551	98%
If yes, does the policy endorse the CLA's Statement on Intellectual Freedom?	88%	12%	294	53%
3. Does your library have a written form for registering objections to or requesting reconsideration of materials?	43%	57%	548	98%
4. Does your library restrict borrowing privileges by age/grade level?	30%	70%	555	99%
5. Does your library require minors to have written parental/guardian consent to consult in-house or to borrow certain individual titles or certain types of materials?	23%	77%	555	99%
6. Other than by age/grade level, does your library restrict in-house access or borrowing privileges to certain individual titles or to certain types of materials?	6%	94%	551	98%
7. During 1985, 1986 or 1987, was your library requested to remove from its collection, or otherwise to restrict access to any book, magazine, or other material?	34%	66%	560	100%
8. Looking back on the objection(s) received, and your experience in handling them, would you have changed your approach generally or in any particular circumstances?	12%	88%	178	94%

continued

	Yes	No	Valid Responses Number	Rate
9. Would you say that the objection(s) received have had any effect on your library's selection, classification, shelving, access, or circulation?	26%	74%	176	93%
10. During 1985, 1986 or 1987, did your library experience loss, theft, defacement, alteration, mutilation, or destruction of any book, magazine, or other material which you suspected was an attempt to prevent or restrict access by others?	11%	64%	543*	97%
11. Has your library been pressured to accept or acquire certain individual titles or certain types of materials, during 1985, 1986 or 1987?	22%	78%	541	97%
12. Does your library have a written policy on donation of materials for the collection?	57%	43%	548	98%
13. Does your library treat potentially controversial or questionable materials differently from other materials in selection, classification, shelving, access, or circulation?	21%	79%	538	96%

*"hard to say" = 26%

Appendix D

Freedom to Read Week
Reading List

Book and Periodical Council 1995 Freedom to Read Week Reading List

Ajzenstat, Sam, and Michaelle McLean. "Censorship: Two Views." *Artviews*, Winter 1984-85.

American Library Association. *Intellectual Freedom Manual.* Third edition. Chicago: Office for Intellectual Freedom, American Library Association, 1989. [author's note: 4th edition published 1992]

Appignanesi, Lisa, and Sara Maitland. *The Rushdie File.* London: Fourth Estate, 1989.

"Art or Obscenity." *Newsweek Magazine*, July 2, 1990.

Berger, Melvin. *Censorship.* New York: Franklin Watts, 1986.

Birdsall, Peter, and Delores Broten. *Mind War: Censorship in English Canada.* Victoria, B.C.: Canlit, 1978.

Boyle, Kevin (ed.). *Article 19 World Report 1988: Information, Freedom and Censorship.* New York: Times Books, 1988.

Books on Trial: A Survey of Recent Cases. New York: National Coalition Against Censorship, 1985.

Booth, David. *Censorship Goes to School.* Toronto: Pembroke Publishers, 1992.

Bosmajian, Haig (ed.). *Censorship, Libraries and the Law.* New York: Neal-Schuman Publishers, 1983.

Brink, André. *Mapmakers: Writing in a State of Siege.* London: Faber, 1983.

British Columbia Library Association (BCLA). *Intellectual Freedom Handbook.* Burnaby, B.C.: BCLA Intellectual Freedom Committee, 1991.

Bryant, Mark (ed.). *Publish and Be Damned: Cartoons for International P.E.N.* London: Heinemann Kingswood, 1988.

Burress, Lee. *Battle of the Books: Literary Censorship in the Public Schools, 1950-1985.* Metuchen, N.J.: Scarecrow Press, 1989.

Burstyn, Varda (ed.). *Women Against Censorship.* Vancouver: Douglas and McIntyre, 1985.

Busha, Charles H. *An Intellectual Freedom Primer.* Littleton, Colo.: Libraries Unlimited, 1977.

Canadian Children's Literature. An issue on Censorship; No. 68. Guelph: Department of English, University of Guelph, December 1992.

Collins, Janet. "Suffer the Little Children." *Books in Canada*, October 1991.

Dean, Malcolm. *CENSORED! Only in Canada.* Toronto: Phenomena Publications, 1981.

de Grazia, Edward. *Censorship Landmarks.* New York: Bowker, 1969.

de Grazia, Edward. *Girls Lean Back Everywhere: The Law of Obscenity and the Assault on Genius.* New York: Random House, 1992.

DelFattore, Joan. *What Johnny Shouldn't Read: Textbook Censorship in America.* Yale University Press, 1992.

Dick, Judith. *Not in Our Schools?!!! School Book Censorship in Canada: A Discussion Guide.* Ottawa: Canadian Library Association, 1982.

Douglas, William O. *Freedom of the Mind.* New York: Doubleday, 1964.

Ernst, Morris, and Allan Schwartz. *Censorship: The Search for the Obscene.* New York: Macmillan U.S.A., 1964.

Greene, Jonathon. *The Encyclopaedia of Censorship.* New York: Facts on File, 1990.

Haight, Ann Lyon. *Banned Books.* Fourth edition. New York: Bowker, 1978.

Hawkins, Ian. "But That's Censorship, Isn't It?" *The Canadian Bookseller*, June/July 1993.

Heins, Marjorie. *Sex, Sin and Blasphemy: A Guide to America's Censorship Wars.* New York: New Press, 1993.

Hendrickson, Robert. *The Literary Life and Other Curiosities.* New York: Viking, 1981.

Hentoff, Nat. *The Day They Came to Arrest the Book.* New York: Laurel-Leaf Dell, 1982.

Hentoff, Nat. *Free Speech for Me — But Not for Thee: How the American Left and Right Relentlessly Censor Each Other.* New York: HarperCollins, 1992.

Index on Censorship. London: Writers & Scholars International Ltd. Issued six times a year.

Jenkinson, David. "Censorship Iceberg — Manitoba." *Canadian Library Journal*, Vol. 43, No. 1, February 1986.

Jenkinson, Edward B. *Censors in the Classroom: The Mindbenders.* New York: Avon Books, 1979.

Jenkinson, Edward B. *The Schoolbook Protest Movement: 40 Questions and Answers.* Bloomington, Ind.: Phi Delta Kappa Educational Foundation, 1986.

Lawrence, D.H. *Sex, Literature and Censorship.* New York: The Viking Press, 1959.

MacDonogh, Steve (ed.). *The Rushdie Letters: Freedom to Speak, Freedom to Write.* Lincoln, Neb.: University of Nebraska Press, 1993.

Marsh, David. Foreword by George Plimpton. *50 Ways to Fight Censorship.* New York: Thunder's Mouth Press, 1991.

McCormack, Thelma. "If Pornography is the Theory, Is Inequality the Practice?" *Philosophy of the Social Sciences*, Vol. 23, No. 3, September 1993.

McCormick, John, and Mairi MacInnes (eds.). *Versions of Censorship.* New York: Doubleday, 1962.

Meade, Jeff. "A War of Words." *Teacher Magazine*, Editorial Projects in Education Inc., November-December 1990.

Mertl, Steve. *Keegstra: The Trial, the Issues, the Consequences.* Saskatoon: Western Producer Prairie Books, 1985.

Mitgang, Herbert. *Dangerous Dossiers: Exposing the Secret War Against America's Greatest Authors.* New York: D.I. Fine, 1988.

Morton, Desmond. "The Wonder of Libraries: Illusion and Reality." *Focus*, Toronto: Ontario Library Association, Winter 1986.

Neill, S.D. "Censorship — a Clash of Values." *Canadian Library Journal*, Vol. 45, No. 1, February 1988.

The New York Public Library. *Censorship: 500 Years of Conflict.* New York: Oxford University Press, 1984.

Newsletter on Intellectual Freedom. Chicago: ALA Intellectual Freedom Committee. Issued six times a year.

Noble, Kimberley. *Bound and Gagged: Libel Chill and the Right to Publish.* Toronto: HarperCollins, September 1992.

Noble, William. *Bookbanning in America: Who Bans Books? — and Why.* Middlebury, Vt.: Paul S. Eriksson, 1990.

Oboler, Eli M. *The Fear of the Word: Censorship and Sex.* Metuchen, N.J.: Scarecrow Press, 1974.

Orr, Lisa. *Censorship: Opposing Viewpoints.* San Diego: Greenhaven Press, 1990.

Peck, Richard. "The Great Library-Shelf Witch Hunt." *Booklist.* Chicago: American Library Association, January 1992.

People for the American Way. *Attacks on Freedom to Learn.* Washington, D.C.: PFAW. (Annual Report)

Perrin, Noel. *Dr. Bowdler's Legacy.* New York: Atheneum, 1969.

Pipes, Daniel. *The Rushdie Affair.* New York: Birch Lane Press, 1990.

Schexnavdre, Linda, and Nancy Burns. *Censorship: A Guide for Successful Workshop Planning.* Phoenix, Ariz.: Oryx Press, 1984.

Schmeiser, D.A. *Civil Liberties in Canada.* London: Oxford University Press, 1964.

Schrader, Alvin. "A Study of Community Censorship Pressures on Canadian Public Libraries." *Canadian Library Journal*, Vol. 49, No. 1, February 1992.

Schrader, Alvin M., and Keith Walker. "Censorship Iceberg — Alberta." *Canadian Library Journal*, Vol. 43, No. 2, April 1986.

Steinhart, Allan L. *Civil Censorship in Canada During World War I*. Toronto: Unitrade Press, 1986.

Theiner, George (ed.). *They Shoot Writers, Don't They*. London: Faber and Faber, 1984.

Thomas, Donald. *A Long Time Burning: A History of Literary Censorship in England*. London: Routledge and Kegan Paul, 1969.

Toronto Arts Group for Human Rights. *The Writer and Human Rights*. Toronto: Lester & Orpen Dennys, 1983.

Vivian, Frederick. *Human Freedom and Responsibility*. London: Chatto & Windus, 1964.

Weatherby, W.J. *Salman Rushdie: Sentenced to Death*. New York: Carroll and Graf, 1990.

West, Mark I. *Trust Your Children: Voices Against Censorship in Children's Literature*. New York: Neal Schuman, 1988.

Whaley, George (ed.). *A Place of Liberty*. Toronto: Clarke, Irwin, 1964.

Reading list provided courtesy of the Book and Periodical Council. Reproduced with permission.

Appendix E

Materials Challenged

1985-87

The works listed here were cited on questionnaires returned by public libraries. Because much of the information came from the memory of library staff or complainants, details were often missing or inaccurate. For the purpose of identifying the works more precisely, every reasonable effort was made to verify authors and titles in current bibliographic sources. Where a distinctive medium was cited on the questionnaires and helped to identify an otherwise very brief entry, it is also included here.

Abby, my love
Abortion in Canada
Abravanel, Elliot D. *Dr. Abravanel's body type program for health, fitness and nutrition*
An act of mercy: euthanasia today
Adams, Richard. *Maia*
Adolf Hitler: pictures from the life of the Führer, 1931-35. Hermann Göring, encomium; Joseph Goebbels, text; Carl Underhill Quinn, translator
Adultery for adults
The adventures of Tom Thumb
The Aga Khans
Aho, Jennifer J. and John W. Petras. *Learning about sex: a guide for children and their parents*
AIE...j'suis menstruée
Alan and Naomi
Alaska
Album Tintin [bande dessinée]
Alexander, Martha. *When the new baby comes, I'm moving out*
A(lexandra) the Great
Algonkians of the Eastern Woodlands
Allard, Harry. *Bumps in the night*
Almost paradise
Alvarez, Walter C. *Nerves in collision*
Alyson, Sasha, ed. *Young, gay and proud*
Ambrus, Victor G. *Son of Dracula*
Anastasia Morningstar and the crystal butterfly
Andersen, Hans Christian. *Big Claus and little Claus*
Andersson, C.D. *Torture tomb*
Andrews, V.C. *Flowers in the attic*
—. *Petals on the wind*
Angel dust blues
Angell, Judie. *What's best for you*
Anglund, Joan Walsh [?]. *Brave cowboy* [?]
Annie on my mind
Apartment three
Arden, Andrew. *The object man*
Are you there, God? It's me, Margaret
Ariel
Armstrong, Louise. *Kiss Daddy goodnight*
L'art du massage
As I went over the water
Asch, Frank. *The last puppy*
—. *Linda*
Asimov, Isaac, Martin H. Greenberg, and Charles G. Waugh, eds. *Young witches & warlocks*
Auel, Jean. *The clan of the cave bear*
Autumn Street
Les aventures de Benji [Disney; sound recording]
Les aventures magiques de Corentin au pays de PipiCaca
Aztec

Baby, baby
Baby taming
Bad Thad
Badjelly the witch
Bailey, Lydia. *The big bang*
Bang bang you're dead
Banks, Lynne Reid. *The writing on the wall*
Bannerman, Helen. *Story of Little Black Sambo*
Barbe-Bleue
Barbour, Douglas, and Stephen Scobie. *The maple laugh forever*
Bardot, Brigitte. *Noonoah, le petit phoque blanc*
Barros, James. *No sense of evil: the espionage case of E. Herbert Norman*
Barth, Edna. *Jack-o'-lantern*
Baskin, Leonard. *Hosie's alphabet*
Bear
The bear and the fly
The bear and the people
Bear goes to town
The beast of Monsieur Racine
Beginner's love
Being invisible
Bell, William. *Crabbe*
Belloc, Hilaire. *Jim, who ran away from his nurse, and was eaten by a lion*
Ben
Benton, John. *Valarie*
Berger, Thomas. *Being invisible*
Bicentennial nigger [sound recording]
Bickham, Jack M. *Ariel*
The big bang
Big, bigger, biggest
Big Claus and little Claus
Big monster
Birch, Beverley. *A question of race*
Bishop, Claire. *The five Chinese brothers*
Bleeks, Sheila J. *Cookies for Luke*
Blodgett, Michael. *Hero and the terror*
Blood sport
Blubber
Blue trees, red sky
Blume, Judy. *Are you there, God? It's me, Margaret*
—. *Blubber*
—. *Deenie*
—. *Forever* [also cited as *Pour toujours*]
—. *It's not the end of the world*

Blume, Judy (*cont.*)
—. *Mo*[?] *Me*[?]
—. *The pain and the great one*
—. *Starring Sally J. Freedman as herself*
—. *Then again, maybe I won't*
—. *Wifey*
Blythe, Ronald. *Dragons and other fabulous beasts*
The body book
The Body politic [periodical]
Bond, Simon. *Unspeakable acts*
Bonsall, Crosby Newell. *Mine's the best*
Bose, Mihir. *The Aga Khans*
Bottner, Barbara. *Nothing in common*
Bouquets for Brimbal
The boy who cried wolf
The boys on the rock
Brandel, Marc. *Murder in the family*
Brave cowboy
Bretecher, Claire. *Les ...* [?]
Briggs, Raymond. *Father Christmas*
—. *Fungus the bogeyman*
—. *The tin-pot foreign general and the old iron woman*
—. *Unlucky Wally*
—. *When the wind blows*
Broken English [sound recording]
Brooks, Robert B. *So that's how I was born!*
The brothers Lionheart
Brown, Cassie. *Death on the ice*
Brown, Jamie. *Superbike!*
Brown, Marc. *The true Francine*
Brown, Margaret Wise. *The dead bird*
Brown, Ruth. *The grizzly revenge*
Browne, Anthony. *Bear goes to town*
—. *Hansel and Gretel*
Brunhoff, Laurent de. *The one pig with horns*
Buckland, Raymond. *Buckland's complete book of witchcraft*
Buckland's complete book of witchcraft
Bumps in the night
Bureau de consultation jeunesse [?]. *AIE...j'suis menstruée*
Buried on Sunday
Burningham, John. *Granpa*
Burstein, John. *Slim Goodbody, the inside story* [?]
Butcher, Geoffrey. *Moses: the escape from Egypt*
The butter battle book
Butz, Arthur R. *The hoax of the twentieth century*
Byars, Betsy C. *Cracker Jackson*

Cabu, Jean. *Cathérine saute au paf!*
Les cadres [?]
Campbell, Giraud W. *A doctor's proven new home cure for arthritis*
Canadian fairy tales
Carlson, Natalie Savage. "several older titles"
Carrick, Carol, and Donald Carrick. *A clearing in the forest*

Castaway
The castrated woman
The cat came back
Cathérine saute au paf!
Un certain malaise
Chamberlain, Elwyn M. *Gates of fire*
Charlie's pillow
Chase, James Hadley. *Consider yourself dead*
Childress, Alice. *A hero ain't nothin' but a sandwich*
A child's garden of verses
Church, Joseph. *Understanding your child from birth to three*
The church mice adrift
The church mice at bay
The church mice in action
Cinderella [several versions]
The clan of the cave bear
A clearing in the forest
Cline, C. Terry, Jr. *Quarry*
A clubbable woman
Coates, Alice. *Horace*
Cohen, Barbara. *I am Joseph*
Cohen, Daniel. *Dealing with the devil*
Cole, Babette. *Poilus, velus, barbus*
Collection: Livres dont vous êtes le héros (Ed. Gallimard)
Collins, Douglas. *Immigration: Parliament vs. the people*
Colville, Alex. *June Noon* [art print]
Comfort, Alex. *The joy of sex*
The companion
Complete guide to punctuation (Press Porcépic, pub.)
Compulsory parenthood
Confessions of a part-time call girl
Congratulations! You're not pregnant
Consider yourself dead
Convard, D. *Les huit jours du diable dans "Super Tintin"*
Cookies for Luke
Cooper, Clarence L., Jr. *The farm*
Coover, Robert. *Gerald's party*
Corrin, Sara, and Stephen Corrin, eds. *Stories for eight-year-olds*
The cowboys
Coyne, John. *The piercing*
Crabbe
Cracker Jackson
Crazy quilt
Creepshow
Croc [periodical]
Crowley, Aleister. *Diary of a drug fiend*
Cudlipp, Edythe. *Furs: an appreciation of luxury, a guide to value*
Cullum, Albert. *You think just because you're big you're right*
Cult movies

Daddy is a monster...sometimes
Daddy's girl

Dahl, Roald. *Dirty beasts*
—. *The enormous crocodile*
—. *Roald Dahl's revolting rhymes*
—. *The witches*
—. *The wonder story of Henry Sugar and six more*
Daley, Robert. *Hands of a stranger*
Dancer of Gor
The dancers of Arun
Dark but full of diamonds
Dark hour of noon
Darling, I am growing old
Daryand, ... [?]. *Pilote et Charlie*
Daughters of Eve
David at Olivet
Davis, Gibbs. *The other Emily*
Davis, Gwen. *Romance*
The day we bombed Utah
The dead bird
Dealing with the devil
Dear garbage man
Death on the ice
Déclic
Deenie
Delporte, Y, and Peyo. "Smurf book"
de Reiser. *Vive les femmes*
Des fleurs sur la neige
De Veaux, Alexis. *Na-ni*
The Devil did it
Devil in the drain
Devils and demons
The Devil's bridge
Diamond, Harvey, and Marilyn Diamond. *Fit for life*
Diary of a drug fiend
Did the sun shine before you were born?
Diet for a strong heart
Dinner at Auntie Rose's
Dirty beasts
The discipline of raising children
Do not open
Dr. Abravanel's body type program for health, fitness and nutrition
Dr. Adder
Dr. Seuss. *The butter battle book*
A doctor's proven new home cure for arthritis
The doctor's wife
The dog crisis
Dolch, Edward. *Big, bigger, biggest*
The doll
Donleavy, J.P. *Fairy tales of New York*
Don't hurt me, Mama
The doomsday gang
Dorothy and the star [16 mm film]
Doyle, Brian. *Rebel angel* [possibly his *Angel square*]
Dragons and other fabulous beasts
Dragonwagon, Crescent. *Wind Rose*

Draves, W. *The word of the Lord brought to mankind by an angel*
Ducks!
Duncan, Lois. *Daughters of Eve*
—. *Killing Mr. Griffin*
Durand, ... [?]. Série "Foc": "Histoires fantastiques"
Durand, René. *Le scalpe et la peau*
Duvoisin, Roger. *Petunia*

Eckankar: compiled writings, vol. 1 [?]
Edgar, Marriot. *The lion and Albert*
Effinger, George Alec. *When gravity fails*
Elisa, T. *Des fleurs sur la neige*
Ellis, Bret Easton. *Less than zero*
Engel, Marian. *Bear*
The enormous crocodile
Evans, George. *Get well soon*
Evidence
Evslin, Barnard. *Heraclea*
Eyerly, Jeannette. *The Phaedra complex*

Fairy tales of New York
Faithfull, Marianne. *Broken English* [sound recording]
Family secrets (Klein)
Family Secrets (Rogers)
The farm
Farmer, P. Jose. *The image of the beast*
Fast Sam, cool Clyde, and stuff
Fast shuffle
Father Christmas
Fatio, Louise. *The happy lion*
Fear and loathing in Las Vegas
Fell's guide to doubling the performance of your car
La femme piégée [?] [bande dessinée]
Fennelly, Tony. *The glory hole murders*
Fighting slave of Gor
Fine things
Finnigan, ... [?] *Newfy* [?] *joke book*
Firerose
Firewater pond
The first deadly sin
Fit for life
Fitzhugh, Louise, and Sandra Scoppettone. *Bang bang you're dead*
The five Chinese brothers
Flick
Flowers in the attic
Flowers of anger
Foley, Louise Munro. *Somebody stole second*
For the glory
Forever
A fortunate catastrophe
The fortunate few
Fowke, Edith. *Sally go round the sun*
Fox, John. *The boys on the rock*

Francoeur, Lucien. *Les rockeurs sanctifiés*
Fraser, L. Craig. *The testament of Adolf Hitler*
Freaky fables
Freddy's book
French, Marilyn. *The women's room*
Friday, Nancy. *Men in love: male sexual fantasies*
The frog prince
Frost, Gavin, and Yvonne Frost. *A witches' grimoire of ancient omens, portents, talismans and charms*
Fuller, John G. *The day we bombed Utah*
Fungus the bogeyman
Furs: an appreciation of luxury, a guide to value

Gachet, Jacqueline. *The ladybug*
Gag, Wanda. *Snow White and the Seven Dwarfs*
Galdone, Paul. *The frog prince*
—. *The greedy old fat man*
—. *King of the cats*
The game
Gantos, Jack, and Nicole Ruben. *The werewolf family*
Garden, Nancy. *Annie on my mind*
Gardner, Joy. *Healing the family*
Gash, Joe. *Priestly murders*
Gates of fire
Gay parenting: a complete guide for gay men and lesbians with children
Gerald's party
Gerbils
Get well soon
Ghosts, witches, and things like that
Gipson, Fred. *Savage Sam*
Girls' and boys' book of etiquette
Girls and sex
The Globe and Mail. "article on Bill C-54"
The glory hole murders
Godard, Christian, and Julio Ribera. *Le vagabond des limbes*
—. *The vagabond of limbo: the ultimate alchemist*
—. *The vagabond of limbo: what is reality, Papa?*
Goffstein, M.B. *My crazy sister*
Going west
Goldsmith, Sharon. *Human sexuality*
Gordon, Sol. *Did the sun shine before you were born?*
—. *The teenage survival book*
Gorky rises
Grands reportages de juin 1988 [revue]
Granpa
Great sex
The greedy old fat man
Greenberg, David. *Slugs*
Greene, Constance C. *A(lexandra) the Great*
—. *I know you, Al*
Greer, Germaine. *The madwoman's underclothes*
The grizzly revenge
The grounding of Group Six
Guide des caresses
The Gunsmith (a series of westerns)

Haeberle, Erwin J. *The sex atlas: a new illustrated guide*
Hag head
Haining, Peter. *Witchcraft and black magic*
The Haj
Hall, Carol. *Northern J. Galloway presents—I been there*
Hall, Lynn. *Flowers of anger*
Hamilton, Wallace. *David at Olivet*
—. *Kevin*
Hamilton, William. *The love of rich women*
Hampton, William. *Fell's guide to doubling the performance of your car*
Hanckel, Frances and John Cunningham. *A way of love, a way of life: a young person's introduction to what it means to be gay*
Handlesman, J.B. *Freaky fables*
Hands of a stranger
Hansel and Gretel
The happy lion
Harranth, Wolf. *My old Grandad*
Harris, Janis. *Alaska*
Harris, Joel Chandler. *Uncle Remus: his songs and his sayings*
Harwood, Richard. *Nuremburg [?] and other war crimes trials*
Hazen, Barbara. *Girls' and boys' book of etiquette*
Healing the family
Heart of the country
Heavy metal magazine [?]
Hector Protector
Helwig, David. *The only son*
Henrie, Fiona. *Gerbils*
Heraclea
A hero ain't nothin' but a sandwich
Hero and the terror
Herriges, Greg. *Someplace safe*
Heymans, Annemie. *The yellow thread adventure*
High wire spider
Hill, Reginald. *A clubbable woman*
Hirschhorn, Richard Clark. *A pride of healers*
L'histoire de Kiki Grabouille
The hoax of the twentieth century
Hogrogian, Nonny. *One fine day*
Holmes, Tom, and Blonnie [?] Holmes, illus. *The story of Henny Penny*
The holocaust: 120 questions and answer
Hoodoo—Conjuration—Witchcraft—Rootwork
Horace
Hosie's alphabet
The hospital in Buwambo
The house of God
Howitt, Mary. *The spider and the fly*
Hughes, Douglas A. *Perspectives on pornography*
Les huit jours du diable dans "Super Tintin"
Human sexuality
Hunt, Bernice Kohn. *Out of the cauldron*
Hunt, Roderick. *Ghosts, witches, and things like that*

Hutchins, H.J. *Anastasia Morningstar and the crystal butterfly*
Hyatt, Harry Middleton. *Hoodoo—Conjuration—Witchcraft—Rootwork*
Hyman, Trina Schart, ed. and illus. *The sleeping beauty*

I am Joseph
I hate school!
I know you, Al
I love you, stupid!
Ice blues: a Donald Strachey mystery
Ignota, B. *Confessions of a part-time call girl*
I'll fix Anthony
The image of the beast
Immigration: Parliament vs. the people
In a dark, dark room and other scary stories
In the night kitchen
Indian summer
Inkeles, Gordon, and Murray Todris. *L'art du massage*
Ipcar, Dahlov Zorach. *The cat came back*
Ireland: a terrible beauty
Iron Maiden. ... [?] [record album]
Irvine, Lucy. *Castaway*
Irwin, Hadley. *Abby, my love*
Isaacs, Susan. *Almost paradise*
Island of Nose
It's not the end of the world
It's not what you'd expect
It's okay if you don't love me
Iznogoud [?] [bande dessinée]

Jack the bear
Jack-o'-lantern
Jacobs, Anita. *Where has Deedie Wooster been all these years?*
Jaensson, Hakan, and Arne Norlin. *Charlie's pillow*
Jagger, Brenda. *A song twice over*
Jennings, ... [?]. *The cowboys*
Jennings, Gary. *Aztec*
Jeschke, Susan. *The Devil did it*
—. *Firerose*
Jessel, Camilla. *The joy of birth: a book for parents and children*
Jetes[?], K.W. *Dr. Adder*
Jim, who ran away from his nurse, and was eaten by a lion
Jitterbug
Johnson, Mendal W. *Let's go play at Adam's*
Johnstone, William W. *The nursery*
Jones, Harold. *Tales to tell*
The joy of birth: a book for parents and children
The joy of football
The joy of life
The joy of sex
Juggling: a novel
Jump from the sky. (Ladybird series)

June Noon [art print]
The Just right family

Kansan
Katz, Welwyn Wilton. *Witchery Hill*
Kaye, Geraldine. *The rotten old car*
Kaye, Marilyn. *Will you cross me?*
Keats, Ezra Jack. *Apartment three*
Keegstra: the trial, the issues, the consequences
Kellogg, Steven. *Won't somebody play with me?*
Kelly, Gary F. *Learning about sex*
Kennedy, Richard. *The porcelain man*
Kennemore, Tim. *The fortunate few*
Kesselman, Wendy Ann. *Flick*
Kevin
Killing Mr. Griffin
Kim, Ashida. *Ninja death touch*
—. *Secrets of the Ninja*
Kimball, Michael. *Firewater pond*
King, Stephen. *Creepshow*
King of the cats
King Stork
Kingdon, Alan. *The joy of life*
Kiss Daddy goodnight
Klein, Norma. *Beginner's love*
—. *Blue trees, red sky*
—. *Family secrets*
—. *It's not what you'd expect*
—. *It's okay if you don't love me*
—. *Naomi in the middle*
—. *Queen of the Whatifs*
Kliban, B. *Two guys fooling around with the moon*
Knebel, Fletcher. *Sabotage*
Krantz, Judith. *Princess Daisy*
Kraus, Robert. *Whose mouse are you?*
Kropp, Paul. *Baby, baby*
Kueshana, Eklal. *The ultimate frontier*
Kushi, Michio. *Diet for a strong heart*

Là-bas [?] [bande dessinée]
Lady Chatterley's lover
The ladybug
Lamia
Lamont, Stewart. *Religion, inc.: the Church of Scientology*
Lampoon [?]
La Salle, Bruno de. *Le petit chaperon rouge*
Last key
The last puppy
Latow, Roberta. *Soft warm rain*
—. *Three rivers*
Lauzier, [?] *Les cadres* [?]
Lauzier, [?] *Un certain malaise*
Lauzier, [?] *Tranches de vie*
Lawrence, D.H. *Lady Chatterley's lover*
Learning about sex

Learning about sex: a guide for children and their parents
Leavitt, David. *The lost language of games* [*cranes*?]
Lee, Dennis. *Lizzy's lion*
Lee, Tanith. *Night's master*
Lehrman, Robert. *Juggling: a novel*
Lenski, Lois. *Let's play house*
Less than zero
Let's go play at Adam's
Let's play house
Levoy, Myron. *Alan and Naomi*
Lianna [video]
Life (June 1985 issue)
Limonov, Edward. *Oscar et les femmes*
Linda
Lindgren, Astrid. *The brothers Lionheart*
The lion and Albert
Littke, Lael. *Trish for president*
Lizzy's lion
Logan, Les. *The game*
The lost language of games [*cranes*?]
The love of rich women
Lovelace, Linda. *Ordeal*
Lowry, Lois. *Autumn Street*
Lundy, Mike. *Raven*
Lusty limericks
Lyle, Katie Letcher. *Dark but full of diamonds*
Lynn, Elizabeth A. *The dancers of Arun*

McBride, Will. *Show me!*
McCaffery, Steve, and B.P. Nichol, eds. *The story so far*
McCall, Dan. *Jack the bear*
McKee, David. *Two monsters*
McNeill, Elizabeth. *Nine and a half weeks*
McPhail, David. *A wolf story*
McQuay, Mike. *Jitterbug*
The madwoman's underclothes
Maia
Major, Kevin. "all titles in general"
Making love: how to be your own sex therapist
Malloy, Judy. *Bad Thad*
Man, myth & magic: the illustrated encyclopedia of mythology, religion and the unknown
The man with seven toes
Manara, Milo. *Déclic*
—. *Le parfum de l'invisible*
Manchete ["Portuguese language periodical"]
Maple, Eric. *Devils and demons*
—. *Witchcraft: the story of man's search for supernatural power*
The maple laugh forever
Maris, Ron. *The Punch and Judy book*
Mark, Jan. *Out of the oven*
Marmouset et Makumba
Martin, Eva. *Canadian fairy tales*
Martin, Jacques. *Barbe-Bleue*

Martinez, Alberto, and Jean-Loup Nory. *Vans: customized vans in colour*
Masters and Johnson on sex and human loving
Masters, William H., and Virginia E. Johnson. *Masters and Johnson on sex and human loving*
Masters, Zeke. *Fast shuffle*
Matthews, Greg. *Heart of the country*
Mayle, Peter. *Baby taming*
—. *What's happening to me?*
—. *Where did I come from?*
Mayle, Peter, and Arthur Robins. *Congratulations! You're not pregnant*
Mazer, Harry. *I love you, stupid!*
Meeting the Mormons
Men in love: male sexual fantasies
Mertl, Steve. *Keegstra: the trial, the issues, the consequences*
Miller, Henry. *Opus pistorum*
Miller, Mitchell, illus. *One misty, moisty morning: rhymes from Mother Goose*
Milligan, Spike. *Badjelly the witch*
Mills, Robert E. *Kansan*
Mine's the best
Mr. and Mrs. Pig's evening out
Mr. Miacca
Mrs. Noah's laundry day
Mitchison, Naomi. *When the bough breaks, and other stories*
Mohr, Nicholasa. *Nilda*
Mon corps est à elles
Monjo, F.N. *Indian summer*
Monnie hates Lydia
"Monty Python"
Moore, Brian. *The doctor's wife*
Moses: the escape from Egypt
Mother Goose nursery rhymes: "specifically the Margery Daw rhyme"
Ms [periodical]
Munsil, Janet. *Dinner at Auntie Rose's*
Murder in the family
Musgrave, Susan and Carol Evans (illus.). *Hag head*
My crazy sister
My old Grandad
Myers, Walter Dean. *Fast Sam, cool Clyde, and stuff*

Na-ni
Naomi in the middle
National Lampoon [periodical] (medical issue)
Nerves in collision
Ness, Evaline. *Mr. Miacca*
Neufeld, John. *Freddy's book*
The new friend
New Internationalist [periodical]
New Musical Express [periodical]
Newman, Shirlee Petkin. *Tell me, Grandma, tell me, Grandpa*
Nicol, Eric, and Dave More. *The joy of football*

Night church
Nightmares: poems to trouble your sleep
Night's master
Nilda
Nine and a half weeks
The Ninja
Ninja death touch
No sense of evil: the espionage case of E. Herbert Norman
Noonoah, le petit phoque blanc
Norman, John. *Dancer of Gor*
—. *Fighting slave of Gor*
Northern J. Galloway presents—I been there
Nothing in common
NOW ["local weekly magazine"]
Nowell, Iris. *The dog crisis*
Nuremburg [?] and other war crimes trials
The nursery

Oakley, Graham. *The church mice adrift*
—. *The church mice at bay*
—. *The church mice in action*
The object man
Ondaatje, Michael. *The man with seven toes*
One fine day
132 ways to earn a living without working (for someone else)
One misty, moisty morning: rhymes from Mother Goose
One on one
The one pig with horns
The only son
Opus pistorum
Ordeal
Oscar et les femmes
Oster, Jerry. *Sweet justice*
The ostrich girl
The other Emily
Out of the cauldron
Out of the oven
Outside over there

The pain and the great one
Le parfum de l'invisible
Paris Match [periodical]
Parker, Robert B. *Taming a sea-horse*
Parrott, E.O. *The Penguin book of limericks*
Paulette
Pearson, Susan. *Monnie hates Lydia*
Peary, Danny. *Cult movies*
Pelrine, Eleanor Wright. *Abortion in Canada*
The Penguin book of limericks
Penney, Alexandra. *Great sex*
Pennington's heir
Perrault, Charles. *Tom Thumb*
Perspectives on pornography
Petals on the wind
Peters, David. *For the glory*

Peterson, Joyce. *Adultery for adults*
Le petit chaperon rouge
Le petit chien
Petit et grand Albert
Petunia
Peyser, Arnold. *The squirrelcage*
Peyton, K.M. *Pennington's heir*
The Phaedra complex
Phillips, Edward. *Buried on Sunday*
Pichard, Georges and Georges Wolinski. *Paulette*
The piercing
Pilote et Charlie
Pinkwater, Daniel. *Devil in the drain*
—. *Ducks!*
Platt, Kin. *The doomsday gang*
Playboar
Playboy [periodical]
Poilus, velus, barbus
Pomeroy, Wardell B. *Girls and sex*
Ponicsan, Darryl. *An unmarried man*
The porcelain man
Pour toujours [Forever]
Prather, Ray. *The ostrich girl*
Prelutsky, Jack. *Nightmares: poems to trouble your sleep*
—. *Rolling Harvey down the hill*
Preussen von den Anfängen bis zur Reichsgründung
Prévert, Jacques. ... [?]
A pride of healers
Priestly murders
Prignaud, Jean. *Le petit chien*
Prince (poster of)
Princess Daisy
Pryor, Richard. *Bicentennial nigger* [sound recording]
The Punch and Judy book
Pyle, Howard. *King Stork*

Quarry
Queen of the Whatifs
A question of race

Rackham, Arthur. *Mother Goose nursery rhymes*: "specifically the Margery Daw rhyme"
Raley, Patricia E. *Making love: how to be your own sex therapist*
Ramaïoli ... [?] and ... [?] Durand. *La terre de la bombe*
The rapist file
Raven
Rayner, Claire. *The body book*
Rayner, Mary. *Mr. and Mrs. Pig's evening out*
Reading, J.P. *Bouquets for Brimbal*
Religion, inc.: the Church of Scientology
Reproduction
Richmond, Sandra. *Wheels for walking*
Riley, Jocelyn. *Crazy quilt*
Roald Dahl's revolting rhymes

Robbins, Harold. *The storyteller*
Robert and Arabella
Roberts, J.R. *The Gunsmith* (a series of westerns)
Robinson, Spider, and Jeanne Robinson. *Stardance*
Les rockeurs sanctifiés
Rogers, Edward S. *Algonkians of the Eastern Woodlands*
Rogers, Lynn. *Family secrets*
Roiphe, Herman, and Anne Roiphe. *Your child's mind: the complete guide to infant and child emotional well-being*
Rolling Harvey down the hill
Romance
Rosenthal, Ed, and Ron Lichtey. *132 ways to earn a living without working (for someone else)*
Ross, Malcolm. *Spectre of power*
—. *Web of deceit*
Ross, Tony. *The boy who cried wolf*
Rotten Island
The rotten old car
Roundhill, Jack. *Meeting the Mormons*
Run, Shelley, run
Ryder, the Tong wars

Sabotage
Sally go round the sun
Samuels, Gertrude. *Run, Shelley, run*
Sanders, Lawrence. *The first deadly sin*
—. *The second deadly sin*
—. *The third deadly sin*
Savage Sam
Le scalpe et la peau
The scarecrows
Scary stories to tell in the dark
Schmidt, Annie M.G. *Island of Nose*
Schreiber, Flora Rheta. *The shoemaker*
Schulenburg, Joy. *Gay parenting: a complete guide for gay men and lesbians with children*
Schwartz, Alvin. *In a dark, dark room and other scary stories*
—. *Scary stories to tell in the dark*
Schwartz, Herbert T. *Tales from the smokehouse*
Schwartz, Joel L. *Upchuck summer*
Scott, R.C. *Blood sport*
Scribner, Charles, Jr. *The Devil's bridge*
The second deadly sin
Secrets of the Ninja
Seigel [Siegel?], Jerry. *One on one*
Sendak, Maurice. *As I went over the water*
—. *Hector Protector*
—. *In the night kitchen*
—. *Outside over there*
—. *Seven little monsters*
—. *Some swell pup*
Serraillier, Ian. *Suppose you met a witch*
Seuling, Barbara. *The teeny tiny woman*
Seven little monsters
The sex atlas: a new illustrated guide

Shakespeare, William. "the complete works"
Shem, Samuel. *The house of God*
Shennan, Victoria. *Ben*
The shoemaker
Show me!
Siegel, Scott. *The companion*
The sleeping beauty
Slim Goodbody, the inside story [?]
Slugs
Smash [periodical]
"Smurf book"
Snow White and the Seven Dwarfs
So that's how I was born!
Soap-box derby (National Film Board) [video]
Soft warm rain
Some swell pup
Somebody stole second
Someplace safe
Sommers, Beverly. *Last key*
Son of Dracula
A song twice over
South African Digest [periodical]
Space station seventh grade
Sparger, Rex. *The doll*
Spectre of power
The spider and the fly
Spinelli, Jerry. *Space station seventh grade*
The squirrelcage
Stanek, Muriel. *Don't hurt me, Mama*
Stardance
Starring Sally J. Freedman as herself
Stay hungry [sound recording]
Steele, Danielle. *Fine things*
Steig, William. *Gorky rises*
—. *Rotten Island*
Steptoe, John. *Daddy is a monster...sometimes*
Stevenson, Richard. *Ice blues: a Donald Strachey mystery*
Stevenson, Robert Louis. *A child's garden of verses*
Stokes, Naomi. *The castrated woman*
Stone, Gene. *Darling, I am growing old*
Stories for eight-year-olds
The story of evolution
The story of Henny Penny
Story of Little Black Sambo
The story so far
The storyteller
Strasser, Todd. *Angel dust blues*
Strieber, Whitley. *Night church*
Superbike!
Suppose you met a witch
Sussman, Les. *The rapist file*
Swaybill, Roger. *Threads*
Swede, George. *High wire spider*
Sweet justice
Szambelan-Strevinsky, Christine. *Dark hour of noon*

Tales from the smokehouse
Tales to tell
Taming a sea-horse
Taylor, Ron. *The story of evolution*
Teddybear postman
The teenage survival book
The teeny tiny woman
Tell me, Grandma, tell me, Grandpa
La terre de la bombe
The testament of Adolf Hitler
Then again, maybe I won't
They came from outer space
The third deadly sin
This is the cocker spaniel
Thomas is different
Thompson, Hunter S. *Fear and loathing in Las Vegas*
Thompson, Julian F. *The grounding of Group Six*
Threads
Three rivers
The three robbers
Thurman, Mark. *Two stupid dummies*
The tin-pot foreign general and the old iron woman
Tom Fox and the apple pie
Tom Thumb
Torture tomb
Tourneur, Dina-K. *Marmouset et Makumba*
Tranches de vie
Travis, Tristan. *Lamia*
Treadwell, M.A. *The discipline of raising children*
Trish for president
Trubo, Richard. *An act of mercy: euthanasia today*
The true Francine
Turin, Adela. *A fortunate catastrophe*
Turkle, Brinton. *Do not open*
Twisted Sister. *Stay hungry* [sound recording]
—. *Under the blade* [sound recording]
Twitchell, Paul. *Eckankar: compiled writings*, vol.1 [?]
Two guys fooling around with the moon
Two monsters
Two stupid dummies

The ultimate frontier
Uncle Remus: his songs and his sayings
Under the blade [sound recording]
Understanding your child from birth to three
Ungerer, Tomi. *The beast of Monsieur Racine*
—. *The three robbers*
—. *Zeralda's ogre*
Ungerer, Tomi. ... [?]
United Church Newsletter [of a local church]
Unlucky Wally
An unmarried man
Unspeakable acts
Upchuck summer
Uris, Jill and Leon Uris. *Ireland: a terrible beauty*

Uris, Leon. *The Haj*
Usborne, Peter [?]. *Witches*

Le vagabond des limbes
The vagabond of limbo: the ultimate alchemist
The vagabond of limbo: what is reality, Papa?
Valarie
Valinieff, Pierre. *Guide des caresses*
Van Lustbader, Eric. *The Ninja*
Vans: customized vans in colour
Vevers, Gwynne. *Reproduction*
Vinton, Anne. *The hospital in Buwambo*
Viorst, Judith. *I'll fix Anthony*
Vive les femmes

Waddell, Martin. *Going west*
Watson, Clyde. *Tom Fox and the apple pie*
Watters, Wendell. *Compulsory parenthood*
A way of love, a way of life: a young person's introduction to what it means to be gay
Web of deceit
Weber, Charles E. *The holocaust: 120 questions and answers*
Webster's New Collegiate Dictionary
Weisman, John. *Evidence*
The werewolf family
Westall, Robert. *The scarecrows*
Weston, Cole. *Ryder, the Tong wars*
What's best for you
What's happening to me?
Wheels for walking
When gravity fails
When the bough breaks, and other stories
When the new baby comes, I'm moving out
When the wind blows
Where did I come from?
Where has Deedie Wooster been all these years?
Whitney, Leon F. *This is the cocker spaniel*
Whose mouse are you?
Wifey
Will you cross me?
Willis, Jeanne, and Margaret Chamberlain. *L'histoire de Kiki Grabouille*
Wind Rose
Winsor, Kathleen. *Robert and Arabella*
Winter, Paula. *The bear and the fly*
Wirths, Claudine G., and Mary Bowman-Kruhm. *I hate school!*
Witchcraft and black magic
Witchcraft: the story of man's search for supernatural power
Witchery Hill
Witches
The witches
A witches' grimoire of ancient omens, portents, talismans and charms

Wolde, Gunilla. *Thomas is different*
A wolf story
Wolinski, Georges. *Mon corps est à elles*
The women's room
The wonder story of Henry Sugar and six more
Won't somebody play with me?
The word of the Lord brought to mankind by an angel
Worthington, Phoebe. *Teddybear postman*
Wright, Freire. *The adventures of Tom Thumb*
The writing on the wall
Wynorski, Jim, ed. *They came from outer space*

The yellow thread adventure
You think just because you're big you're right

Young, gay and proud
Young witches & warlocks
Your child's mind: the complete guide to infant and child emotional well-being

Zarowny, Shane. *Big monster*
Zeralda's ogre
Zimnik, Reiner. *The bear and the people*
Zion, Gene. *Dear garbage man*
Zolotow, Charlotte. *The new friend*
Zoom [periodical]

Index

Index

A list of titles cited on questionnaires returned by respondents appears as Appendix E. Only those titles mentioned in the text are indexed.

Abby, My Love (Irwin), 74
Abortion in Canada (Pelrine), 72
Abortion, materials on, 103
    challenges against, 101, 106-8
Abravanel, Elliott D. *Dr. Abravanel's Body Type Program for Health, Fitness and Nutrition,* 87
Academic libraries
    censorship research in, 21
Access policies, 37-57, 113, 117
    acquisition pressure and, 105
    controversial materials ownership and, 50
    differential treatment of materials and, 44
    minors' access restrictions and, 42
    rates of challenges and, 61
    response to challenges and, 91
Access restrictions, 12, 122. *See also* Differential treatment of materials; Removal of materials; Withdrawal of materials
    age-related. *See* Age-related access
    on challenged materials, 83
AC/DC (heavy metal group)
    challenges to, 65, 67
Acquisition of materials, 15. *See also* Selection
Acquisition pressure, 105-10, 115
    controversial materials ownership and, 50, 51
    definition of, 59, 105
    rates of challenges and, 61
An Act of Mercy (Trubo), 72, 86, 88
Adams, Richard. *Maia,* 69
Administrative levels, in resolving challenges, 84
Adolf Hitler: Pictures from the Life of the Führer (Quinn), 72
Adultery for Adults (Peterson), 71
Adults. *See also* Parents
    depicted in children's books, 74-76
    fiction
        challenges against, 69-70
    materials
        retention rates of, 85
Adventures of Tom (Wright), 77
Affective filter (social learning theory), 120-21
The Aga Khans (Bose), 62, 72
Age of sexual consent, censorship and, 118
Age-related access
    borrowing restrictions, acquisition pressure and, 105
    differential treatment of materials and, 44, 69
    restrictions, 40-44, 81-82, 113, 117-18
        rates of challenges and, 61

Agnostic materials, pressure to acquire, 108
Aho, Jennifer. *Learning About Sex,* 79
AIDS, materials on
    defacement of, 103
    pressure to acquire, 108
Alan and Naomi (Levoy), 78
Alberta
    access policies in, 40
    challenges in, 22
    controversial materials ownership in, 52
    public library governance in, 29
    rate of covert incidents in, 99
    rates of challenges in, 61, 62
    survey respondents in, 29
    withdrawal of materials in, 83
Alcoholics Anonymous, 106, 108
Alexander, Martha. *When the New Baby Comes, I'm Moving Out,* 75
A(lexandra) the Great (Greene), 79
Algonkians of the Eastern Woodlands (Rogers), 86
Allard, Harry. *Bumps in the Night,* 76
Alvarez, Walter. *Nerves in Collision,* 72, 87
Alyson, Sasha. *Young, Gay and Proud,* 79
American Association of University Professors. *Liberty and Learning in the Schools,* 118
American Civil Liberties Union, 68
American Library Association, 13-14
    Intellectual Freedom Committee, 15
        response to Bill C-54, 54
    Intellectual Freedom Manual, 15, 38
    Library Bill of Rights, 156 (reproduced)
        age-related restrictions and, 117
    Office for Intellectual Freedom, 38
And the Band Played On, 108
Andersen, Hans Christian. *Big Claus and Little Claus,* 76
Andersson, C.D. *Torture Tomb,* 88
Andrews, V.C., 38, 65, 67
    Flowers in the Attic, 51 (table), 65, 66 (table)
Angel Dust Blues (Strasser), 65 (table), 67, 74
Angell, J. *What's Best for You,* 74
Anglund, Joan Walsh. *Brave Cowboy,* 86
Annie on My Mind (Garden), 52, 73, 86, 91
Anthropological theory, 121
Anthropology, materials on
    covert censorship of, 114
Archer, Jeffrey. *Kane and Abel,* 102
Are You There God? (Blume), 73

Ariel (Bickham), 73
Armstrong, Louise. *Kiss Daddy Goodnight,* 70
Asch, Frank, 67 (table). *The Last Puppy,* 74
Asheim, Lester, 13-14, 122
Ashley, Edwin, 120
Association des bibliothécaires du Québec, 28
Association pour l'avancement des sciences et des techniques de la documentation (ASTED), 28
ASTED, 28
Astérix, 93
Astrology, materials on
    complaints regarding, 65
Auel, Jean
    Clan of the Cave Bear, 67, 69
    Valley of the Horses, 49, 51 (table)
Authors challenged, 67. See also names of individual authors
Les Aventures de Benji, 78
Les Aventures magiques de Corentin au pays de PipiCaca, 74, 86

Bad Thad (Malloy), 75
Badjelly the Witch (Milligan), 78
Baha'i faith
    acquisition pressure and, 107, 108
Baigent, M. *Holy Blood Holy Grail,* 51 (table), 53
Bailey, Lydia. *The Big Bang,* 79
Balanced collection concept (Berelson), 121-22
Bandes dessinées, 93
Bannerman, Helen. *Little Black Sambo,* 46, 78
Baptist material, pressure to acquire, 108
Barbe-bleue (Martin), 74, 88
Barbour, Douglas. *The Maple Laugh Forever,* 72
Barros, James. *No Sense of Evil,* 72
Bear (Engel), 11, 65 (table), 69
The Beast of Monsieur Racine (Ungerer), 65 (table), 76
Beginner's Love (Klein), 73, 102
Bell, William. *Crabbe,* 76-77
Bellairs, J. *Figure in the Shadows,* 51 (table), 53
Belloc, Hilaire. *Jim Who Ran Away from His Nurse and Was Eaten by a Lion,* 74
Ben (Shennon), 75
Benton, John. *Valarie,* 66 (table)
Bercuson, David and Douglas Wertheimer. *Trust Betrayed,* 95
Berelson, Bernard, 121-22
Bernadette. *Cinderella,* 78
Bertalanffy, Ludwig von, 120
Beta Associates, 22
Bicentennial Nigger (Pryor), 71
Bickham, Jack M. *Ariel,* 73
The Big Bang (Bailey), 79
Big Bigger Biggest (Dolch), 86
Big Claus and Little Claus (Andersen), 76
Big Monster (Zarowny), 77
Bill C-54, 54-57, 119
Birch, Beverly. *A Question of Race,* 79
Birdsall, Peter, 117
Bishop, Claire. *Five Chinese Brothers,* 77
Blasphemy, defacement of materials containing, 100
Bleeks, Sheila J. *Cookies for Luke,* 75
Blodgett, Michael. *Hero and the Terror,* 70
Blubber (Blume), 78
Blue Trees, Red Sky (Klein), 65 (table), 78

Blume, Judy, 40, 43, 67
    Are You There God?, 73
    Blubber, 78
    Deenie, 66 (table), 67, 73
    Forever
        challenges against, 26, 51 (table), 65, 66, 67
        differential treatment of, 40, 48
        intended audience of, 69
        reasons for challenges, 80
        results of challenges, 82, 85, 87
    Starring Sally J. Freedman as Herself, 66 (table), 74, 78
    Then Again, Maybe I Won't, 46, 51 (table)
    Wifey
        challenges against, 26, 51 (table)
        differential treatment of, 40, 42, 49
        intended audience of, 69, 80, 82, 85
        reasons for challenges, 80
        results of challenges, 82, 85, 87
The Body Book (Rayner), 79, 102
The Body Politic (periodical), 65 (table), 86, 87
Bond, Simon. *Unspeakable Acts,* 71
Bonsall, Crosby. *Mine's the Best,* 76
Book and Periodical Council, 119. See also Book and Periodical Development Council
    Freedom of Expression Committee
        Bill C-54 and, 57
        The Freedom of Expression and the Freedom to Read, 154-55 (reproduced)
Book and Periodical Development Council, 11-12. See also Book and Periodical Council
Book of Predictions (Wallechinsky), 100
Book reviews
    age levels cited in, 69
    use in selection, 45, 92
Book Selection and Intellectual Freedom (Merritt), 14
Booth, David
    Censorship Goes to School, 21
    Impressions reading series, 21
Borrowers
    client confidentiality, 118
    registered
        access policies and, 39
        as complainants, 62, 63
Bose, Mihir. *The Aga Khans,* 62, 72
Bottner, Barbara. *Nothing in Common,* 74
Bouquets for Brimbal (Reading), 73
Boys and Sex (Pomeroy), 41
The Boys on the Rock (Fox), 73, 87
Brancato, Robin. *Facing Up,* 46
Brandel, Marc. *Murder in the Family,* 66 (table), 86, 87
Brave Cowboy (Anglund), 86
Briggs, Raymond 67
    Father Christmas, 66 (table), 75, 87
    Fungus the Bogeyman, 87, 91
    The Tin-Pot Foreign General and the Old Iron Woman, 65 (table), 73-74
    Unlucky Wally, 70
    When the Wind Blows, 87
British Columbia
    acquisition pressure in, 106
    controversial materials ownership in, 52

public library governance in, 29
school libraries, reasons for challenges, 68
survey respondents in, 29
British Columbia Library Association
Intellectual Freedom Committee, 38
Statement on Intellectual Freedom, 153 (reproduced)
Broten, Delores, 117
The Brothers Lionheart (Lindgren), 75, 86
Brown, Margaret Wise. *The Dead Bird,* 75-76
Browne, Anthony, 67 (table)
Buckland, Raymond. *Buckland's Complete Book of Witchcraft,* 71
Bumps in the Night (Allard), 76
Buried on Sunday (Phillips), 69
Burton, Melody, 84
Busha, Charles, 21, 121
Butcher, Geoffrey. *Moses—The Escape from Egypt,* 76
The Butter Battle Book (Seuss), 51 (table), 53, 65, 76
Butz, Arthur R. *The Hoax of the Twentieth Century,* 65 (table), 72, 88, 109
Byars, Betsy. *Cracker Jackson,* 74

Cabu, Jean. *Cathérine saute au paf!*, 86, 87
Caldicott, Helen. *Missile Envy,* 101
Calgary (proclaims Freedom to Read Week), 119
Campbell, Giraud W. *A Doctor's Proven New Home Cure for Arthritis,* 72
Canadian Book Publishers Council, 21, 22
Canadian Dimensions (periodical), 100
Canadian Library Association
Committee on Undesirable Literature, 119
Information and Telecommunication Access Principles, 148 (reproduced)
intellectual freedom and, 119
response to Bill C-54, 54
Statement on Intellectual Freedom, 28, 147 (reproduced)
age-related restrictions and, 117-18
book selection policies and, 38-39
differential treatment of materials and, 44
and minors' access restrictions, 41-42
Canadian Library Journal, 119
Canadian Society of Children's Authors, Illustrators and Performers, 119
CANSCAIP Minus-30, 119
Carlson, Natalie Savage, 65, 67
Carnovsky, Leon, 13
The Castrated Family, 102
The Castrated Woman (Stokes), 72
The Cat Came Back (Ipcar), 79
Cathérine saute au paf! (Cabu), 86, 87
Caywood, Carolyn, 121
Censorship, 11-12. *See also* Intellectual freedom; Self-censorship
acquisition pressure and, 105
context of, 16
covert. *See* Covert censorship
definition of, 15
incidents. *See* Challenges
"justifiable," 89
overt. *See* Overt challenges
and the public library, 115-16
research, 21-23
selection of materials and, 13, 89

staff attitudes toward, 31, 115. *See also* Staff
stages of, 16-17
weeding of materials and, 89
Censorship Activities in Public and Public School Libraries (National Commission on Libraries and Information Science), 12
Censorship Goes to School (Booth), 21
Challenges. *See also* Complaints
authors frequently challenged, 67
vs. complaints, 16, 22
controversial materials ownership and, 50, 51
covert. *See* Covert challenges
definition of, 15-16, 22
effect on institutional policies, 90-97
formal, 22
forms for, 38, 40
overt. *See* Overt challenges
policies regarding, 85, 89
and withdrawals, 86-87
procedures for, 38
publicization of, 123
rates of
in Alberta, 22
in Manitoba, 22
and retention rates, 85
reasons for, 67-81
and permanent withdrawals, 84
responses of staff to, 83-86, 90-92
titles frequently challenged, 65-66
verbal, 31, 60
written, 22
Chamberlain, Margaret. *L'Histoire de Kiki Grabouille,* 87
Chambers, Aidan. *Introducing Books to Children,* 120
Charlie's Pillow (Jaenssen and Worlin), 76
Charte des droits du lecteur, 28, 40, 150 (reproduced)
Childbirth, materials on
restrictions on, 118
Children. *See also* Minors
access restrictions on, 40-44, 113
A Children's Almanac of Words at Play (Espy), 95
Children's elementary materials, retention rates of, 85
Children's fiction, complaints about, 73-78
Children's literature
age levels in reviews of, 69
as subversive, 118-19
censorship of, 21
Children's non-fiction, complaints about, 78-79
Children's Own, 106
A Child's Garden of Verses (Stevenson), 78
Chinese Destiny (Smedley), 52 (tables)
The Chocolate War (Cormier), 67
The Christian Socratic (periodical), 106
Church, Joseph. *Understanding Your Child from Birth to Three,* 71
The Church Mice at Bay (Oakley), 76
Church of Scientology
acquisition pressure and, 106, 107, 108
challenges and, 117
covert censorship of materials on, 100
Cinderella, 86
Cinderella (Bernadette), 78
Cinderella (Suddon), 51 (table), 53

Circulation rates
    access policies and, 39
City of Gold and Other Stories from the Old Testament (Dickinson), 52 (table), 53
Civil rights, 122
Clan of the Cave Bear (Auel), 67, 69
Classification of materials. *See also* Differential treatment of materials
    access restrictions and, 46
    effect of challenges on, 81, 92
Client confidentiality, 118
Cohen, B. *I Am Joseph*, 51 (table)
Cole, Babette. *Poilus, Vélus, Barbus*, 87
Collection: Livres dont vous êtes le héros, 66 (table)
Collections
    balanced, 13, 121-22
        acquisition/selection and, 45-46
    development policies, 117
    multilingual
        response to challenges and, 95
    pressure to alter, 16
    representative, 13
    vulnerability of, 49-54, 113
    weeding from, 68-69
Collins, Jackie
    Girls in High Places, 102
    Hollywood Husbands, 102
Comfort, Alex
    The Joy of Sex, 40, 47, 48, 49, 102
    The Illustrated Joy of Sex, 47
    More Joy of Sex, 47, 48, 102
Comic books, 65
    covert censorship of, 102
Comics Notebook (periodical), 102
Committee on Undesirable Literature. *See under* Canadian Library Association
Committees, selection of materials by, 38
Community
    cultural mix in, censorship and, 120
    demands of, 13
    interests, and the library, 115
    knowledge of, 91-92
    language of, 35-36
    pressures, 12
    rights, 122-23
    values, 68, 120
The Companion (Siegel), 82
Complainants, 62-63, 81-82
Complaints. *See also* Challenges
    as censorship incidents, 22
    vs. challenges, 16, 22
    definition of, 15-16
    formal, 37
    forms for, 64
    verbal, 63, 82
    written, 63, 82
Compleat Mother (periodical), 106
Complete Guide to Punctuation, 72
Compulsory Parenthood (Watters), 70
Conference on Intellectual Freedom, 2nd, 13-14
Consent for minors. *See under* Parents

Controversial materials
    differential treatment of, 44-49
    labelling of
        effect of challenges on, 92
    potentially, 15
Controversial materials checklist, 25-26, 49-54, 113, 121
    ownership of titles, 51
        acquisition pressure and, 106
        differential treatment of materials and, 50, 51
        rates of challenges and, 61
        retention rates and, 85
Convard, D. *Les huit jours du diable dans "Super Tintin,"* 76
Conway, Flo. *Holy Terror*, 101
Cookies for Luke (Bleeks), 75
Cooper, Clarence L., jr. *The Farm*, 70
Cormier, Robert, 94
    The Chocolate War, 67
Corporation des bibliothécaires professionnels du Québec, 28
Councillors, as complainants, 62, 63
Covert censorship, 16, 99-103, 114-15
    covert challenges, definition of, 59
    definition of, 99
    incidents, rate of, 99
    reasons for, 99-100
    types of materials affected, 99
Coyne, John. *The Piercing*, 70
Crabbe (Bell), 76-77
Cracker Jackson (Byars), 74
Creationism, materials on
    pressure to acquire, 108, 114
Creepshow (King), 65 (table), 87, 89
Croc (periodical), 66 (table), 89
Crowley, Aleister. *Diary of a Drug Fiend*, 87
Crucial incidents, 23
Cudlipp, Edythe. *Furs*, 71
Cullum, Albert. *You Think Just Because You're Big You're Right*, 86
Cults, 100
Cults. *See* Religion
Cunningham, John. *A Way of Love, a Way of Life*, 66 (table), 79
Curious George (Rey), 95

D&D. *See* Dungeons and Dragons
Daddy is a Monster...Sometimes (Steptoe), 74, 86
Dahl, Roald, 67
    Dirty Beasts, 86
    The Enormous Crocodile, 66 (table), 77
    Roald Dahl's Revolting Rhymes, 78, 86
    The Witches, 74
Daley, Robert. *Hands of a Stranger*, 66 (table), 69
Dancer of Gor (Norman), 66 (table), 86
Dancers of Arun (Lynn), 102
Dark but Full of Diamonds (Lyle), 73
Darling, I Am Growing Old (Stone), 69
Davis, Adelle. *Let's Have Healthy Children*, 47-48
Davis, Gibbs. *The Other Emily*, 75
Davis, Gwen. *Romance*, 69
The Day We Bombed Utah (Fuller), 72
Dayee, F. *Private Zone*, 51 (table), 52 (table)
The Dead Bird (Brown), 75-76
Dear Garbageman (Zion), 78
Decision making, in resolving challenges, 84

Deenie (Blume), 66 (table), 67, 73
Defacement of materials
  access policies and, 48-49
  as censorship, 99
Defusing Censorship (Jones), 15-16
de la Salle, Bruno. *See* La Salle, Bruno de
Delaware Library Association. Intellectual Freedom and Open Access Committee, 22
The Devil Did It (Jeschke), 66 (table), 76, 86
Devils and Demons (Maple), 87
Devils in the Castle (Lareuse), 52 (tables)
Diamond, Harvey. *Fit for Life,* 72, 87
Diamond, Marilyn. *Fit for Life,* 72, 87
Dianetics (Hubbard), 108
Diary of a Drug Fiend (Crowley), 87
Dickinson, P. *City of Gold and Other Stories from the Old Testament,* 52 (table), 53
Did the Sun Shine Before You Were Born? (Gordon), 79, 86
Diet for a Strong Heart (Kushi), 72
Differential treatment of materials, 44-49, 113, 121. *See also* Classification of materials; Labelling of materials; Removal of materials; Shelving, differential; Withdrawal of materials
  acquisition pressure and, 105-106
  controversial materials ownership and, 50, 51
  rates of challenges and, 61
Dinner at Aunt Rose's (Munsil), 74
Direct challenges. *See* Overt challenges
Dirty Beasts (Dahl), 86
The Discipline of Raising Children (Treadwell), 70, 86
Diversity, of points of view, 13, 121
The Diviners (Laurence), 96
Dr. Abravanel's Body Type Program for Health, Fitness and Nutrition (Abravanel), 87
Dr. Seuss. *The Butter Battle Book,* 51 (table), 53, 65, 76
Doctors of Death, 103
A Doctor's Proven New Home Cure for Arthritis (Campbell), 72
Doerkson, M. *Jazzy,* 51 (table), 52 (table)
The Dog Crisis (Nowell), 71
Dolch, Edward. *Big Bigger Biggest,* 86
Donations
  acquisition pressure and, 106
  policy, and retention rates, 85
Donleavy, J.P. *Fairy Tales of New York,* 37, 66 (table), 69
Don't Hurt Me, Mama (Stanek), 66 (table), 73, 82
Don't Tell the Grownups (Lurie), 118-19
Draves, W. *The Word of the Lord Brought to Mankind by an Angel,* 71, 88
Drugs, materials on
  challenged, 65
  covert censorship of, 114
Duberman, Martin, 116
Due process, 122
  in collection challenges, 117
Dungeons and Dragons, 100, 114
Durand, René, 67 (table). *La Terre de la bombe,* 70

Eckankar, pressure to acquire materials on, 107
Eckankar: Compiled Writings, 71
Edmonton (proclaims Freedom to Read Week), 119
Edmonton Public Library, 26, 119

Elementary materials. *See* Children's elementary materials
Ellis, Bret Easton. *Less than Zero,* 70
Encyclopedia of Witchcraft and Magic (Newall), 102
Engel, Marian. *Bear,* 11, 65 (table), 69
England, Claire, 21, 22, 60
English-language institutions. *See also* Language of institution
  retention rates in, 85
English-language provinces. *See also* names of individual provinces and territories
  survey respondents in, 30
The Enormous Crocodile (Dahl), 66 (table), 77
Espy, William R. *A Children's Almanac of Words at Play,* 95
Evslin, Bernard. *Heraclea,* 73
The Exorcist, 41

Facing Up (Brancato), 46
Fairy Tales of New York (Donleavy), 37, 66 (table), 69
Families, depicted in children's books, 74-76
Family Secrets (Klein), 73
The Farm (Cooper), 70
Farmer, P. Jose. *Image of the Beast,* 88
Father Christmas (Briggs), 66 (table), 75, 87
Fatio, Louise. *Happy Lion,* 66 (table)
Fear and Loathing in Las Vegas (Thompson), 69
Fear of Flying (Jong), 51 (table), 53
Feliciter, coverage of freedom of expression in, 119
Fell's Guide to Doubling Performance of Your Car (Hampton), 86, 88
La femme piégée, 87
Ferry, J. *The Olson Murders,* 51 (table), 52 (table)
Fiction. *See also under* Adults; Children's fiction; Young adult fiction
  challenges against, 64
  covert censorship of, 114
Figure in the Shadows (Bellairs), 51 (table), 53
Fighting Slave of Gor (Norman), 70
Films, access to, 42
Fire Rose (Jeschke), 76
The First Deadly Sin (Sanders), 66 (table)
Fiske, Marjorie, 14-15, 21, 121
Fit for Life (Diamond and Diamond), 72, 87
Five Chinese Brothers (Bishop), 77
Flick (Kesselman), 73
Flowers in the Attic (Andrews), 51 (table), 65, 66 (table)
Foley, Louise Munro. *Somebody Stole Second,* 88
Follett, Ken. *Lie Down with Lions,* 101
Forever (Blume)
  challenges against, 26, 51 (table), 65, 66, 67
  differential treatment of, 40, 48
  intended audience of, 69
  reasons for challenges, 80
  results of challenges, 82, 85, 87
Forms
  for challenges, 38, 40
  for complaints, 64
A Fortunate Catastrophe (Turin), 77
Foster, M. *Not So Gay World,* 102
Fowke, Edith. *Sally Go Round the Sun,* 77
Fox, John. *The Boys on the Rock,* 73, 87
Francoeur, Lucien. *Les Rockeurs Sanctifiés,* 87, 100
Freddy's Book (Neufeld), 52 (tables), 52-53, 78

Freedom of choice, 14, 122. *See also under* Access
Freedom of expression, 122. *See also* Intellectual freedom
Freedom of Expression Committee (Book and Periodical Council)
 Bill C-54 and, 57
Freedom to Read: Don't Take It for Granted! (video), 119
Freedom to Read Week, 11-12, 119
Freemasonry, pressure to acquire materials on, 106
French-language institutions. *See also* Language of institution
 access policies and, 39
 controversial materials ownership and, 52
Friday, Nancy. *Men in Love,* 48, 70, 86
Frog Prince (Galdone), 78
Frost, Gavin and Yvonne. *A Witches' Grimoire,* 71, 100
Fuller, John G. *The Day We Bombed Utah,* 72
Fungus the Bogeyman (Briggs), 87, 91
Furs (Cudlipp), 71

Gag, Wanda. *Snow White and the Seven Dwarfs,* 77
Galdone, Paul, 67 (table)
 Frog Prince, 78
 The Greedy Old Fat Man, 77
Gantos, Jack. *The Werewolf Family,* 65 (table), 77, 86
Garden, Nancy. *Annie on My Mind,* 52, 73, 86, 91
Gardner, Joy. *Healing the Family,* 72, 87
Gay, Marie-Louise. *Lizzy's Lion*
 challenges against, 65 (table), 66, 115
 reasons for challenges, 80
 results of challenges, 82, 84, 86, 87
Gay and Lesbian Library Service (Gough and Greenblatt), 121
Gay Parenting (Schulenberg), 70
Gays. *See* Homosexuality
GED (General Education Development Test) study programs, 48
General systems theory (Bertalanffy), 120
Gerbils (Henrie), 79
Gipson, Fred. *Savage Sam,* 77
Girls and Boys Book of Etiquette (Hazen), 79, 88
Girls and Sex (Pomeroy), 41, 79
Girls in High Places (Collins), 102
Go Ask Alice, 67
Godard, Christian, 67 (table)
 Le Vagabond des Limbes, 87, 91
 The Vagabond of Limbo, 66 (table), 78, 87
Goffstein, M.B. *My Crazy Sister,* 75
Goldsmith, Sharon. *Human Sexuality,* 71
Goodbye Janette (Robbins), 51 (table), 52 (table)
Gordon, Sol, 67 (table)
 Did the Sun Shine Before You Were Born?, 79, 86
 The Teenage Survival Book, 79
Gorky Rises (Steig), 65 (table), 75
Gough, Cal. *Gay and Lesbian Library Service,* 121
The Greedy Old Fat Man (Galdone), 77
Greenberg, David. *Slugs,* 46, 65 (table), 66, 80-81, 82, 85
Greenblatt, Ellen. *Gay and Lesbian Library Service,* 121
Greene, Constance C., 67 (table)
 A(lexandra) the Great, 79
 I Know You, Al, 78
Greer, Germaine. *The Mad Woman's Underclothes,* 69
Groups. *See also* names of particular groups
 complaints from, 62, 63
Growing and Changing (McCoy), 46
Guide des caresses (Valinieff), 87

Guns Illustrated, 48
The Gunsmith series (Roberts), 65, 66 (table)

Haeberle, Erwin J. *The Sex Atlas,* 70
Hag Head (Musgrave), 48, 66 (table), 76
Haining, Peter. *Witchcraft and Black Magic,* 88
The Haj (Uris)
 challenges against, 51 (table), 65, 66
 reasons for challenges, 53, 81
 results of challenges against, 82, 85, 87
Halifax City Regional Library, 119
Hall, Carol. *I Been There,* 78
Hamilton, Wallace, 67 (table)
 Kevin, 11
Hamilton, William. *The Love of Rich Women,* 66 (table)
Hampton, William. *Fell's Guide to Doubling the Performance of
 Your Car,* 86, 88
Hanckel, Frances. *A Way of Love, a Way of Life,* 66 (table), 79
Handbook of Secret Organizations (Whalen), 102
Hands of a Stranger (Daley), 66 (table), 69
Happy Lion (Fatio), 66 (table)
Hare Krishna, 108
Harranth, Wolf. *My Old Grandad,* 75
Harris, Joel Chandler. *Uncle Remus,* 87
Harwood, Richard. *Nuremberg and Other War Crimes Trials,* 101
Hazen, Barbara. *Girls and Boys Book of Etiquette,* 79, 88
Healing the Family (Gardner), 72, 87
Health, materials on, 46-47, 48
Heart of the Country (Matthews), 70
Heavy metal groups, complaints regarding, 65
Hector Protector (Sendak), 74
Hemming, James, 46
Henrie, Fiona. *Gerbils,* 79
Heraclea (Evslin), 73
Hero and the Terror (Blodgett), 70
High Wire Spider (Swede), 75
Hinton, S.E., 94
Hirschhorn, Richard Clark. *A Pride of Healers,* 70
L'Histoire de Kiki Grabouille (Willis and Chamberlain), 87
Histoires fantastiques, 66 (table)
Hite, Shere. *The Hite Report,* 41
The Hite Report (Hite), 41
The Hoax of the Twentieth Century (Butz), 65 (table), 72, 88, 109
Hold Fast (Major), 51 (table)
Hollywood Husbands (Collins), 102
Holmes, Tom. *The Story of Henny Penny,* 66 (table), 77
The Holocaust: 120 Questions and Answers (Weber), 101
Holocaust revisionist materials, 48, 114
 acquisition pressure and, 109
Holy Blood Holy Grail (Baigent), 51 (table), 53
Holy Terror (Conway and Siegelman), 101
Homosexuality, materials on
 challenges to, 65
 differential treatment of, 49
Homosexuals, library service to, 121
Hoodoo Conjuration Witchcraft Rootwork (Hyatt), 82
Hopkins, Dianne McAfee, 21
 challenges vs. complaints, 16, 22
 rates of challenges, 60
 reasons for challenges, 68
 removal of materials, 83

retention rates and, 85
selection policies, 40, 84
titles challenged, 67
verbal vs. written challenges, 64
Hubbard, Ron. *Dianetics*, 108
Hughes, Douglas A. *Perspectives on Pornography*, 70
Les huit jours du diable dans "Super Tintin" (Convard), 76
Human Sexuality (Goldsmith), 71
Hunt, Beatrice Kohn. *Out of the Cauldron*, 79
Hyatt, Harry Middleton. *Hoodoo Conjuration Witchcraft Rootwork*, 82

I Am Joseph (Cohen), 51 (table)
I Been There (Hall), 78
I Know You, Al (Greene), 78
Ice Blues, 69
I'll Belly Your Button in a Minute (O'Huigin), 48
I'll Fix Anthony (Viorst), 66 (table), 76
The Illustrated Joy of Sex (Comfort), 47
Image of the Beast (Farmer), 88
Impressions reading series (Booth), 21
In the Night Kitchen (Sendak), 26, 51 (table), 65, 74, 102-3
Indian Summer (Monjo), 65 (table), 72, 77
Indirect challenges. *See* Covert challenges
Institute for Historical Review, 109
Institutions
    culture of, and censorship, 120
    governance of, and censorship, 120
    language of. *See* Language of institutions
    policies of
        effect of challenges on, 92
        in resolution of challenges, 83-84
        retention rates and, 85
    responding to survey, 35-36
Intellectual freedom
    Canadian Library Association and, 119
    community and, 15, 123
    management practices and, 37
    public awareness of, 92, 119-20
    public library community and, 119
Intellectual Freedom Manual (American Library Association), 15
Introducing Books to Children (Chambers), 120
Inventions, materials on
    pressure to acquire, 108
Inwood, D. *The Olson Murders*, 51 (table), 52 (table)
Ipcar, Dahlov. *The Cat Came Back*, 79
Iran, materials on
    covert censorship of, 100
Ireland (Uris and Uris), 72
Irwin, Hadley. *Abby, My Love*, 74
Israel, materials on
    covert censorship of, 100
It's Not What You'd Expect (Klein), 73
It's Okay if You Don't Love Me (Klein), 51 (table)

J'accuse ma ... de victorien Theoret [?], 109
Jackson, Shirley [title not specified], 100
Jacobs, Anita. *Where Has Deedie Wooster Been All These Years?*, 66 (table), 74
Jacques the Woodcutter (Macklem), 48
Jaenssen, Haken. *Charlie's Pillow*, 76

Jazzy (Doerkson), 51 (table), 52 (table)
Jehovah's Witnesses, acquisition pressure and, 106, 107, 108
Jenkinson, David, 21, 22, 89
Jeschke, Susan
    The Devil Did It, 66 (table), 76, 86
    Fire Rose, 76
Jessel, Camilla. *The Joy of Birth*, 79
Jewish-Nazi relations in literature, covert censorship of, 101
Jim Who Ran Away from His Nurse and Was Eaten by a Lion (Belloc), 74
Johnson, C. and E. Johnson. *Love and Sex and Growing Up*, 52 (table)
Johnson, Mendal W. *Let's Go Play at Adam's*, 76, 86
Johnson, Virginia E. and William H. Masters. *Masters & Johnson on Sex & Human Loving*, 108
Johnstone, William W. *The Nursery*, 88
Joint public/school library facilities
    access policies and, 48
    response to challenges in, 95
Jones, Frances M. *Defusing Censorship*, 15-16
Jones, Harold. *Tale to Tell*, 77
Jong, E. *Fear of Flying*, 51 (table), 53
The Joy of Birth (Jessel), 79
The Joy of Life (Kingdon), 87
The Joy of Sex (Comfort), 40, 47, 48, 49, 102
Juggling (Lehrman), 66 (table), 74
Jump from the Sky, 77-78
Jurisdictions. *See also* names of individual provinces and territories
    access policies in, 39-40
    acquisition pressure in, 106
    controversial materials ownership by, 51-52
    effects of challenges in, 92
    rates of challenges in, 61
    rates of covert incidents in, 99
The Just Right Family, 75
"Justifiable" censorship, 89

Kane and Abel (Archer), 102
Kansan (Mills), 11
Katz, Welwyn Wilton. *Witchery Hill*, 66 (table), 87
Kaye, Geraldine. *The Rotten Old Car*, 75
Kaye, Marilyn. *Will You Cross Me*, 75
Keegstra (Mertl and Ward), 72, 101
Keene, Carolyn. *Nancy Drew*, 45
Kellogg, Steven. *Won't Somebody Play with Me*, 78
Kelly, Gary F. *Learning About Sex*, 79
Kesselman, Wendy. *Flick*, 73
Kevin (Hamilton), 11
Kim, Ashida, 67 (table)
    Ninja Death Touch, 71, 86
    Secrets of the Ninja, 71, 87
King, Stephen, 38. *Creepshow*, 65, 87, 89
King of the Cats (Jacobs), 66 (table)
King Stork (Pyle), 66 (table), 77
Kingdon, Alan. *The Joy of Life*, 87
Kiss Daddy Goodnight (Armstrong), 70
Kitzinger. *Woman's Experience of Sex*, 48
Klein, Norma, 67
    Beginner's Love, 73, 102
    Blue Trees, Red Sky, 65 (table), 78
    Family Secrets, 73

Klein, Norma (*cont.*)
   It's Not What You'd Expect, 73
   It's Okay if You Don't Love Me, 51 (table)
   Love is One of the Choices, 46
   Naomi in the Middle, 65 (table), 73, 87, 89
   Queen of What If, 82
Knives Illustrated, 48
Knowing About Sex (Hemming), 46
Koontz, Dean, 38
Kosinski, J. *The Painted Bird,* 51 (table)
Krantz, Judith. *Princess Daisy,* 70
Kropp, Paul, 93
Kueshana, Eklal. *The Ultimate Frontier,* 86
Kushi, Michio. *Diet for a Strong Heart,* 72

Là-bas (comic book), 87, 88
Labelling of controversial materials, 49, 81-82
   effect of challenges on, 92
Lambs for Dinner (Maestro), 52 (tables), 53
Lamia (Travis), 86
Lamont, Stewart. *Religion Inc.,* 66 (table), 71
Lampoon, 87
Language of institution
   access policies and, 39
   Bill C-54 and, 54
   children's access in, 41
   controversial materials ownership and, 50, 52
   differential treatment of materials and, 44
   rates of challenges and, 61
   survey responses and, 35-36
Lareuse, J. *Devils in the Castle,* 52 (tables)
La Salle, Bruno de. *Le petit chaperon rouge,* 74, 86
The Last Puppy (Asch), 74
Laurence, Margaret. *The Diviners,* 96
Lauzier [?], 67 (table)
Learning about Sex (Aho), 79
Learning about Sex (Kelly), 79
Learning to Read Music (Lilienfeld), 100
Lee, Dennis. *Lizzy's Lion*
   challenges against, 65 (table), 66, 115
   reasons for challenges, 80
   results of challenges, 82, 84, 86, 87
Lehrman, Robert. *Juggling,* 66 (table), 74
Lenski, Lois. *Let's Play House,* 77
Lesbians. *See* Homosexuality; Homosexuals
Less than Zero (Ellis), 70
Let's Go Play at Adam's (Johnson), 76, 86
Let's Have Healthy Children (Davis), 47-48
Let's Play House (Lenski), 77
Let's Visit Pakistan, 101
Levine, Sylvia and Joseph Koenig. *Why Men Rape,* 47-48
Levoy, Myron. *Alan and Naomi,* 78
Liberty and Learning in the Schools (American Association of University Professors), 118
Libraries. *See* Institutions; Public libraries
Library Association of Alberta. Intellectual Freedom Committee, 119
Library materials. *See* Materials
Library staff. *See* Staff
Library trustees, as complainants, 62, 63
Lichtey, R. *132 Ways to Earn a Living without Working for Someone Else,* 71

Lie Down with Lions (Follett), 101
Life (periodical), 71
Lilienfeld, Robert. *Learning to Read Music,* 100
Lindgren, Astrid. *The Brothers Lionheart,* 75, 86
Linguistic grouping. *See* Language of institution
Littke, Lael. *Trish for President,* 11
Little Black Sambo (Bannerman), 46, 78
Lizzy's Lion (Lee)
   challenges against, 65 (table), 66, 115
   reasons for challenges, 80
   results of challenges, 82, 84, 86, 87
Locksmithing, materials on
   complaints regarding, 48
Love and Sex and Growing Up, 52 (table)
Love is One of the Choices (Klein), 46
The Love of Rich Women (Hamilton), 66 (table)
Lovelace, Linda. *Ordeal,* 51 (table), 66 (table), 70, 102
Lurie, Alison. *Don't Tell the Grownups,* 118-19
Lyle, Katie Letcher. *Dark but Full of Diamonds,* 73
Lynn, Elizabeth. *Dancers of Arun,* 102

McBride, Will. *Show Me,* 48, 102
McCoy, Kathy, 46
   The Teenage Body Book, 51 (table), 52 (table)
McGrady, M. *Ordeal,* 51 (table)
McKee, Richard, 121
Macklem, Michael. *Jacques the Woodcutter,* 48
McNeill, Elizabeth. *Nine and a Half Weeks,* 86
McPhail, David. *A Wolf Story,* 78
The Mad Woman's Underclothes (Greer), 69
Madden, Susan, 119
Madonna. *Sex,* 119
Maestro, Betsy. *Lambs for Dinner,* 52 (tables), 53
Magic, materials on
   complaints regarding, 65
Maia (Adams), 69
Major, Kevin, 11, 65, 67
   Hold Fast, 51 (table),
Malinowski, Bronislaw. *The Sexual Life of Savages in North-Western Melanesia,* 101
Malloy, Judy. *Bad Thad,* 75
Man and Woman: Encyclopedia of Adult Relationships, 48
The Man with Seven Toes (Ondaatje), 70
Manera, Milo, 67 (table)
Manitoba
   challenges in, 21, 22
   public library governance in, 29
   rates of challenges in, 61, 62
   rate of covert incidents in, 99
   school libraries
      reasons for challenges, 68
   survey respondents in, 30
   withdrawal of materials in, 83
Mann, Ron. *The Punch and Judy Book,* 77
Maple, Eric, 67 (table)
   Devils and Demons, 87
The Maple Laugh Forever (Barbour), 72
Mark, Jan. *Out of the Oven,* 65 (table), 76
Marmouset et Makumba (Tourneur), 87
Martin, Jacques. *Barbe-bleue,* 74, 88
Martinez, Alberto. *Vans,* 71
Mass media. *See* Media

Masters & Johnson on Sex & Human Loving (Masters and Johnson), 108
Masters, William H. and Virginia E. Johnson. *Masters & Johnson on Sex & Human Loving*, 108
Materials. *See also under* Adults; Children; Young adult
　access to. *See* Access policies
　acquisition guidelines for, 15
　circulation rates
　　survey responses and, 30
　controversial. *See* Controversial materials
　demand for
　　influence on acquisition and selection, 45
　differential treatment of. *See* Differential treatment of materials
　language of, and response to survey, 35-36
　pressure to add, 16
　pressure to remove/restrict, 16
　removal of, 12, 82
　restriction of access to. *See under* Access
　selection of. *See* Selection of materials
　separate areas for, 40
　types challenged, 64-67
　　retention rates of, 85-86
　types most affected in covert censorship, 99
　withdrawal of, 82
Matthews, Greg. *Heart of the Country,* 70
Mayle, Peter, 67 (table)
　What's Happening to Me?, 65 (table), 79
　Where Did I Come From?, 11, 65 (table), 66-67, 81, 82, 85, 86
Measurement of Melody (Millar), 100
Media
　censorship issues and the, 120
　coverage of challenges, 84
　　and retention rates of materials, 85
　　and withdrawal of materials, 87
　non-print, challenges against, 64
Meeting the Mormons (Roundhill), 71, 86
Men in Love (Friday), 48, 70, 86
Menstruation, materials on
　complaints regarding, 11
Merritt, LeRoy Charles. *Book Selection and Intellectual Freedom,* 14
Mertl, Steve. *Keegstra,* 72, 101
Millar, G. *Measurement of Melody,* 100
Milligan, Spike. *Badjelly the Witch,* 78
Mills, Robert E. *Kansan,* 11
Mine's the Best (Bonsall), 76
Minors. *See also* Children; Young adults
　access restrictions on, 42
　intellectual freedom policy for, 117
　parental consent for. *See under* Parents
Missile Envy (Caldicott), 101
Mr. and Mrs. Pig's Evening Out (Rayner), 65 (table), 77
Mr. Chips 101 Plans, 48
Mon corps est à elles (Wolinski), 86, 87
Monjo, F.N. *Indian Summer,* 65 (table), 72, 77
More Joy of Sex (Comfort), 47, 48, 49, 102
Morgentaler (Pelrine), 101
Mormon Church, materials on
　covert censorship of, 100
Mormons, acquisition pressure and, 108

Moses—The Escape from Egypt (Butcher), 76
Ms (periodical), 70
Multi-branch systems, 29
　access policies and, 39
　acquisition pressure and, 105
　censorship research and, 23
　children's access in, 41
　controversial materials ownership and, 50
　differential treatment of materials in, 44
　rates of challenges and, 60-61
　rate of covert incidents in, 99
　response to Bill C-54, 54
　retention rates in, 85
　survey responses and, 27, 35, 36
Multilingual collections
　response to challenges and, 95
Municipalities, population of. *See also* Small communities
　access policies and, 39
　acquisition pressure and, 105
　density, and survey responses, 35
　differential treatment of materials and, 44
　opposition to Bill C-54 and, 54
　rates of challenges and size of, 60-62
　and retention rates, 85
　size, and survey responses, 36
Munsil, Janet. *Dinner at Auntie Rose's,* 74
Murphy, Eddie, 45
Murder in the Family (Brandel), 66 (table), 86, 87
Muscle building, materials on
　covert censorship of, 114
Musgrave, Susan. *Hag Head,* 48, 66 (table), 76
My Crazy Sister (Goffstein), 75
My Old Grandad (Harranth), 75

Nancy Drew series (Carolyn Keene), 45
Naomi in the Middle (Klein), 65 (table), 73, 87, 89
National Commission on Libraries and Information Science. *Censorship Activities in Public and Public School Libraries,* 12
National Film Board. *Soap-Box Derby,* 78
National Lampoon (periodical), 86, 90
Natural Motherhood (periodical), 109
Nazism, materials on
　covert censorship of, 114
Nerves in Collision (Alvarez), 72, 87
Neufeld, John. *Freddy's Book,* 52 (tables), 52-53, 78
New Brunswick
　access policies in, 40
　acquisition pressure in, 106
　effect of challenges in, 92
　public library governance in, 29
　rates of challenges in, 62
　rate of covert incidents in, 99
New Friend (Zolotow), 75
New Internationalist (periodical), 72, 88
Newall, V. *Encyclopedia of Witchcraft and Magic,* 102
Newfoundland
　access policies in, 40
　public library governance in, 29
　rates of challenges in, 61, 62
　rate of covert incidents in, 99
Nightmares: Poems to Trouble Your Sleep (Prelutsky), 11

Nine and a Half Weeks (McNeill), 86
Ninja Death Touch (Kim), 71, 86
No Sense of Evil (Barros), 72
Non-fiction
    adult, challenges against, 70-73
    children's, 78-79
    weeding of, 69
    young adult, 78-79
Non-print media, challenges against, 64
Norman, John, 67 (table)
    Dancer of Gor, 66 (table), 86
    Fighting Slave of Gor, 70
Northwest Territories
    access policies in, 40
    acquisition pressure in, 106
    controversial materials ownership in, 52
    effect of challenges in, 92
    public library governance in, 29
    rates of challenges in, 61, 62
    rate of covert incidents in, 99
Nory, Jean-Loup. *Vans*, 71
Nostradamus Prophecies, 100
Not So Gay World (Foster), 102
Nothing in Common (Bottner), 74
Nova Scotia
    public library governance in, 29
    rates of challenges in, 62
    rate of covert incidents in, 99
Novels, covert censorship of, 114
Now (periodical), 66 (table)
Nowell, Iris. *The Dog Crisis*, 71
Nuremberg and Other War Crimes Trials (Harwood), 101
The Nursery (Johnstone), 88

Oakley, Graham, 67 (table). *The Church Mice at Bay*, 76
Objections. *See* Challenges
Occult, materials on
    challenges against, 65
    complaints against, 76
    covert censorship of, 100, 114
    pressure to acquire, 108
Offending material. *See* Controversial materials
O'Huigin, Sean. *I'll Belly Your Button in a Minute*, 48
The Olson Murders (Ferry and Inwood), 51 (table), 52 (table)
Ondaatje, Michael. *The Man with Seven Toes*, 70
101 Uses for a Cabbage Patch Head Doll, 101
132 Ways to Earn a Living without Working for Someone Else (Rosenthal and Lichtey), 71
One on One (Seigel), 75
Ontario
    access policies in, 40
    controversial materials ownership in, 52
    public libraries
        censorship in, 60
    public library governance in, 29
    rates of challenges in, 61, 62
    rate of covert incidents in, 99
Ontario Library Association
    Statement on the Intellectual Rights of the Individual, 151 (reproduced)
Ordeal (Lovelace), 51 (table), 66 (table), 70, 102

Oregon Intellectual Freedom Clearinghouse, 22
The Other Emily (Davis), 75
Our Bodies, Ourselves, 41, 43
Out of the Cauldron (Hunt), 79
Out of the Oven (Mark), 65 (table), 76
Outside Over There (Sendak), 65 (table), 66-67, 81, 82, 85
Overt challenges, 16, 59-97, 114
    definition of, 59
    rates of, 59-62

The Painted Bird (Kosinski), 51 (table)
Palestinians, materials on
    covert censorship of, 100
Parapsychology, materials on
    challenges against, 65
Parents
    as complainants, 62-63
    consent, for minors, 41, 43-44, 118
        acquisition pressure and, 105
        retention rates and, 85
Paris Match (periodical), 87
Parker, Robert. *Taming a Sea-Horse*, 69
Parrott, E.O. *The Penguin Book of Limericks*, 66 (table), 71, 87
Pascal, Francine. *Sweet Valley High* series, 38
Patron access. *See* Access policies
Paulette (Pichard and Wolinski), 86, 87
Pelrine, Eleanor Wright
    Abortion in Canada, 72
    Morgentaler, 101
The Penguin Book of Limericks, 66 (table), 71, 87
Pennington's Heir (Peyton), 75
Pentecostals, acquisition pressure and, 106
Perrault, Charles. *Tom Thumb*, 74
Perspectives on Pornography (Hughes), 70
Peterson, Joyce. *Adultery for Adults*, 71
Le Petit chaperon rouge (La Salle), 74, 86
Le Petit chien (Prignaud), 75
Petit et grand Albert, 86
Peyton, K.M. *Pennington's Heir*, 75
Phillips, Edward. *Buried on Sunday*, 69
Pichard, Georges. *Paulette*, 86, 87
The Piercing (Coyne), 70
Pinkwater, Daniel, 67 (table)
The Plain Truth, 106, 108
Playboar (periodical), 70, 87
Playboy (periodical), 70, 91, 96
Poilus, Vélus, Barbus (Cole), 87
Political groups, acquisition pressure from, 106, 109-10
Political materials, covert censorship of, 100-1, 114
Pomeroy, Wardell B
    Boys and Sex, 41
    Girls and Sex, 41, 79
Pope, Michael. *Sex and the Undecided Librarian*, 117
Poppel, Norman, 120
Popular novels, covert censorship of, 101-2, 114
Population
    of censorship research, 23
    of municipalities. *See under* Municipalities
    of survey, 26
Potentially controversial materials. *See* Controversial materials checklist

Potok, Chaim. *Wanderings,* 93
Prelutsky, Jack, 67 (table)
    Nightmares: Poems to Trouble Your Sleep, 11
Prestin, John. *Safe Sex,* 47
Preussen, von den Anfangen bis zur Reichsgründung, 72
A Pride of Healers (Hirschhorn), 70
Prignaud, Jean. *Le petit chien,* 75
Prince (poster of), 79
Prince Edward Island
    access policies in, 40
    acquisition pressure in, 106
    controversial materials ownership in, 52
    effect of challenges in, 92
    public library governance in, 29
    rates of challenges in, 61, 62
    rate of covert incidents in, 99
Princess Daisy (Krantz), 70
Private Zone (Dayee), 51 (table), 52 (table)
Profanity in literature
    complaints about, 78
Pro-choice groups. *See* Abortion
Pro-life groups
    acquisition pressure and, 106-8
Pro-Life Society, 107
Pryor, Richard. *Bicentennial Nigger,* 71
Public libraries
    freedom of choice and, 14
    governance of, 28-29, 113
    institutional culture of, 120
    joint public/school facilities, 95
    materials. *See* Materials
    purpose of, 13
    responding, 35-36
    response to Bill C-54, 54
    social change and political values, 14
    staff. *See* Staff
Publishing industry
    censorship issues and, 120
The Punch and Judy Book (Mann), 77
Pyle, Howard. *King Stork,* 66 (table), 77

Quebec Library Association, 28
Quebec (province)
    access policies in, 40
    controversial materials ownership in, 52
    public library governance in, 29
    rate of covert incidents in, 99
    survey respondents in, 30
Queen of What If (Klein), 82
A Question of Race (Birch), 79
Questionnaire, pre-testing of, 26
Quinn, Carl Underhill. *Adolf Hitler: Pictures from the Life of the Führer,* 72

Racism in literature, 121
    challenges against, 77-78
Rage of Angels (Sheldon), 102
Rajneeshism, materials on
    pressure to acquire, 106
Ramïoli. *La terre de la bombe,* 70
The Rapist File (Sussman), 66 (table), 71, 87, 102

Rayner, Claire. *The Body Book,* 79, 102
Rayner, Mary. *Mr. and Mrs. Pig's Evening Out,* 65 (table), 77
Reader response theory, censorship and, 120
Reading, effect on attitudes and behaviour, 120
Reading, J.P. *Bouquets for Brimbal,* 73
Reclassification of material. *See* Classification of materials
Registered borrowers. *See* Borrowers, registered
Religion
    in literature
        complaints against, 76
    materials on
        covert censorship of, 100, 114
Religion Inc. (Lamont), 66 (table), 71
Religious groups
    acquisition pressure and, 106-7, 108
Relocation of offending material. *See* Classification of materials; Shelving, differential
Removal of materials, 81-82. *See also* Withdrawal of materials
    acquisition pressure and, 105
    requests for
        acquisition pressure and, 106
    temporary, of challenged materials, 83
Reproduction (Vevers), 87
Responses to survey, 27-31
Restricted access, age-based. *See* Age-related access restrictions
Retention rates, of challenged materials, 85-86
Revisionism, Holocaust, 48
    acquisition pressure and, 109
Rey, H.A. *Curious George,* 95
Ribera, Julio, 67 (table)
    Le Vagabond des Limbes, 87, 91
    The Vagabond of Limbo, 66 (table), 78, 87
Richmond, Sandra. *Wheels for Walking,* 74
Roald Dahl's Revolting Rhymes (Dahl), 78, 86
Robbins, Harold, 65, 67, 101
    Goodbye Janette, 51 (table)
    The Storyteller, 70
Roberts, J.R. *The Gunsmith* series, 65, 66 (table)
Roberts, Oral, 107
Les Rockeurs Sanctifiés (Francoeur), 87, 100
Rockwell, T. *The Thief,* 52 (tables)
Rogers, Edward. *Algonkians of the Eastern Woodlands,* 86
Rohmer, Richard. *Starmageddon,* 101
Roiphe, Herman. *Your Child's Mind,* 71
Romance (Davis), 69
Romances, covert censorship of, 114
Rosenthal, E. *132 Ways to Earn a Living without Working for Someone Else,* 71
Rosicrucians, acquisition pressure and, 106
Ross, Malcolm, 67 (table)
    Spectre of Power, 72, 87
    Web of Deceit, 65 (table), 72, 87, 101
The Rotten Old Car (Kaye), 75
Roundhill, Jack. *Meeting the Mormons,* 71, 86
Rubel, Nicole. *The Werewolf Family,* 65 (table), 77, 86
Run, Shelley, Run (Samuels), 73
Ryder, the Tong Wars (Weston), 88

Safe Sex (Prestin), 47
Sally Go Round the Sun (Fowke), 77
Samuels, Gertrude. *Run, Shelley, Run,* 73

Sanders, Lawrence, 67 (table)
    The First Deadly Sin, 66 (table)
Saskatchewan
    access policies in, 40
    acquisition pressure in, 106
    controversial materials ownership in, 52
    public library governance in, 29
    rates of challenges in, 61, 62
    rate of covert incidents in, 99
    survey respondents in, 29
Saskatchewan Library Association
    statement on intellectual freedom, 152 (reproduced)
Satanic Bible, 100
Savage Sam (Gipson), 77
Scary Stories to Tell in the Dark (Schwartz), 66 (table)
Scheer, Robert. *With Enough Shovels*, 101
School libraries
    censorship research in, 21
    rates of challenges in, 60
    selection policies in, 40
School Library Journal, 66, 121
School staff
    complaints from, 62, 63
School-housed facilities, 35. *See also* Joint public/school library facilities
Schools on Trial: A Positive Alternative, 108
Schulenberg, Joy. *Gay Parenting*, 70
Schwartz, Alvin, 67 (table)
    Scary Stories to Tell in the Dark, 66 (table)
Schwartz, Herbert T. *Tales from the Smokehouse*, 48, 79, 88
Schwartz, Joel L. *Upchuck Summer*, 66 (table)
Science and the Supernatural (Taylor), 100
Scientology. *See* Church of Scientology
Secrets of the Ninja (Kim), 71, 87
Seigel, Jerry. *One on One*, 75
Selection of materials, 15
    vs. censorship, 13, 89
    by committee, 38
    effect of challenges on, 92
    policies, 37-40, 38-39
        acquisition pressure and, 105, 106
        and challenges to content, 68
        response to challenges and, 91
    prior restraint in, 31
    selectors vs. users, 14
    self-censorship in, 44-45
Self-censorship, 12, 31, 121. *See also* Censorship
    checklists and, 26
    in selection of materials, 44-45, 117
    studies of, 21
Sendak, Maurice, 67
    Hector Protector, 74
    In the Night Kitchen, 26, 51 (table), 65, 74, 102-3
    Outside Over There, 65 (table), 66-67, 81, 82, 85
    Seven Little Monsters, 87
    Some Swell Pup, 76
Serebnick, Judith, 13
Seuling, Barbara. *The Teeny Tiny Woman*, 77
Seven Little Monsters (Sendak), 87
Sex, 114. *See also* Sex education
    and violence, 113

Sex (Madonna), 119
Sex and the Undecided Librarian (Pope), 117
The Sex Atlas (Haeberle), 70
Sex education, 114, 118
Sexism in literature
    challenges against, 77-78
Sexual abuse, materials on
    restrictions on, 118
Sexual depictions, in adult fiction, 69-70
The Sexual Life of Savages in North-Western Melanesia (Malinowski), 101
The Sexual Side of Love, 48
Sheldon, Sydney. *Rage of Angels*, 102
Shelving, differential. *See also* Differential treatment of materials
    children's access restrictions and, 47
    for controversial materials, 46
Shennon, Victoria. *Ben*, 75
Show Me (McBride), 48, 102
Siegel, Scott. *The Companion*, 82
Siegelman, Jim. *Holy Terror*, 101
Single-unit libraries, 29
    access policies in, 39
    acquisition pressure in, 105
    children's access in, 41
    controversial materials ownership in, 50
    differential treatment of materials in, 44
    rates of challenges in, 60-61
    response to Bill C-54, 54
    survey responses from, 35, 36
Slang dictionaries, 48
Slugs (Greenberg), 46, 65 (table), 66, 80-81, 82, 85
Small communities. *See also* Municipalities
    and minors' access restrictions, 42
    response to challenges in, 95-96
Smedley, A. *Chinese Destiny*, 52 (table)
Snow White and the Seven Dwarfs (Gag), 77
Soap-Box Derby (National Film Board), 78
Social class, controversial materials ownership and, 53
Social learning theory, censorship and, 120-21
Some Swell Pup (Sendak), 76
Somebody Stole Second (Foley), 88
South African Digest, 87
Spectre of Power (Ross), 72, 87
"Sponge theory," of reading, 120
The Spotlight (periodical), 109-110
Staff. *See also* School staff
    children's access restrictions and, 41
    as complainants, 62, 63
    in loco parentis, 42-43, 82, 118
    institutional policies and, 37
    requests for punishment of, 81-82
    response to challenges, 83-86
    response to pressures, 12
    training of, and response to complaints, 37
Stanek, Muriel. *Don't Hurt Me, Mama*, 66 (table), 73, 82
Starmageddon (Rohmer), 101
Starring Sally J. Freedman as Herself (Blume), 66 (table), 74, 78
State control, 118
Steig, William, 67 (table). *Gorky Rises*, 65 (table), 75
Steptoe, John. *Daddy is a Monster...Sometimes*, 74, 86
Stevenson, Robert Louis. *A Child's Garden of Verses*, 78

Stokes, Naomi. *The Castrated Woman,* 72
Stone, Gene. *Darling, I Am Growing Old,* 69
The Story of Henny Penny (Holmes), 66 (table), 77
The Storyteller (Robbins), 70
Strasser, Todd. *Angel Dust Blues,* 65 (table), 67, 74
Suddon, A. *Cinderella,* 51 (table), 53
Suicide: Directions, 45
Survey
    controversial materials checklist. *See* Controversial materials checklist
    limitations of, 31
    non-respondents, 31
    participation rates of jurisdictions, 30
    population of, 26
    questionnaire, 25, 129-44 (reproduced)
    responses to, 27-31, 159-60 (reproduced)
    study questions, 19-20
Sussman, Les. *The Rapist File,* 66 (table), 71, 87, 102
Swaggart, Jimmy, 107
Swede, George. *High Wire Spider,* 75
Sweet Valley High series (Pascal), 38
Swindoll, Charles. *You and Your Child,* 41, 43

Tale to Tell (Jones), 77
Tales from the Smokehouse (Schwartz), 48, 79, 88
Taming a Sea-Horse (Parker), 69
Taylor, T. *Science and the Supernatural,* 100
Teddybear Postman (Worthington), 77
The Teenage Body Book (McCoy and Wibbelsman), 51 (table), 52 (table)
The Teenage Survival Book (Gordon), 79
Teenagers. *See* Young adults
The Teeny Tiny Woman (Seuling), 77
Tell Me, Grandma, Tell Me, Grandpa, 73
La Terre de la bombe (Ramïoli and Durand), 70
Theft of materials
    access policies and, 48-49
    as censorship, 99
Then Again, Maybe I Won't (Blume), 46, 51 (table)
The Thief (Rockwell), 52 (tables)
This is South Africa, 100
This is the Cocker Spaniel (Whitney), 72, 88
Thomas Is Different (Wolde), 78
Thompson, Hunter S. *Fear and Loathing in Las Vegas,* 69
Thunder Bay Public Library, 119
Thurman, Mark. *Two Stupid Dummies,* 76
Time coverage, in censorship research, 22
Time required for resolution of challenges, 84
The Tin-Pot Foreign General and the Old Iron Woman (Briggs), 65 (table), 73, 74
Titles. *See also* specific titles
    challenged, 64-67, 169-74 (complete list)
    withdrawn, 86-89
TM, acquisition pressure and, 106
Tom Fox and the Apple Pie (Watson), 75
Tom Thumb (Perrault), 74
Torture Tomb (Andersson), 88
Tourneur, Dina-K. *Marmouset et Makumba,* 87
Tranches de vie, 66 (table)
Transcendental Meditation. *See* TM
Travis, Tristan. *Lamia,* 86

Treadwell, M.A. *The Discipline of Raising Children,* 70, 86
Trish for President (Littke), 11
Trubo, Richard. *An Act of Mercy,* 72, 86, 88
The True Cross (Wildsmith), 51 (table), 52 (table)
Trust Betrayed (Bercuson and Wertheimer), 95
Trustees, library
    as complainants, 62, 63
Turin, Adela. *A Fortunate Catastrophe,* 77
Twisted Sister, 65, 67
Two Stupid Dummies (Thurman), 76

UFOs (Unidentified Flying Objects), pressure to acquire materials on, 108
The Ultimate Frontier (Kueshana), 86
Uncle Remus: His Songs and His Sayings (Harris), 87
Understanding Your Child from Birth to Three (Church), 71
Ungerer, Tomi, 67 (table). *The Beast of Monsieur Racine,* 65 (table), 76
United Church Newsletter, 73
Universal Declaration of Human Rights, 122
Unlucky Wally (Briggs), 70
Unspeakable Acts (Bond), 71
Upchuck Summer (Schwartz), 66 (table)
Uris, Jill and Leon Uris. *Ireland,* 72
Uris, Leon. *The Haj*
    challenges against, 51 (table), 65, 66
    reasons for challenges, 53, 81
    results of challenges, 82, 85, 87
Usborne, Peter. *Witches,* 87
Users of materials vs. selectors, 14

Le Vagabond des Limbes (Godard and Ribera), 87, 91
The Vagabond of Limbo (Godard and Ribera), 66 (table), 78, 87
Valarie (Benton), 66 (table)
Valinieff, Pierre. *Guide des caresses,* 87
Valley of the Horses (Auel), 49, 51 (table)
Values
    community, 68
    literature and, 120
Vans (Martinez and Nory), 71
Verbal challenges. *See under* Challenges
La ... vérité (periodical), 109
Vevers, Gwynne. *Reproduction,* 87
Videocassettes
    patron access to, 42
Violence in literature
    complaints against, 76-77
Viorst, Judith. *I'll Fix Anthony,* 66 (table), 76

Walker, Keith, 22
Wallechinsky, D. *Book of Predictions,* 100
Wanderings (Potok), 93
Ward, John. *Keegstra,* 101
Washington Conference on Intellectual Freedom, 14
Washington (state), challenges in, 22
Watchtower, 108
Watson, Clyde. *Tom Fox and the Apple Pie,* 75
Watters, Wendell. *Compulsory Parenthood,* 70
A Way of Love, a Way of Life (Hanckel and Cunningham), 66 (table), 79
Web of Deceit (Ross), 65 (table), 72, 87, 101

Weber, Charles E. *The Holocaust: 120 Questions and Answers,* 101
Webster's New Collegiate Dictionary, 11, 87
Weeding of materials, 68-69, 89. *See also* Removal of materials; Withdrawal of materials
    vs. censorship, 89
The Werewolf Family (Gantos and Rubel), 65 (table), 77, 86
Wertheimer, Douglas and David Bercuson. *Trust Betrayed,* 95
Western Guard (newspaper), 109
Westerns, 65, 94
    covert censorship of, 101, 114
Weston, Cole. *Ryder, the Tong Wars,* 88
Whalen, William J. *Handbook of Secret Organizations,* 102
What's Best for You (Angell), 74
What's Happening to Me (Mayle), 65 (table), 79
Wheels for Walking (Richmond), 74
When the New Baby Comes, I'm Moving Out (Alexander), 75
When the Wind Blows (Briggs), 87
Where Did I Come From? (Mayle), 11, 65 (table), 66-67, 81, 82, 85, 86
Where Has Deedie Wooster Been All These Years? (Jacobs), 66 (table), 74
Whitney, Leon F. *This is the Cocker Spaniel,* 72, 88
Why Men Rape (Levine and Koenig), 47-48
Wibbelsman, C. *The Teenage Body Book,* 51 (table), 52 (table)
Wifey (Blume)
    challenges against, 26, 51 (table)
    differential treatment of, 40, 42, 49
    intended audience of, 69, 80, 82, 85
    reasons for challenges, 80
    results of challenges, 82, 85, 87
Wildsmith, B. *The True Cross,* 51 (table), 53
Will You Cross Me (Kaye), 75
Willis, Jeanne. *L'Histoire de Kiki Grabouille,* 87
Witchcraft
    in literature for children and young adults
        complaints against, 76
    materials on
        challenges to, 65
        covert censorship of, 100, 114
Witchcraft and Black Magic (Haining), 88
Witchery Hill (Katz), 66 (table), 87
Witches (Usborne), 87
The Witches (Dahl), 74
A Witches' Grimoire (Frost and Frost), 71, 100
With Enough Shovels (Scheer), 101
Withdrawal of materials, 83, 86-89. *See also* Removal of materials; Weeding of materials
    permanent, reasons for challenges and, 84

Wolde, Gunilla. *Thomas Is Different,* 78
A Wolf Story (McPhail), 78
Wolinski, Georges, 67 (table)
    Mon corps est à elles, 86, 87
    Paulette, 86, 87
Woman Alive (series), 48
Woman's Experience of Sex (Kitzinger), 48
Won't Somebody Play with Me (Kellogg), 78
The Word of the Lord Brought to Mankind by an Angel (Draves), 71, 88
Worlin, Arne. *Charlie's Pillow,* 76
Worthington, Phoebe. *Teddybear Postman,* 77
Wright, Freire. *Adventures of Tom,* 77
Writers Guild of Alberta, 119

You and Your Child (Swindoll), 41, 43
You Think Just Because You're Big You're Right (Cullum), 86
Young adult fiction, complaints about, 73-78
Young adult literature
    censorship of, 21
    responding libraries, 35-36
    suitability of, 69
Young adult non-fiction, 78-79
Young adult sections, effect of challenges on, 93-94
Young adults. *See also* Minors
    access restrictions on, 40-44, 113
    reading habits of, 38
Young, Gay and Proud (Alyson), 79
Your Child's Mind (Roiphe), 71
Yukon
    access policies in, 40
    acquisition pressure in, 106
    controversial materials ownership in, 52
    effect of challenges in, 92
    public library governance in, 29
    rates of challenges in, 61, 62
    rate of covert incidents in, 99

Zarowny, Shane. *Big Monster,* 77
Zindel, Paul, 94
Zion, Gene. *Dear Garbageman,* 78
Zolotow, Charlotte. *New Friend,* 75
Zoom, 87
Zundel, Ernst, materials on
    covert censorship of, 100

About the Author

Alvin M. Schrader is a professor in the School of Library and Information Studies at the University of Alberta. He joined the school in 1982 while completing his doctoral studies at Indiana University in Bloomington, Indiana. His professional experience includes two years as a special librarian in Toronto and two years as the manager of public library reference services for the City of Brampton Public Library and Art Gallery in Brampton, Ontario.

He was elected for a two-year term (1993-95) to the Board of Directors of the Library Association of Alberta, and he is a long-time member both of the Intellectual Freedom Committee of the Library Association of Alberta and of the Advisory Committee on Intellectual Freedom of the Canadian Library Association. He has written several articles about censorship and intellectual freedom, and he is a committed opponent of state censorship. Dr. Schrader is a native of Alberta, born at Bentley and raised on a farm near Rimbey.